Dedicated to ...

My Beloved Husband

Chandraprakash Bokhare

...... Mrs. Ashwini

Dedicated to ...

My Beloved Son

Aariv Ingale

...... Mrs. Vaishali

A TEXT BOOK OF

ARTIFICIAL INTELLIGENCE

(ELECTIVE - V)

FOR

SEMESTER – VI

THIRD YEAR (T.Y.) B. TECH COURSE IN COMPUTER ENGINEERING

Strictly According to New Revised Credit System Syllabus of Babasaheb Ambedkar Technological University (BATU), Lonere, (Dist. Raigad) Maharashtra,

(w.e.f. June 2019-20)

Dr. Mrs. ASHWINI C. BOKHARE
M.E. Ph.D
Associate Professor
Deptt. of Information Technology
Army Institute of Technology,
Dighi, PUNE.

Mrs. VAISHALI S. INGALE
M.E. Computer
Assistant Professor
Deptt. of Information Technology
Army Institute of Technology,
Dighi, PUNE.

NIRALI PRAKASHAN
ADVANCEMENT OF KNOWLEDGE

N1125

ARTIFICIAL INTELLIGENCE (COMP., BATU) **ISBN : 978-93-89944-10-5**

First Edition : **February 2020**

Published By :
NIRALI PRAKASHAN
Abhyudaya Pragati, 1312 Shivaji Nagar
Off J.M. Road, PUNE 411005
Tel : (020) 25512336/37/39
Email : niralipune@pragationline.com

➢ DISTRIBUTION CENTRES

PUNE

Nirali Prakashan (Local) : 119 Budhwar Peth, Jogeshwari Mandir Lane, Pune 411002, Maharashtra
Tel : (020) 2445 2044, Mobile : 9657703145, Email : niralilocal@pragationline.com

Nirali Prakashan (Outstation) : S. No. 28/27 Dhayari, Near Asian College, Dhayari, Pune 411041, Maharashtra
Tel : (020) 2469 0204, Fax : (020) 2469 0316, Mobile : 9657703143
Email : bookorder@pragationline.com

MUMBAI

Nirali Prakashan : 385 S.V.P. Road, Rasadhara Co-op. Hsg. Society Ltd., Girgaum, Mumbai 400004, Maharashtra
Tel : (022) 2385 6339 / 2386 9976, Fax : (022) 2386 9976, Mobile : 9320129587
Email : niralimumbai@pragationline.com

➢ DISTRIBUTION BRANCHES

JALGAON

Nirali Prakashan : 34 V. V. Golani Market, Navi Peth, Jalgaon 425001, Maharashtra
Tel : (0257) 222 0395, Mob : 94234 91860, Email : niralijalgaon@pragationline.com

KOLHAPUR

Nirali Prakashan : New Mahadvar Road, Kedar Plaza 1st Floor, Opp. IDBI Bank
Kolhapur 416012, Maharashtra. Mobile : 9850046155
Email : niralikolhapur@pragationline.com

NAGPUR

Nirali Prakashan : Above Maratha Mandir, Shop No 3, Second Floor,
Rani Jhanshi Square, Sitabuldi, Nagpur 440012, Maharashtra
Tel : (0712) 254 7129, Email : niralinagpur@pragationline.com

DELHI

Nirali Prakashan : 4593/15 Basement, Agarwal Lane, Ansari Road, Daryaganj
Near Times of India Building, New DelhiV 110002 Mobile : 8505972553
Email : niralidelhi@pragationline.com

BENGALURU

Nirali Prakashan : Maitri Ground Floor, Jaya Apartments, No. 99, 6th Cross, 6th Main,
Malleswaram, Bengaluru 560003, Karnataka
Mobile : 9449043034, Email : niralibangalore@pragationline.com

PREFACE

It gives us great pleasure to present the book **"Artificial Intelligence" (Elective - V)** for the students of **Semester VI Third Year (T.Y.) B. Tech. Course Computer Engineering of Dr. Babasaheb Ambedkar Technological University (BATU), Lonere, Dist. Raigad (Maharashtra).** This book is strictly as per the new revised syllabus 2019-20 Pattern, effective from the Academic Year July 2019-20.

In New Revised Syllabus, there will Class Assessment (CA) 20 Marks, Mid Sem. Exam. (MSE) 20 Marks and End Sem. Exam. (ESE) 60 Marks. End Sem. Exam. will be based on all Six units and each unit will carry 20 Marks.

The Theory Course will have 3 Credits.

The basic objective of this book is to bridge the gap between the vast contents of the reference books, written by the renowned International Authors and the concise requirements of Undergraduate Students. This book has been written in a comprehensive manner using Simple and Lucid language, keeping in mind students' requirements. The main emphasis has been given on exploring the basic concepts rather than merely the Information. Solved Examples and Exercises have been provided throughout the book and at the end of the Unit. Also we have given **Model Question Papers** for practice at the end of book.

Our special thanks to our family members, students and all those who directly or indirectly supported us in this project.

We also take this opportunity to express our sincere thanks to Shri. Dineshbhai Furia, Shri. Jignesh Furia, Mrs. Nirali Verma, Shri. M. P. Munde and entire team of Nirali Prakashan, namely Mrs. Deepali Lachake (Co-ordinator), and her colleagues who really have taken keen interest and untiring efforts in publishing this text.

The advice and suggestions of our esteemed readers to improve the text are most welcome and will be highly appreciated.

Pune **Authors**

SYLLABUS

Unit I :

Introduction

Introduction, What Is AI?, The Foundations of Artificial Intelligence, The History of Artificial Intelligence, The State of the Art.

Intelligent Agents

Agents and Environments Good Behavior: The Concept of Rationality, The Nature of Environments, The Structure of Agents.

Unit II : Problem-Solving

Solving Problems by Searching, Problem-Solving Agents, Example Problems, Searching for Solutions, Uninformed Search Strategies, Informed (Heuristic) Search Strategies, Heuristic Functions.

Unit III : Constraint Satisfaction Problems

Defining Constraint Satisfaction Problems, Constraint Propagation: Inference in CSPs, Backtracking Search for CSPs, Local Search for CSPs, The Structure of Problems.

Unit IV : Game Playing

Adversarial Search, Games, Optimal Decisions in Games, Alpha–Beta Pruning.

Unit V :

Logical Agents

Knowledge-Based Agents, The Wumpus World, Logic, Propositional Logic: A Very Simple Logic, Propositional Theorem Proving, Effective Propositional Model Checking, Agents Based on Propositional Logic

First-Order Logic

Representation Revisited Syntax and Semantics of First-Order Logic, Using First-Order Logic, Knowledge Engineering in First-Order Logic, Inference in First-Order Logic, Propositional vs. First-Order Inference, Unification and Lifting, Forward Chaining, Backward Chaining, Resolution.

Unit VI : Uncertainty

Quantifying Uncertainty, Acting under Uncertainty, Basic Probability Notation, Inference Using Full Joint Distributions, Independence, Bayes' Rule and Its Use, The Wumpus World Revisited, Probabilistic Reasoning, Representing Knowledge in an Uncertain Domain, The Semantics of Bayesian Networks, Efficient Representation of Conditional Distributions Exact Inference in Bayesian Networks, Approximate Inference in Bayesian Networks, Relational and First-Order Probability Models, and Other Approaches to Uncertain Reasoning.

CONTENTS

◈◈◈

UNIT I

INTELLIGENT AGENTS

A : INTRODUCTION

1.1 INTRODUCTION

- Artificial Intelligence is a new field of Computer Science. AI began in earnest with the emergence of modern computer during 1940–1950. It was the ability of new electronic machines to store large amount of information and process it at very high speeds that gave researchers the vision of building systems which could emulate some human abilities.

1.1.1 Reason for Studying AI

- AI strives to build intelligent entities as well as to understand them.
- AI constructed interesting intelligent entities and useful in their own right.
- AI produced many significant and impressive products.
- Computer with human level intelligence (or better) would have a huge impact on our everyday lives and on the future course of civilization.
- AI currently encompasses a huge variety of subfields:
  - ➢ General purpose area:
    - (i) Perception
    - (ii) Logical reasoning
  - ➢ Specific task:
    - (i) Playing chess
    - (ii) Proving mathematical theorems
    - (iii) Writing poetry
    - (iv) Diagnosing diseases

1.2 WHAT IS AI ?

- The definitions of AI vary along two main dimensions concerned with:
  1. Thought process and reasoning
  2. Behaviour.
- In definition, each dimension measures success in terms of:
  1. Human performance.
  2. Rationality i.e. ideal concept of intelligence system is rational if it does the right thing.
- Thus, we have four possible goals to pursue in artificial intelligence.

Definitions of AI:

1. Concerned with the dimension, thought process and reasoning measure success in terms of human performance.

(i) "The exciting new effort to make computer think ... machines with mind, in the full and literal sense"

... by Haugeland, 1985.

(ii) "(The automation of) activities that we associate with human thinking, activities such as decision-making, problem solving, learning ..."

– By Bellman, 1978.

According to definitions (i) and (ii) systems think like human.

2. Concerned with the dimension thought process and reasoning measure success in terms of rationality.

(iii) "The study of mental faculties through the use of computational models".

– By Charniak and McDermott, 1985.

(iv) "The study of the computation that makes it possible to perceive, reason and act".

– By Winston, 1992.

According to definitions (iii) and (iv) systems think rationally.

3. Concerned with the dimension behaviour, measure success in terms of human performance.

(v) "The art of creating mics that perform functions that require intelligence when performed by people". *– By Kurzweil, 1990.*

(vi) "The study of how to make computers do things at which, at the moment, people are better".

– By Rich and Knight, 1991.

According to definitions (v) and (vi) system act like humans

4. Concerned with the dimension, behaviour measure success in terms of rationality.

(vii) "A field of study that seeks to explain and emulate intelligent behaviour in terms of computational process." *– By Schalkoff, 1990.*

(viii)"The branch of computer science that is concerned with the automation of intelligent behaviour".

– By Luger and Stubblefield, 1993.

- According to definitions (vii) and (viii) system act rationally. People may have the confusion between approaches centered.
- A human centered approach must be an empirical science, involving hypothesis and experimental conformation.
- A rationalist approach involves a combination of mathematics and engineering.

1.3 THE FOUNDATION OF ARTIFICIAL INTELLIGENCE

- There are various disciplines that contribute ideas, viewpoints and techniques to AI, as follows:
  1. **Philosophy:**
     Deals with
     (a) Rules used to draw valid conclusions.
     (b) Theory of how mental mind arises from a physical brain.
     (c) The source of knowledge.
     (d) How does knowledge lead to action?
  2. **Mathematics:**
     Deals with
     (a) Formal rules to draw valid conclusion.
     (b) What can be computed?
     (c) How do we reason with uncertain information?
  3. **Economics:**
     Deals with
     (a) How to make decisions to maximize payoff?
     (b) How should we do this when others may not go along?
     (c) How should we do this when the payoff may be far in future?
  4. **Neuroscience:**
     Deals with how brain processes information.
  5. **Psychology:**
     How humans and animals think and act.
  6. **Computer Engineering:**
     Deals with how we can build an efficient computer.
  7. **Control Theory and Cybernetics:**
     Deals with how artifacts can operate under their own control.
  8. **Linguistics:**
     Deals with how language relates to thought.

- Modern linguistics and AI were "born" at about the same time and grew up together, it was an intersection in a hybrid field called computational linguistics or natural language processing.
- Understanding language requires an understanding of the structure of sentences.
- Most of the early work in knowledge representation was tied to language and informed by research in linguistics. For artificial intelligence to succeed, we need two things:
  1. Intelligence
  2. Artifact
- The modern digital electronic computer was invented independently and almost simultaneously by scientists in three countries embattled in World War II. The first operational computer was the electromechanical computer. Heath Robinson, built in 1940 by Alan Turing's team for a single purpose: deciphering German messages.
- In 1943, the same group developed the colossus, a powerful general-purpose machine based on vacuum tubes.
- In the half-century, each generation of computer hardware brought an increase in speed and capacity and a decrease in price. Performance doubled every 18 months or so with a decade or two to go at this rate of increase. After that, we will need molecular engineering or some other new technology.
- AI also owes debt to the software side of computer science, which has supplied the operating systems, programming languages and tools needed to write modern programs. But in this one area where the debt has been repaid work in AI has pioneered many ideas that have made their way back to mainstream computer science, including time sharing, interative interpreters, personal computers with windows and mice, rapid development environments, the linked list data type, automatic storage management, and key concept of symbolic, functional and dynamic object--oriented programming.

1.4 THE HISTORY OF ARTIFICIAL INTELLIGENCE

The contributions of other fields to the development of AI is seen by many as so important that they consider the history of AI cannot be recounted without including the discussion of history of knowledge that dates back to Aristotle.

We discuss the history of Artificial intelligence covering the following points:

1. The gestation of artificial intelligence (1943-1955)
2. The birth of artificial intelligence (1956)
3. Early enthusiasm, great expectations (1952-1969)
4. A dose of reality (1966-1973)
5. Knowledge-based systems: The key to power? (1969-1979)
6. AI becomes an industry (1980-present)
7. The return of neural networks (1986-present)
8. AI becomes a science (1987-present)
9. The emergence of intelligent agents (1995-present)

1. The Gestation of Artificial Intelligence (1943-1955):

- The first work that is now generally recognized as AI was done by Warren McCulloch and Walter Pitts (1943).

  They drew on two sources:

  (i) Knowledge of basic physiology

  (ii) Functions of neurons in the brain.
- Warren McCulloch and Walter Pitts (1943) gave the concept of artificial neural networks. They suggested that suitably defined networks could learn. Donald Hebb (1949) demonstrated a simple learning rule, now called **Hebbian Learning,** for modifying the connection strengths between neurons.
- Alan Turing was the first to put forward a complete vision of AI in his 1950 article "Computing Machinery and Intelligence." Therein, he introduced the turing test, machine learning, genetic algorithms and reinforcement learning.
- Two graduate students in the Princeton mathematics department, Marvin Minsky and Dean Edmonds, built the first neural network computer in 1951 called SNARC.

2. The Birth of Artificial Intelligence (1956):

- U.S. researchers interested in automata theory, neural nets, and the study of intelligence were brought together in a workshop at Dartmouth in the summer of 1956 where John McCarthy proposed the name for the field as "**Artificial Intelligence.**"

3. Early Enthusiasm, Great Expectations (1952-1969):

- Starting in 1952, Arthur Samuel wrote a series of programs for checkers (draughts) that eventually learned to play at a strong amateur level.
- McCarthy in 1958 defined a high level language LISP, a dominant AI programming language. In the same year McCarthy and others at MIT invented time sharing. Also in 1958, McCarthy published a paper entitled *Programs with Common Sense,* in which he described the Advice Taker, a hypothetical program that can be seen as the first complete AI system.
- At IBM, Nathaniel Rochester and his colleagues produced some of the first AI programs. Herbert Gelernter (1959) constructed the Geometry Theorem Prover.
- Newell and Simon developed Logic Theorist (1963a) and General Problem Solver (1963b).
- James Slagle's SAINT program (1963a) solved integration problems.
- Tom Evans's ANALOGY program (1968) solved geometric analogy problems.
- Daniel Bobrow's STUDENT program (1967) solved algebra story problems.
- Hebb's learning methods were enhanced by Bemie Widrow (Widrow and Hoff, 1960; Widrow. 1962), who called his networks **adalines,** and by Frank Rosenblatt (1962) with his **perceptrons.** Rosenblatt proved the **perceptron convergence theorem.**

4. A Dose of Reality (1966-1973):

- In 1966 the failure of machine translation project brought an end to the US government's funding of the project.
- Minsky and Papert's book: '*Perceptrons*' (1969) proved that although perceptrons (a simple form of neural network) could be shown to learn anything they were capable of representing, they could represent very little.
- In 1973 Lighthill report entailed cutting of British funding to AI research in most of the universities in the Great Britain.

5. Knowledge-Based Systems: The Key to Power? (1969-1979):

- The DENDRAL program (1969) solved the problem of inferring molecular structure from the information provided by a mass spectrometer.
- MYCIN was developed in mid 1970s at Stanford that diagnosed blood infections.

6. AI Becomes an Industry (1980-Present):

- The first successful commercial expert system R1 began operation at the Digital Equipment Corporation (McDermott, 1982).

- Nearly every major U.S. corporation had its own AI group and was either using or investigating expert systems.
- In 1981, the Japanese announced the "Fifth Generation" project, a 10-year plan to build intelligent computers running Prolog.
- United States formed the Microelectronics and Computer Technology Corporation (MCC) as a research consortium.
- Alvey report reinstated the funding that was cut by the Lighthill report.
- The AI industry boomed from a few million dollars in 1980 to billions of dollars in 1988. Soon after that came a period called the "AI Winter" in which many companies suffered as they failed to deliver on extravagant promises.

7. The Return of Neural Networks (1986-Present):

- In the mid-1980s at least four different groups reinvented the back-propagation learning algorithm first found in 1969 by Bryson and Ho.

8. AI Becomes a Science (1987-Present):

- Judea Pearl's (1988) *Probabilistic Reasoning in Intelligent Systems* led to a new acceptance of probability and decision theory in AI.

9. The Emergence of Intelligent Agents (1995-Present):

- The work of Allen Newell, John Laird, and Paul Rosenbloom on SOAR (Newell. 1990: Laird el al., 1987) is the best-known example of a complete agent architecture.
- AI technologies underlie many Internet tools, such as search engines, recommender systems, and Web site construction systems.

1.5 APPLICATIONS OF ARTIFICIAL INTELLIGENCE

The two most fundamental concerns of AI researchers are knowledge representation and search like most sciences. AI is decomposed into a number of sub-disciplines that, while sharing an essential approach to problem solving, have concerned themselves with different application.

The following are major application areas of AI:

1. Game Playing:

- Most of the early research in state space search was done using common board games such as checkers, chess and the 8-puzzle.
- Most games are played use well-defined set of rules, this makes it easy to generate the search space and frees the researcher from many ambiguities and complexities inherent in the less structured problem.
- The board configuration used in playing these games are easily represented on a computer, requiring none of the complex formalisms needed to capture the semantic subtleties of more complex problem domain.
- Game-playing programs, in spite of their simplicity, offer their own challenges, including an opponent moves may not be reliably anticipated.

2. Automated Reasoning and Theorem Proving:

- Automatic theorem proving is the oldest branch of artificial intelligence. A wide variety of problems can be attacked by representing the problem description and relevant background information as logical axioms and treating problem instances as theorems to be proved. Automatic theorem systems are not capable of solving extremely complex problems independently without human assistance.

3. Expert Systems:

- Expert knowledge is a combination of a theoretical understanding of the problem and a collection of heuristic problem-solving rules that experience has shown to be effective in the domain.
- Expert systems are constructed by obtaining this knowledge from a human expert and coding it into a form that a computer may apply to similar problems.
- This reliance on the knowledge of a human domain expert for the system's problem-solving strategies is a major feature of the expert systems.

4. Natural Language Understanding and Semantic Modeling:

- One of the long-standing goals of artificial intelligence is the creation of programs that are capable of understanding human language. Not only the ability to understand natural language seems to be one of the most fundamental aspects of human intelligence, but also its successful automation would have an incredible impact on the usability and effectiveness of computer themselves. Much efforts has been put into writing programs that understand natural language.
- Although these programs have achieved success within restricted contexts, systems that can use natural language with the flexibility and generality that characterize human speech are beyond current methodologies.

5. **Modelling Human Performance:**

- The design of systems that explicitly model some aspects of human solving has been the fertile area of research in both artificial intelligence and psychology. Human performance modelling, in addition to providing AI with much of its basic methodology, has proved to be a powerful tool for formulating and testing theories of human cognition.

1.6 THE STATE OF THE ART

These days there are so many activities. So many subfields exist in AI. Not magic are science friction but rather science, engineering and mathematics.

- **Speech Recognition :** A traveler calling airlines to book a flight can have entire conversion guided by an automatically speech recognition and dialog management system.
- **Autonomous Planning and Scheduling :** A hundred million miles from earth, NASA's remote agent program become first on-board autonomous planning program to control the scheduling operations for a spacecraft.
- **Game Playing :** IBM's DEEP BLUE become the first computer program to deflect the world champion in a chess match when it bested Garry Kasparov by a score of 3.5 to 2.5 in an exhibition match.
- **Spam Fighting :** Each day, learning algorithm classify over a billion messages as spam, saving the recipient from having to waste time deleting. The spammers are continually updating their tactics, it is difficult for a static programmed approach to keep up, and learning algorithms work best.
- **Logistics Planning :** During the Persian Gulf exists of 1991, V.S. forces deployed a Dynamic Analysis and Re-planning Tool, DART, to do automated logistic planning and scheduling for transportation. This involved up to 50000 vehicles, cargo and people at a time, and had to account for starting points, destinations, routes and conflict resolution of all parameters.

  The AI planning techniques generated in hours a plan that would have taken weeks with older methods.
- **Robotics :** The iRobot corporation has sold over two million roomba robotic vacuum cleaners for home use. The company also deploys the more rugged PackBot to Ireq and Afghanistan, where it is used to handle hazardous materials, clear explosives and identify the location of snipers.
- **Machine Translation :** A computer program automatically translates from one languages to other languages.

  The program uses a statistical model built from examples of language translations (e.g. Marathi to English) and from examples of English text totaling two trillion words.

B : INTELLIGENCE AGENTS

1.7 AGENTS AND ENVIRONMENTS

- An agent is anything that can be viewed as perceiving its **environment** through **sensor** and acting upon that environment through **actuators** as shown in Fig. 1.1.

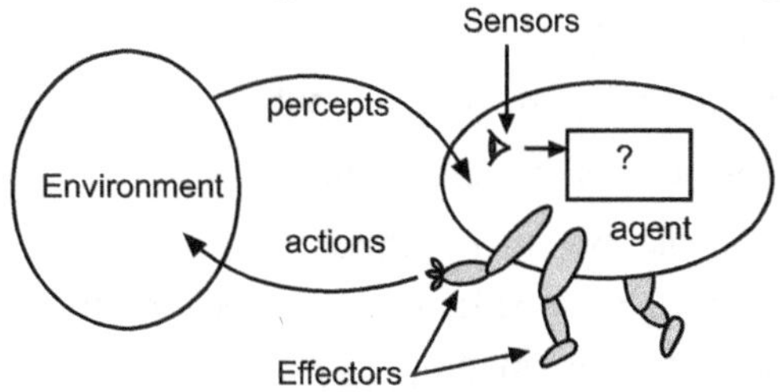

Fig. 1.1

- A human agent has eyes, ears and other organs for sensor, one has hands, legs, mouth and other body parts for actuators.
- A robotic agent might have cameras and infrared range finders for sensors and robot arms for actuators.
- A software agent receives keystrokes, file contents and network packets as sensory inputs and acts on the environment by displaying on the screen, writing files and network packets, (i.e. actuators)

1.8 GOOD BEHAVIOR

- The rational agent is one that does the right thing. We will say that the right action is the one that will cause the agent to be most successful and that leaves us with the problem of deciding how and when to evaluate the agent's success.
- We use the term 'percept' to refer to the agent's perceptual inputs at any given instant. An agent's percept sequence is the complete history of everything the agent has ever perceived.
- An agent's choice of action at any given instant can depend on the entire percept sequence observed till date.

- We say that an agent's behaviour is described by the agent function that maps any given percept sequence to an action.
- Performance measure uses criteria that determine how successful an agent is. Obviously, there is not one fixed measure suitable for all agents, so we will say performance measure is an objective that defines degree of success.
- An intelligent agent should always do what is actually the right thing depending on four things:
  1. The performance measure that defines degree of success.
  2. Everything that the agent has perceived so far. We will call this complete perceptual history, the percept sequence.
  3. What the agent knows about the environment.
  4. The actions that the agent can perform.
- The intelligent agent should be able to operate successfully in a wide variety of environments, given sufficient time to adapt.

1.9 THE CONCEPT OF RATIONALITY

What is rational at any given time depends on four things:

1. The performance measure that defines the criterion of success.
2. The agent's prior knowledge of the environment.
3. The actions that the agent can perform.
4. The agent's percept sequence to date.

This leads to a definition of a rational agent.

- For each possible percept sequence, a rational agent should select an action that is expected to maximize its performance measure, given the evidence provided by the percept sequence and whatever built-in knowledge the agent has.
- Consider the simple vacuum cleaner agent that cleans a square if it is dirty and moves to the other square if not dirty, this agent function tabulated in (Fig. 1.2).

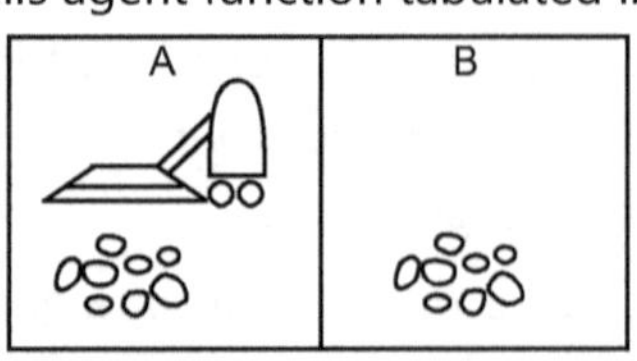

Fig. 1.2: A Vacuum-cleaner World with Just Two locations

Table 1.1 : Partial Tabulation of Simple Agent Function for Vacuum-Cleaner World Shown in Fig. 1.2

Percept Sequence	Action
[A, Clean]	Right
[A, Dirty]	Suck
[B, Clean]	Left
[B, Dirty]	Suck
[A, Clean] [A, Clean]	Right
[A, Clean] [A, Dirty]	Suck
⋮	⋮
[A, Clean], [A, Clean], [A, Clean]	Right
[A, Clean], [A, Clean], [A, Dirty]	Suck

Let us assume the following:

- The performance measure awards one point for each clean square at each time step over a "lifetime" of 1000 time steps.
- The "Geography" of the environment is known a prior (Fig. 1.2) but the dirt distance distribution and the initial location of the agent are not clean squares stay clean and sucking cleans the current square. The left and right action move the agent left and right except when this would take the agent outside the environment, in which case the agent remains where it is.
- The only available action are left Right, Suck and NoOp (do nothing).
- The agent correctly perceives its location and whether that location contains dirt.
- We claim that under these circumstances the agent is indeed rational; its expected performance is at least as high as any other agent's.
- But same agent would be irrational under different circumstances. For example, once all the dirt is cleaned up, it will oscillate needlessly back and forth; if the performance measure includes a penalty of one point for each movement left or right, the agent will fare poorly.
- A better agent for this case would do nothing once it is sure that all squares are clean. If clean squares can become dirty again, the agent should occasionally check and re-clean them if needed. If the Geography of the environment is unknown the agent will need to explore it rather than stick to squares A and B.

Omniscience, Learning and Autonomy:

- An omniscient agent knows the actual outcome of its actions and can act accordingly, but omniscience is impossible in reality.

  For Example: I am walking along Viman Nagar one day I saw an old friend across the street. There is no traffic nearby and I am not otherwise engaged, so, being rational, I start to cross the street. Meanwhile, at 33,000 feet, a cargo door falls off a passing airliner and before I make it to other side of the street I am flattened.

  Was I irrational to cross the street?
- This example shows that rationality is not the same as perfection.
- Rationality maximizes expected performance, while perfection maximizes actual performance. Rationality does not require omniscience, then, because the rational choice depends only on the percept sequence to date.
- A rational agent not only to gather information, but also to learn as much as possible from what it perceives. The agent's initial configuration could reflect some prior knowledge of the environment, but as the agent gains experience this may be modified and augmented. There are extreme cases in which the environment is completely known as priori. In such cases, the agent need not perceive or learn, it simply act correctly.
- Successfully agents split the task of computing the agent function into three different periods. When the agent is being designed, some of the computation is being designed, some of computation is done by its designers, when it is deliberating on its next action, the agent does more computation and as it learns from experience, it does even more computation to decide how to modify its behaviour.
- To the extent that an agent relies on the prior knowledge of its designer rather than on its own percepts, the agent lacts autonomy.
- A rational agent should be autonomous, it should learn what it can to compensate for partial or incorrect prior knowledge.

  For Example : A vacuum cleaning agent that learns to foresee where and when additional dirt will appear will do better than one does not.

1.10 THE NATURE OF ENVIRONMENTS

- The task environment are essentially the "Problems", to which rational agents are the "Solutions". The task environment comes in a variety of flavours. The flavours of the task environment directly affect the appropriate design for the agent program.
- For defining rationality of the agent, we have to specify the **P**erformance measure, the **E**nvironment and the agent's **A**ctuators and **S**ensors (PEAS).
- In designing an agent, the first step must always be to specify the task environment as fully as possible.
- Consider the problem automated taxi driver PEAS environment is given below.

Table 1.2

Agent Type	Performance Measure	Environment	Actuators	Sensors
Taxi driver	Safe, fast, legal, comfortable trip, maximize profits	Roads, other traffic, customers	Steering accelerator, brake, signal, horn, display	Cameras, sonar, speedometer, GPS, odometer, accelerometer, engine sensor, keyboards

- **The Performance Measure** of the automated driver depends on the following qualities:
  - ➢ Getting to the correct destination
  - ➢ Minimizing fuel consumption
  - ➢ Minimizing trip time and/or cost
  - ➢ Minimizing violations of traffic laws and disturbances to the other drivers
  - ➢ Maximizing safety and passenger comfort
  - ➢ Maximizing profits
- **The Environment** that the taxi will face.
  - ➢ Any taxi driver must deal with a variety of roads, ranging from rural to urban areas, roads containing traffic like Mumbai or less traffic like Nagpur.
  - ➢ The taxi must also interact with potential and actual passengers.
- **The Actuators** available to an automated taxi will be more or less the same as those available to a human driver. Control over the engine through the accelerator and control over steering and brakes. In addition, it will need output to a display screen or voice synthesizer to talk back to the passengers and perhaps some way to communicate with other vehicles.

- **The Sensors:** To achieve its goals in the driving environment, the taxi will need to know where it is, what else is on the road, and how fast it is going.

  Its basic sensor should therefore include one or more controllable TV cameras, the speedometer and the odometer. To control the vehicle properly, especially on curves, it should have an accelerometer.

1.10.1 Properties of Task Environment

- **Fully Observable V/s. Partially Observable:**
  - ➢ If an agent's sensor gives it access to the complete state of the environment at each point in time, then we say that the task environment is fully observable.
  - ➢ A task environment is fully observable if the sensor detects all the aspects that are relevant to the choice of action that depends on performance measures. Fully observable environments are convenient because the agent need not maintain any internal state to keep track of the world.
  - ➢ An environment might be partially observable because of the noisy and inaccurate sensors or because parts of the state are simply missing from the sensor data.

    For Example:

    1. Vacuum agent with only a local dirt sensor cannot tell whether there is dirt in other squares.
    2. An automated taxi will not be able to know what other drivers are thinking.
- **Deterministic V/s. Stochastic:**
  - ➢ If the next state of the environment is completely determined by the current state and the action executed by the agent, then we say the environment is deterministic.
  - ➢ If the next state of the environment is not completely determined, then we say the environment is stochastic.
  - ➢ Environment is deterministic or stochastic depending on whether it is fully observable or partially observable. Fully observable environment is deterministic. Partially observable environment is stochastic.
- **Episodic V/s. Sequential:**
  - ➢ In an episodic task environment, the agent's experience is divided into atomic episodes. Each episode consists of the agent perceiving and then performing a single action.
  - ➢ Critically, the next episode does not depend on action taken in previous episodes. In the episodic environment, the choice of action in each episode depends only on the episode itself.

    For Example: An agent that has to spot defective parts on an assembly line.

    In sequential environment, the current decision could affect all future decisions.

    For Example: Chess and taxi driving.
- **Static V/s. Dynamic:**
  - ➢ If the environment can change while an agent is deliberating, then the environment is dynamic for the agent; otherwise, it is static.
  - ➢ Static environment is easy to deal with as compared to dynamic because of continuously asking the agent what it wants to do.
  - ➢ If the environment itself does not change with the passage of time but the agent's performance score does, then we say the environment is semi dynamic.
- **Discrete V/s. Continuous:**
  - ➢ The discrete/continuous distinction can be applied to the state of the environment, to the way time is handled, and to the precepts and actions of the agent.

    For Example: Chess game has a finite number of distinct states and also has a discrete set of precepts and actions.

    Taxi driving is a continuous-state and continuous-time problem.
- **Single Agent V/s. Multi-agent:**
  - ➢ It depends upon the required single agent or multi-agent.

    For Example: Solving a crossword puzzle is a single agent environment and playing chess is in a two agent environment i.e. multi-agent.

1.11 THE STRUCTURE OF AGENTS

- The job of AI is to design the agent program that implements agent function mapping precepts to actions. We assume this program will run on some sort of computing device with physical sensors and actuators. We call this the architecture.

  agent = architecture + program
- The program we choose has to be one that is appropriate for the architecture.

For Example: If the program is going to recommend action like walk, the architecture must have legs. The architecture might be just an ordinary PC, or it might be a robotic car with several onboard computers, cameras and other sensors. In general, the architecture makes the percepts from the sensors available to the program and feeds the program's action choices to the actuators as they are generated.

1.11.1 Agent Programs

- The agent program take the current percept as input from the sensors and returns an action to the actuators. If the agent's actions depend on the entire percept sequence, the agent will have to remember the percepts.
- The key challenge for AI is to find out how to write programs that produce rational behaviour from a small amount of code rather than from a large number of table entries.
- The following are four basic kinds of agent program:
    1. Simple reflex agents.
    2. Mode-based reflex agents.
    3. Goal-based agents.
    4. Utility-based agents.

1. Simple Reflex Agents:

- The simplest kind of agent is the simple reflex agent. These agents select actions on the basis of the current percept, ignoring the rest of the percept history.

  For Example: The vacuum agent, whose agent function is a simple reflex agent because its decision is based only on the current location and on whether that contains dirt.

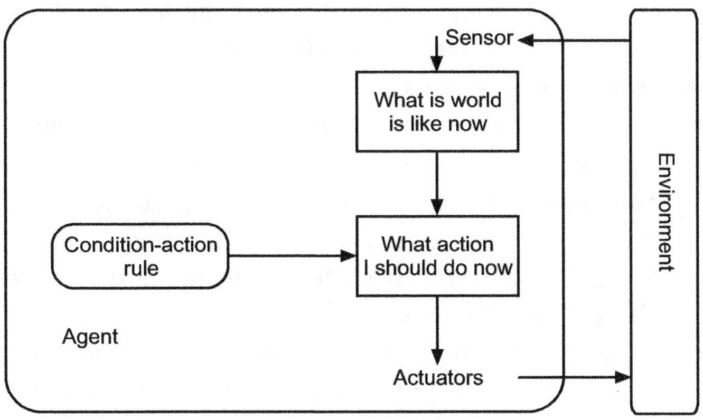

Fig. 1.3 : Simple reflex agent

Note:

(rectangles) : To represent the current internal state of the agent's decision process.

(ovals) : To represent the background information used in the process.

Program 1.1: A simple reflex agent. It acts according to a rule whose condition matches the current state, as defined by the percept

```
Function: SIMPLE - REFLEX - AGENT (percept)
        returns an action.
Static: Rules, a set of condition - action rules.
        State  ← INTERPRET - INPUT (percept)
        Rule   ← RULE - MATCH (state, rules)
        Action ← RULE - ACTION (rule)
Return Action
```

- The condition-action rules allow the agent to make the connection from percept to action.

  For Example: The driver of the automated taxi condition is "the car is in the front speed breaker". Then agent program to the action initiate breaking" written as,

  If car-in-front-speed breaker **then** initiate-braking.

- Program 1.1 the **INTERPRET-INPUT** function generates an abstracted description of the current state from the percept.
- **RULE-MATCH** function returns the first rule in the set of rules that matches the given state description. The description in terms of the "rules" and "matching" is purely conceptual, actual implementations can be as a collection of logic gates implementing a Boolean circuit.
- Simple reflex agents have the admirable property of being simple, but they turn out to be of very limited intelligence. The simple reflex agent will work only if the correct decision can be made on the basis of only the current percept that is, only if the environment is fully observable. Even a little bit of unobservability can cause serious trouble.

2. Model-Based Reflex Agents:

- The most effective way to handle partial observability is for the agent to keep track of the part of the world it can't see now. That is, the agent should maintain some sort of internal state that depends on the percept history and thereby reflects at least some of the unobserved aspects of the current state.

  For Example: Driving task such as changing lanes, the agent needs to keep track of where the other cars are if it can't see them all at once.

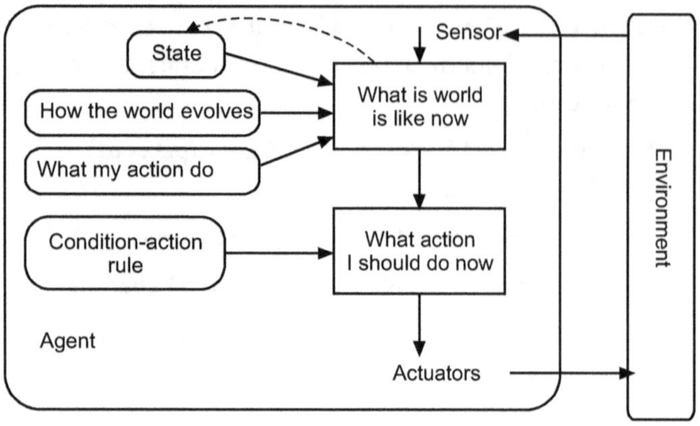

Fig. 1.4 : A model-based reflex agent

Program 1.2: A model-based reflex agent. It keeps track of the current state of the world using an internal model. It then chooses an action in the same way as the reflex agent

Function: REFLEX - AGENT WITH - STATE (percept) **returns** an action.

Static: State, a description of the current world state.

rules, a set condition-action rules.

action, the most recent action, initially none.

State ← UPDATE - STATE (state, action, percept)

Rule ← RULE - MATCH (state, rules)

Action ← RULE - ACTION (rule)

Return Action

- Updating this internal state information as time goes by requires two kinds of knowledge to be encoded in the agent program.
  - ➢ We need some information about how the world evolves independently of the agent.

  For Example : Overtaking car generally will be closer behind that it was a moment ago.
- We need some information about how the agent's own action would affect the world.

  For Example, when the agent turns the steering wheel clockwise, the car turns to the right.
- Program 1.2 gives the structure of the model-based reflex agent with internal state, showing how the current percept is combined with the old internal state to generate the updated description of the current state.
- Fig 1.5 shows the agent program. The function **UPDATE-STATE** is responsible for creating the new internal state description.

3. Goal-Based Agents

- Knowing about the current state of the environment is not always enough to decide what to do.

  For Example: At a road junction, the taxi can turn left, turn right, or go straight. The correct decision depends on where the taxi trying to get to. The agent needs some sort of goal information that describes situations that are desirable, i.e. depending upon the passenger's destination.
- The agent program can combine this with information about the result of possible action in order to choose actions that achieve the goal.
- In the goal-based agent decision-making is fundamentally different from the condition-action rule, in goal-based it involves consideration of the future both "what will happen if I do such and such?" and "will that make me happy?".

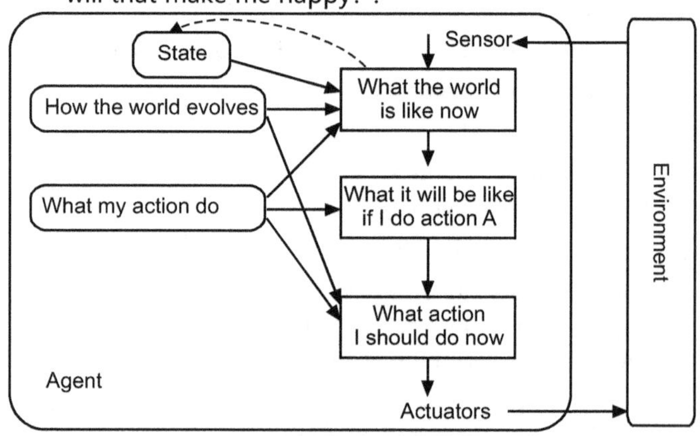

Fig. 1.5 : A model-based, goal based agent. It keeps track of the world state as well as a set of goals it is trying to achieve and chooses an action that will (eventually) lead to the achievement of its goals

4. Utility Based Agents:

- Goals alone are not really enough to generate high-quality behaviour in most environments.

  For Example: There are many action sequences that will get the taxi to its destination (thereby achieving the goal), but some are quicker, safer, more reliable, or cheaper than the others.
- Goals just provide a crude binary distinction between "happy" and "unhappy" states, whereas a more general performance measure should allow a comparison of different world states according to exactly how happy they would make the agent if they could be achieved. Because "happy" does not sound very scientific, the customary terminology is to say that if one world state is preferred to another, then it has higher **utility** for the agent.

- A **utility function** maps a state (or a sequence of states) onto a real number, which describes the associated degree of happiness.
- A complete specification of utility function allows rational decisions in two kinds of cases where, goals are inadequate.
  - ➢ When there are conflicting goals i.e. only some of them can be achieved.

    For Example, speed and safety.

  A utility function specifies the appropriate trade off.
- When there are several goals that the agent can aim for none of which can be achieved with certainty, utility provides a way in which the likelihood of success can be weighted up against the importance of the goals.

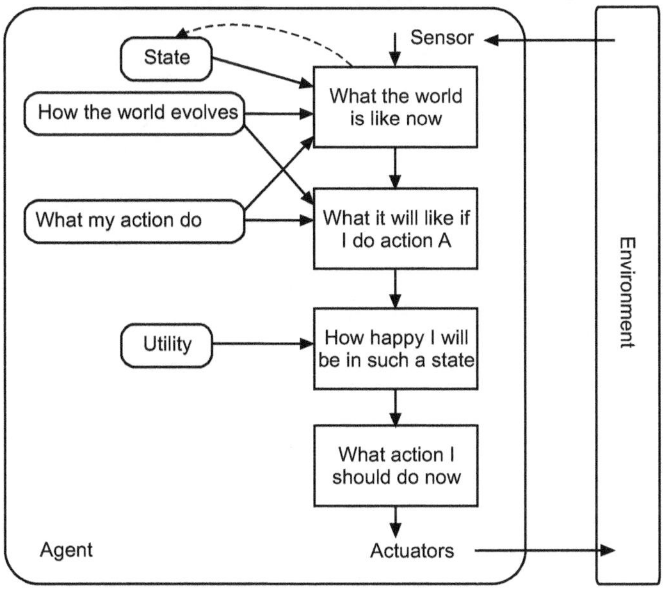

Fig. 1.6 : A model-based, utility-based agent

- It uses a model of the world, along with a utility function that measures its performances among the state of the worlds. Then it chooses the action that leads to the best expected utility, where expected utility is computed by taking the average of overall possible outcome states, weighted by the probability of the outcome.

5. Learning Agents:

- Turing (1950) considers the idea of actually programming his intelligent machines by hand. The method he proposes is to build learning machines and then to teach them. In many areas of AI, this is now the preferred method for creating state of the art system. Learning allows the agent to operate in initially unknown environments and to become more competent than its initial knowledge might allow.

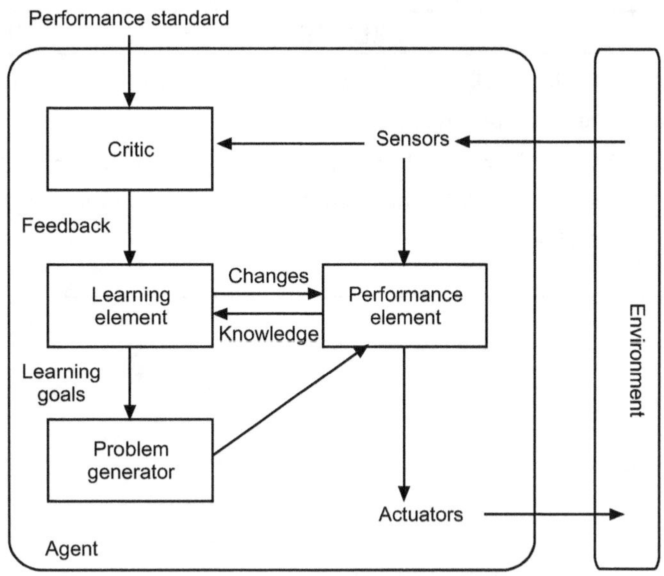

Fig. 1.7 : A general model of learning agent

- A learning agent can be divided into four conceptual components, as shown in Fig. 1.7.
  - ➢ **Learning Element:** Learning element is responsible for making improvements.
  - ➢ **Performance Element:** Performance element is a responsible external action. The performance element takes in percepts and decides on actions.
  - ➢ **Critic:** The learning element uses feedback from the critic on how the agent is doing and determines how the performance element should be modified to do better in the future.
- The critic tells the learning element how well the agent is doing with respect to a fixed performance standard.
- The critic is necessary because the percepts themselves provide no indication of the agent's success.
- **Problem Generator:** The last component of the learning agent is the problem generator. It is responsible for suggesting actions that will lead to new and informative experiences. The point is that if the performance element had its way, it would keep doing the actions that are best, given what it knows. But if the agent is willing to explore a little and do some perhaps suboptimal actions in the short run, it might discover much better actions for the long run. The problem generator's job is to suggest these exploratory actions.

EXERCISE

1. Explain desirables properties of AI internal representation and AI software.
2. What is artificial Intelligence? Explain how an AI system is different from a conventional computing system.
3. What is AI? State various characteristics of AI?
4. Explain the nature and scope of AI. Why game playing problems are considered as AI problem.
5. Explain the structure of agents in AI.
6. Explain the concept of Rationality.
7. Explain properties of task environment.

✠ ✠ ✠

UNIT II

PROBLEM-SOLVING

2.1 SOLVING PROBLEMS BY SEARCHING

- Reflex agents are the simplest agent, which base their actions on a direct mapping from state to actions.
- Such agents can not operate well in environments for which this mapping would be too large to store and would take too long to learn.
  - ➢ Goal based agents consider future actions and the desirability of their outcomes.
  - ➢ The goal based agents called a problem-solving agent.
  - ➢ Problem-solving agent use atomic representations, that is states of the world are considered as wholes, with no internal structure visible to the problem solving algorithms.
  - ➢ Goal based agents, that use more advanced factored or structured representations are usually called planning agents.

2.2 PROBLEM-SOLVING AGENTS

- Intelligent agents are supposed to maximize their performance measure. The goal-based agent is called a problem-solving agent. Problem-solving agents decide what to do by finding sequences of actions that lead to desirable states.
- Goals help organize behaviour by limiting the objectives that the agent is trying to achieve. Goal formulation, based on the current situation and the agents performance measure, is the first step in problem-solving.
- Consider goal to be a set of world states. It consists of exactly those states in which the goal is satisfied. The agents task is to find out which sequence of actions will get it to a goal state. Before this, it needs to decide what sort of actions and states to consider because at this level of details there is too much uncertainty in the world and there would be too many states to consider, given a goal. Problem formulation is the process of deciding what actions and states to consider, given a goal.
- An agent with several immediate options of unknown value can decide what to do by first examining different possible sequences of actions that leads to states of unknown value and then choosing the best sequence.
- The process of looking for such a sequence is called a **search**. A search algorithm takes a problem as an input and returns a solution in the form of an action sequence. Once a solution is found, the actions it recommends can be carried out. This is called the execution phase. Thus, a simple "formulate search, execute" design for the agent is shown in Program 2.1.

Program 2.1 : A simple problem-solving agent. It first formulates a goal and a problem, searches for a sequence of action that would solve the problem and then executes the actions one at a time. When this is complete, it formulates another goal and starts over. Note that when it is executing the sequence it ignores its percepts, it assumes that the solution it has found will always work

```
Function: SIMPLE-PROBLEM-SOLVING-AGENT (percept) returns an action
Inputs:   percept, a percept
Static:   Seq, an action sequence, initially empty
          State, some description of the current world state
          goal, a goal initially null
          problem, a problem formulation
   State ← UPDATE - STATE (State, percept)
   if seq is empty then do
          goal ← FORMULATE - GOAL (state)
          problem ← FORMULATIVE - PROBLEM (state, goal)
      seq ← SEARCH (problem)
   action ← FIRST (seq)
   seq ← REST (seq)
   return action
```

- After formulating a goal and a problem to solve, the agent calls a search procedure to solve it. It then uses the solution to guide its actions, doing whatever the solution recommends as the next thing to do typically, the first action of the sequence and then removing that step from the sequence. Once the solution has been executed, the agent formulates a new goal.
- Consider the example of driving a car from Bucharest to Arad, as shown in Fig. 2.1.

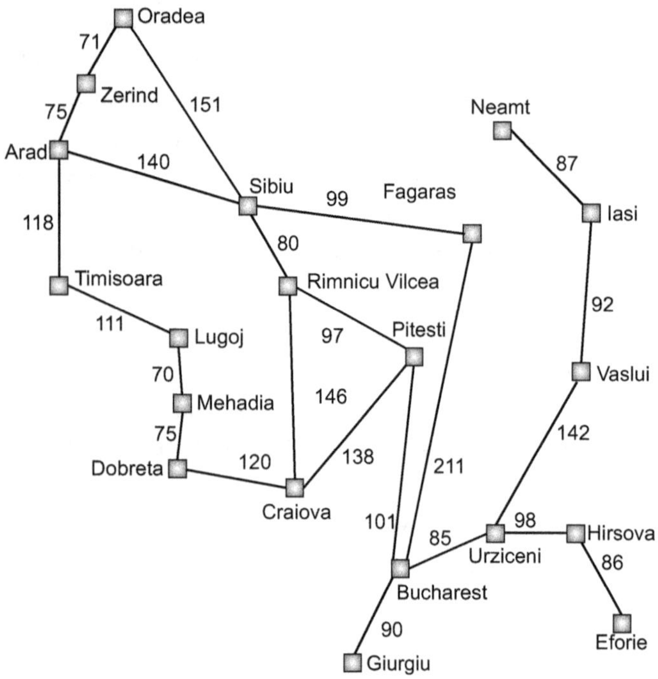

Fig. 2.1 : A Simplified Road Map of Part of Romania

1. Well-Defined Problems and Solutions:

A **problem** can be defined formally by four components:

(i) The **Initial State** that the agent starts in e.g. the initial state for our agent is Bucharest.

(ii) A description of the possible **actions** available to the agent. The most common formulation uses a **successor function**. Give a particular state x, SUCCESSOR-FN(x) returns a set of {action, successor} ordered pairs, where each action is one of the legal actions in the state x and each successor is a state that can be reached from x by applying the action. For example, from the state in (Bucharest), the successor function for the Arad problem would return.

{{Go (Giurgiu), In(Guirgiu)}, {Go(Urziceni), In(Urziceni)}, {Go(Pitesti), In(Pitesti)}}

Together, the initial state and successor function implicitly define the **state space** of the problem - the set of all states reachable from the initial state. The state space from the graph in which modes are states and the arcs between nodes are actions. A **path** in the state space is a sequence of states connected by a sequence of action.

(iii) The Goal Test, which determines whether a given state is a goal state. Sometimes there is an explicit set of possible goal states and the test simply checks whether the given state is one of them. The agent's goal in Arad is the singleton set `{In (Arad)}`. Sometimes the goal is specified by an abstract property rather than by an explicitly enumerated set of states. For example, in chess, the goal is to reach a state called "checkmate", where the opponent's king is under attack and can't escape.

(iv) A Path Cost function is a function that assigns a numeric cost to each path. The problem-solving agent chooses a cost function that reflects its own performance measure. For the agent trying to get to "Pitesti", time is of the essence, so the cost of a path can be described as the sum of the costs of the individual actions along the path. The **step cost** of taking action a to go from state x to state y is denoted by C(x, a, y).

2. Formulating Problems:

- Here is a formulation of the problem of getting to Arad in terms of the initial state, successor function, goal test and path cost. This formulation seems reasonable, yet it omits a great many aspects of the real world. Compare the simple state description, we have chosen. In (Bucharest), to an actual cross-country trip, where the state of the world includes so many things, the travelling companions, what is on the radio, the scenery out of the window, whether there are any law enforcement officers nearby, how far it is to be the next rest stop, the condition of the road, the weather and so on. All these considerations are left out of our state descriptions because they are irrelevant to the problem of finding a route to Arad. The process of removing detail from a representation is called abstraction.
- In addition to abstracting the state description, we must abstract the actions themselves. A driving action has many effects. Besides changing the location of the vehicle and its occupants, it takes-up time, consumes fuel, generates pollution and changes the agents. Formulation takes into account only the change in location. Also, there are many actions that omit altogether, turning on the radio,

looking out of the window, slowing down for low enforcement officers and so on. And no need to specify actions at the level of "turn steering wheel to the left by the three degrees".

- The choice of good abstraction thus involves removing as much detail as possible while retaining validity and ensuring that the abstract actions are easy to carry out. Were it not for the ability to construct useful abstraction, intelligent agents would be completely swamped by the real world.

2.3 EXAMPLE PROBLEMS

The problem solving approach has been applied to a vast array of task environment.

The best known are:

1. **Toy Problem:**

- A toy problem is intended to illustrate or exercise various problem-solving methods.
- It can be given a concise, exact description. It can be used easily by different researchers to compare the performance of algorithm.

2. **Real-World Problem:**

- A real-world problem is one whose solutions people actually care about.
- They tend not to have a single agreed-upon description, but attempt to give the general flavour of their formulations.

Examples of each problems are given below:

2.3.1 Examples of Toy Problem

1. **Vacuum-Cleaner World:**

This problem shown in Fig. 2.2 having only two locations: squares A and B. The vacuum agent perceives which square it is in and whether there is dirt in the square. It can choose to move left, move right, suck-up the dirt, or do nothing.

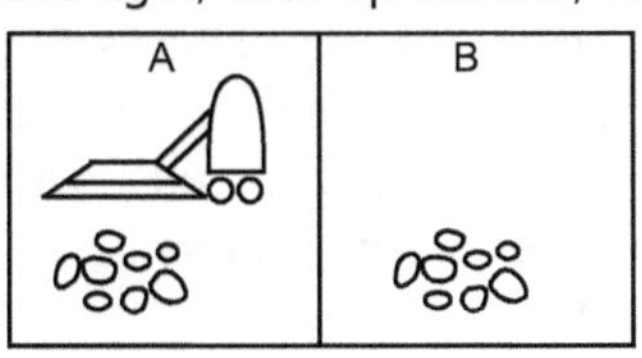

Fig. 2.2

The standard formulation is as follows:

- **States:** The agent is in one of two locations, each of which might or might not contain dirt. Thus there are $2 \times 2^2 = 8$ possible world states.
- **Initial State:** Any state can be designated as the initial state.
- **Successor Function:** This generates the legal states that result from trying the three actions (Left, Right and Suck). The complete state space is shown in Fig. 2.3.
- **Goal Test:** This checks whether all the squares are clean.
- **Path Cost:** Each step costs 1, so the path cost is the number of steps in the path.

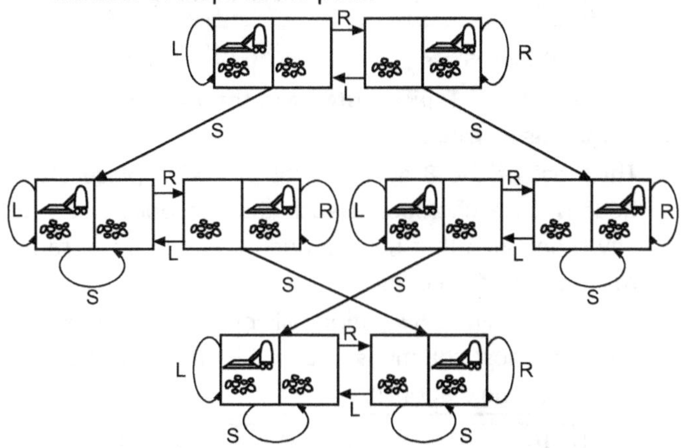

Fig. 2.3 : The State Space for the Vacuum World. Arcs Denote Actions: L = Left, R = Right, S = Suck

- Compared with real world, this toy problem has discrete locations, discrete dirt, reliable cleaning, and it never gets messed up once cleaned.
- State is determined by both the agent location and the dirt locations. A larger environment with n locations has $n2^n$ states.

2. **The 8-Puzzle:**

An instance of 8-puzzle is shown in Fig. 2.4, consists of a 3×3 board with eight numbered tiles and a blank space can slide into the space. The object is to reach a specified goal state as shown in Fig. 2.4.

- **States:** A state description specifies the location of each of the eight tiles and the blank in one of the nine squares.
- **Initial State:** Any state can be designated as the initial state. Note that any given goal can be reached from exactly half of the possible initial states.
- **Successor Function:** This generates the legal states that result from trying the four actions (blank moves to left, right, up or down).
- **Goal Test:** This checks whether the state matches the goal configuration shown in Fig. 2.4.
- **Path Cost:** Each step costs 1, so the path cost is the number of steps in the path.

The actions are abstracted to their beginning and final states, ignoring the intermediate locations where the block is sliding. We have abstructed away actions such as shaking the board when pieces get stuck, or extracting the pieces with a knife and putting them back again.

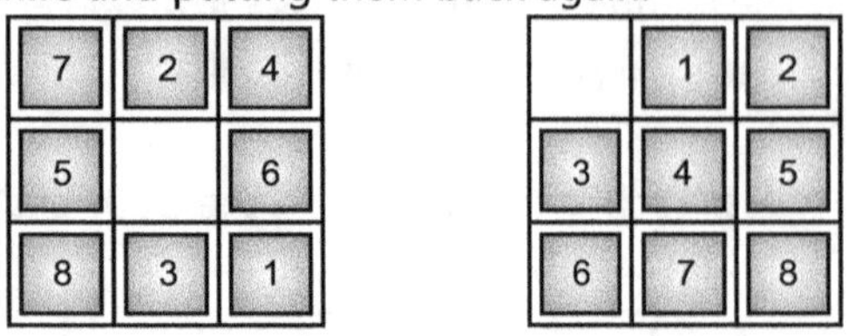

(a) Start State **(b) Goal State**

Fig. 2.4 : A Typical Instance of the 8-Puzzle

3. **8-Queens Problem:**

- The goal of the 8-queens problem is to place eight queens on a chessboard such that no queen attacks any other such that no two queens can place in same row, column or diagonal.
- As shown in Fig. 2.5 solution fails because the queen in the right most column is attacked by the queen at the top left (same diagonal).

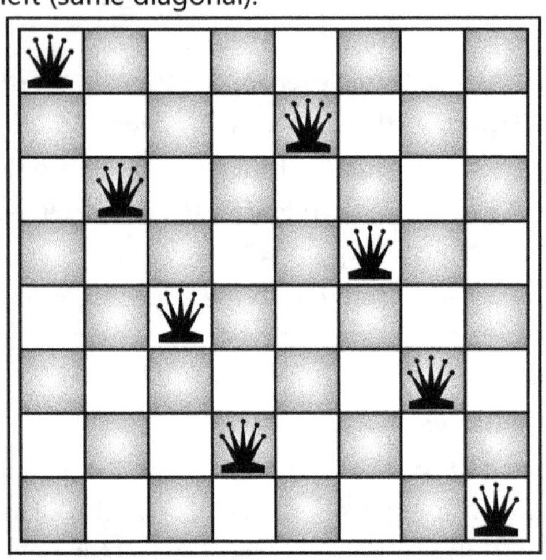

Fig. 2.5 : Almost a Solution to the 8-Queens Problem

This problem can be solved by two ways:

1. **An Incremental Formulation:** This involves operators that argument the state description, starting with an empty state for 8-queens problem, each action adds a queen to the state.
2. **A Complete State Formulation:** This starts with all 8-queens on the board and moves them around.

   In both the cases, the path cost is of no interest because only the final counts.

   8-queens problem can be solved by incremental formulation as follows:

- **States:** Any arrangement of 0 to 8 queens on the board is a state.
- **Initial:** No queens on the board.
- **Successor Function:** Add a queen to any empty square.
- **Goal Test:** 8-queens are on the board, none attacked.

In this formulation, $64 . 63 \ldots 57 \approx 3 \times 10^{14}$ possible sequences to investigate. A better formulation would prohibit placing a queen in any square that is already attacked.

This formulation reduces the 8-queens state space from 3×10^{14} to just 2,057, and solutions are easy to find.

2.3.2 Examples of Real-World Problem

1. **Route-Finding Problem:**

- This problem is defined in terms of specified locations and transitions along links between them. Route-finding algorithms are used in a variety of applications, such as routing in computer networks, and air-line travel planning systems.

Consider an airline travel problem specified as follows:

- **States:** Each is represented by a location (for example, an airport) and the current time.
- **Initial State:** This is specified by the problem.
- **Successor Function:** This returns the states resulting from taking any scheduled flight, leaving later than the current time plus within airport transit time, from the current airport to another.
- **Goal Test:** Are we at the destination by some pre-specified time?
- **Path Cost:** This depends on monetary cost, waiting time, flight time, customs and immigration procedures, seat quality, time of day, type of airplane, frequent-flyer mileage awards, and so on.

2. **The Travelling Salesperson Problem (TSP):**

- TSP is a touring problem in which each city must be visited exactly once. The aim is to find the shortest tour. The problem is known to be NP-hard, but an enormous amount of effort has been expended to improve the capabilities of TSP algorithms. In addition to planning trips for travelling salespersons, these algorithms have been used for task such as planning movements of automatic circuit-board drills and of stocking machines on shop floors.

3. **A VLSI Layout:**

- This problem requires positioning millions of components and connections on a chip to minimize area, minimize circuit delays, minimize stray capacitances and maximize manufacturing yield. The layout problem comes after the logical design phase, and it split into two parts:

  (i) Cell layout. (ii) Channel routing.

(i) Cell Layout: In cell layout, the primitive components of the circuit are grouped into cells, each of which performs some recognized functions.

Each cell has a fixed footprint (size and shape) and requires a certain number of connections to each of the other cells.

The aim is to place cells on the chip so that they do not overlap and so that there is room for the connecting wires to be placed between the cells.

(ii) Channel Routing: Channel routing finds a specific route for each wire through the gaps between the cells.

2.4 SEARCHING FOR SOLUTIONS

- Some problems are already formulated, now need to solve them. This is done by search through the state space. Search techniques uses an explicit search tree that is generated by the initial state and the successor function that together define the state space. When one state can be reached from multiple paths then that search tree is graph.
- Fig. 2.6 shows some of the expansions in the search tree for finding a route from Arad and Bucharest.
- The root of the search tree is a search node corresponding to the initial state, In (Arad).
- The first step is to test whether this is a goal state, if this is not a goal state, we need to consider some other states. This is done by expanding the current state that is applying the successor function to the current state, that generates a new set of states.

In this example, we get three new states:

1. In (Sibiu) 2. In (Timisoara) 3. In (Zerind)

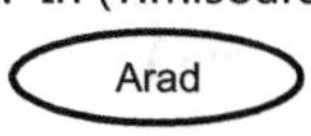

(a) The initial state

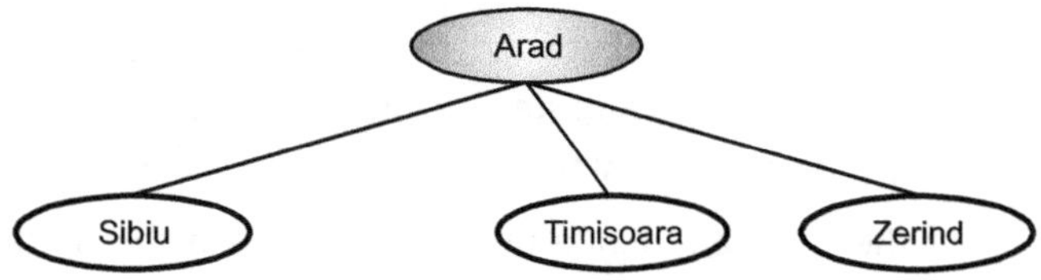

(b) After expanding Arad

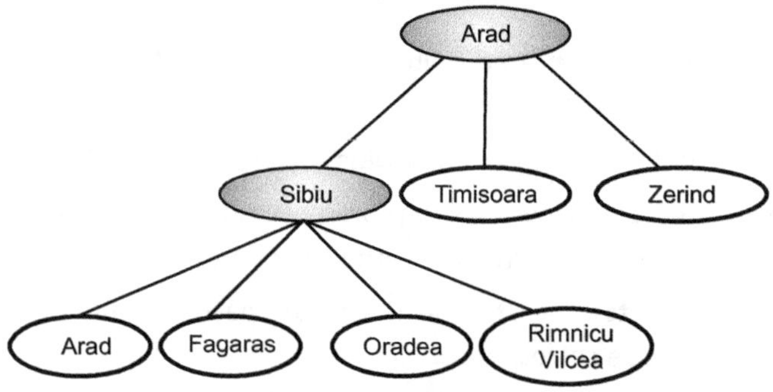

(c) After expanding Sibiu

Fig. 2.6 : Partial search trees for finding a route from Arad to Bucharest. Nodes that have been expanded are shaded; nodes that have been generated by not yet expanded are outlined in bold; nodes that have not yet been generated are shown in faint dashed lines.

- Now we must choose one option and putting the others aside for later. In this case, the first choice does not lead to a solution. Suppose we choose Sibiu first, we check whether it is a goal state, if not then expand the state to get.
- In (Arad), In (Fagaras), In (Oradea) and In (Rimnicu Vilcea).
- Now we can choose any of these four or go back and choose Timisoara or Zerind.
- We continue choosing, testing and expanding until either a solution is found or there are no more states to be expanded.
- The choice of which state to expand is determined by the search strategy. The general tree-search algorithm is shown in Program 2.2.

Program 2.2 : An Informal Description of the General Tree-Search Algorithm

```
function TREE-SEARCH (problem, strategy) returns a solution, or failure
    initialize the search tree using the initial state of problem
        loop do
        if there are no candidates for expansion then return failure
        choose a leaf node for expansion according to the strategy
        if the node contains a goal state then return the corresponding solution
        else expand the node and add the resulting nodes to the search tree
```

- There is difference between the state space and the search tree. For the route finding problem, there are only 20 states in the state space, one for each city.
- But there are an infinite number of paths in this state space, so the search tree has an infinite number of nodes.

  For Example: Arad - Sibiu, Arad - Sibiu - Arad, Arad - Sibiu - Arad - Sibiu.
- Good search algorithm avoids such repeated paths.
- There are many ways to represent nodes, we defined a node is a data structure with five components.
  1. **State:** The state in the state space to which the node corresponds.
  2. **Parent-Node:** The node in the search tree that generated this node.
  3. **Action:** The action that was applied to the parent to generate the node.
  4. **PAT-Cost:** The cost, traditionally denoted by g(n), of the path from the initial state to the node, as indicated by the parent pointers, and
  5. **Depth:** The number of steps along the path from the initial state.

Difference between Nodes and States:

Node:

- A node is a book-keeping data structure used to represent the search tree.
- Nodes are on the particular paths, as defined by PARENT-NODE pointers.
- Two different nodes can contain the same world state, if that state is generated via two different search paths.
- The node data structure is shown in Fig. 2.7.

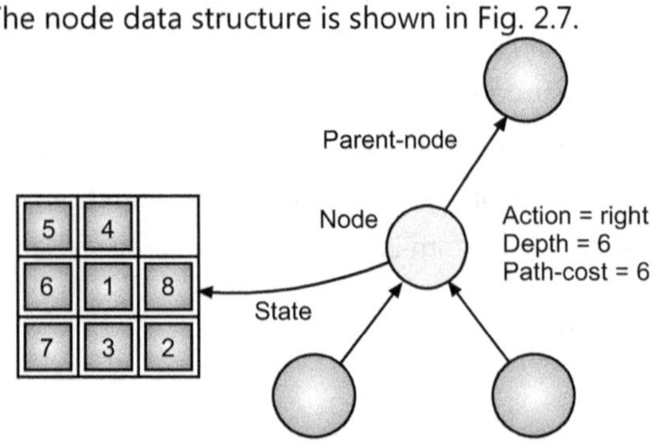

Fig. 2.7 : Nodes are the Data Structures from which the Search Tree is Constructed. Each has a Parent, a State and Various Book-keeping Fields. Arrows Point from Child to Parent

State:

- A state corresponds to a configuration of the world.
- States are not on particular paths.
- The nodes that have been generated by not yet expanded. The collection of these nodes is called as a **fringe**.
- Each element of the fringe is a leaf node in the tree.
- Fig. 2.6 shows the fringe of each tree consists of those nodes with bold ovales. The simplest representation of the fringe would be a set of nodes.
- The search strategy then would be a function that selects the next node to be expanded from this set.
- Selecting the next node to be expanded is computationally expensive, because the strategy function have to look at every element of the set to choose the best one.

Therefore, the collection of fringe nodes is implemented as a queue. The operations on a queue are as follows:

- **MAKE-QUEUE (element, ...):**

  Creates a queue with the given element(s).
- **EMPTY? (queue):**

  Returns true only if there are no more elements in the queue.
- **FIRST (queue):**

  Returns the first element of the queue.
- **Remove-First (queue):**

  Returns FIRST (queue) and removes it from the queue.
- **INSERT (element, queue):**

  Inserts an element into the queue and returns the resulting queue.
- **INSERT-ALL (elements, queue):**

  Insert a set of elements into the queue and returns the resulting queue.

With these definitions, we can write the general tree-search algorithm shown in Program 2.3.

Program 2.3 : The general tree-search algorithm. (Note that the fringe argument must be an empty queue, and the type of the queue will affect the order of the search). The SOLUTION function returns the sequence of actions obtained by the following parent pointers back to the root

```
function TREE-SEARCH (problem, fringe) returns a solution, or failure
    fringe ← INSERT (MAKE-NODE(INITIAL-STATE[problem]), fringe)
    loop do
        if EMPTY? (fringe) then return failure
        node ← REMOVE-FIRST (fringe)
        if GOAL-TEST [problem] applied to STATE [node] succeeds
            then return SOLUTION (node)
        fringe ← INSERT-ALL (EXPAND (node, problem), fringe)
```

```
function EXPAND (node, problem) returns a set of nodes
    successors ← the empty set
    for each (action, result) in SUCCESSOR-FN [problem] (STATE [node]) do
        s ← a new NODE
        STATE[s] ← result
        PARENT-NODE[s] ← node
        ACTION[s] ← action
        PATH-COST[s] ← PATH-COST[node] + STEP-COST (node, action, s)
        DEPTH[s] ← DEPTH [node] + 1
        add s to successors
    return successors
```

Measuring Problem - Solving Performance:

- The output of a problem-solving algorithm is either failure or a solution. The performance of an algorithm can evaluated in four ways:
  1. **Completeness:** Is the algorithm guaranteed to find a solution when there is one?
  2. **Optimality:** Does the strategy find the optimal solution?
  3. **Time Complexities:** How long does it take to find a solution?
  4. **Space Complexity:** How much memory is needed to perform the search.
- Time and space complexities are always considered with respect to some measure of the problem difficulty.
- The graph is represented implicitly by the initial state successor function and is frequently infinite, space complexity is expressed in terms of three quantities:
  1. The branching factor 'b' or maximum number of successors of any node.
  2. The depth 'd' of the shallowest goal node.
  3. The maximum length 'm' of any path in the state space.
- Time complexity is often measured in terms of number of nodes generated during the search.

2.5 UNINFORMED SEARCH STRATEGIES

- The uninformed search strategies are also called as blind search.
- This search have no additional information about the states beyond that provided in the problem definition. It generates successors and distinguish a goal state from a non-goal state.

2.5.1 Breadth-First Search

- Breadth-first search is a simple strategy in which the root node is expanded first, then all the successors of the root node are expanded next, then their successors and so on. That is all the nodes at a given depth are expanded before expanding any node at the next level, as shown in Fig. 2.8.

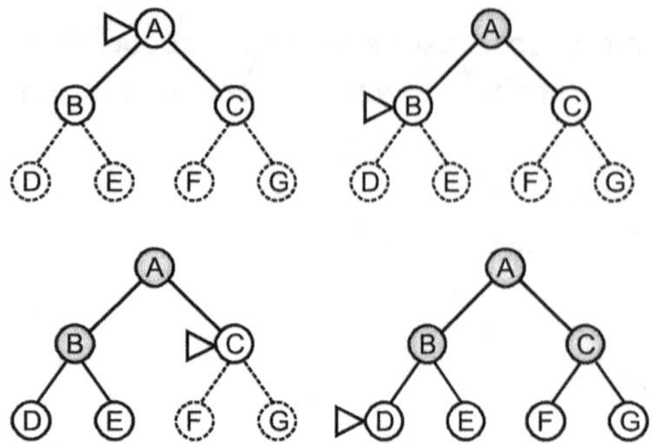

Fig. 2.8 : Breadth-First Search on a Simple Binary Tree. At Each Stage, the Node to be Expanded Next is Indicated by a Marker

- Breadth-first search gives the complete solution, if the shallowest goal node is at some finite depth 'd', after expanding all shallower nodes.
- Breadth-first search gives optimal result if the path cost is a non-decreasing function of the depth of the node, i.e. when all actions have same cost.
- Consider a hypothetical state space where every state has 'b' successors.
  - ➢ The root of the search tree generates b nodes at the first level.
  - ➢ Each children i.e. successors of root node generates 'b' more nodes, so total nodes at the second level is b^2.
  - ➢ Each of these generates b more nodes, yielding b^3 nodes at the third level and so on.
- Now, suppose that the solution is at depth d. In worst case, we would expand all nodes except last node at level 'd' (since last node is goal and is not expanded), generates $b^{d+1} - b$ nodes at level d + 1. Then the total number of nodes generated is

$$b + b^2 + b^3 + \ldots + b^d + (b^{d+1} - b) = 0(b^{d+1})$$

- Every nodes that generated must remain in memory, because it is either part of the fringe or is an ancestor of a fringe node.
- The space complexity is, therefore, the same as the time complexity (plus one node for the root).
- As we have seen time complexity is exponential. Complexity search problems cannot be solved by uninformed methods. It is better for small state space.

2.5.2 Uninform-Cost Search

- Bread-first search is optimal when all step costs are equal, because it always expands the shallowest unexpanded node.
- Uniform-cost search is optimal with any step cost function. Instead of expanding the shallowest node, uniform-cost search expands the node n with the lowest path cost. If all step costs are equal, this search algorithm is identical to breadth-first search.
- Uniform-cost search does not care about the number of step, a path has, but only about their total cost.
- It will get stuck in an infinite loop if it ever expands a node that has a zero-cost leading back to the same state.
- Optimality is ensured, if the cost of every step is greater than or equal to some small positive constant $\in$.
- Uniform-cost search is guided by path costs rather than depths, so its complexity cannot easily be characterized in terms of 'b' and 'd'.
- Let C* be the cost of the optimal solution, assume that every action costs at least ε.
- Then algorithm's worst-case time and space complexity is $0\ (b^{\lceil C^*/\in \rceil})$, which can be much greater than b^d.

2.5.3 Depth-First Search

- Depth-first search always expands the deepest node in the current fringe of the search tree. The progress of the search is illustrated in Fig. 2.9. The search proceeds immediately to the deepest level of the search tree, where the nodes have no successors. As those nodes are expanded, they are dropped from the fringe, so then search "backs up" to the next shallowest node that still has unexplored successors.
- This strategy can be implemented by TREE-SEARCH with a last-in-first-out (LIFO) known as a stack. Program 2.4 shows DFS algorithm. (A recursive depth-first algorithm incorporating a depth limit).

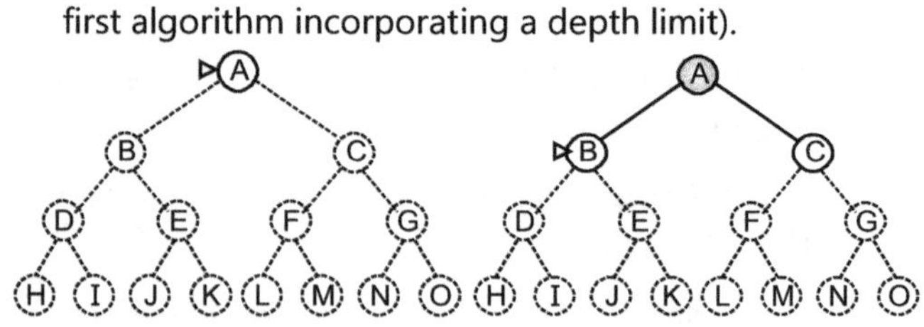

(a)

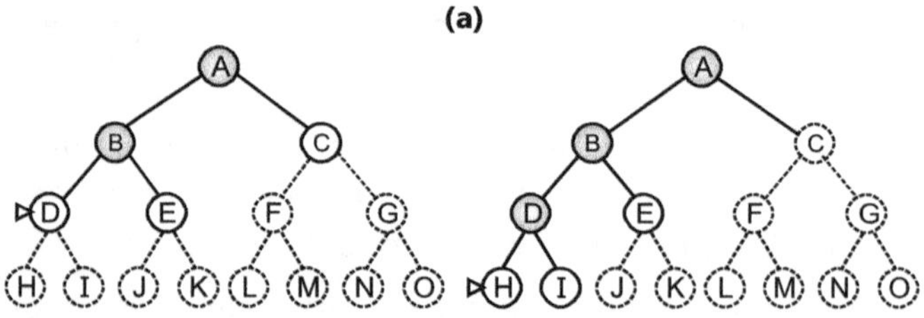

(b)

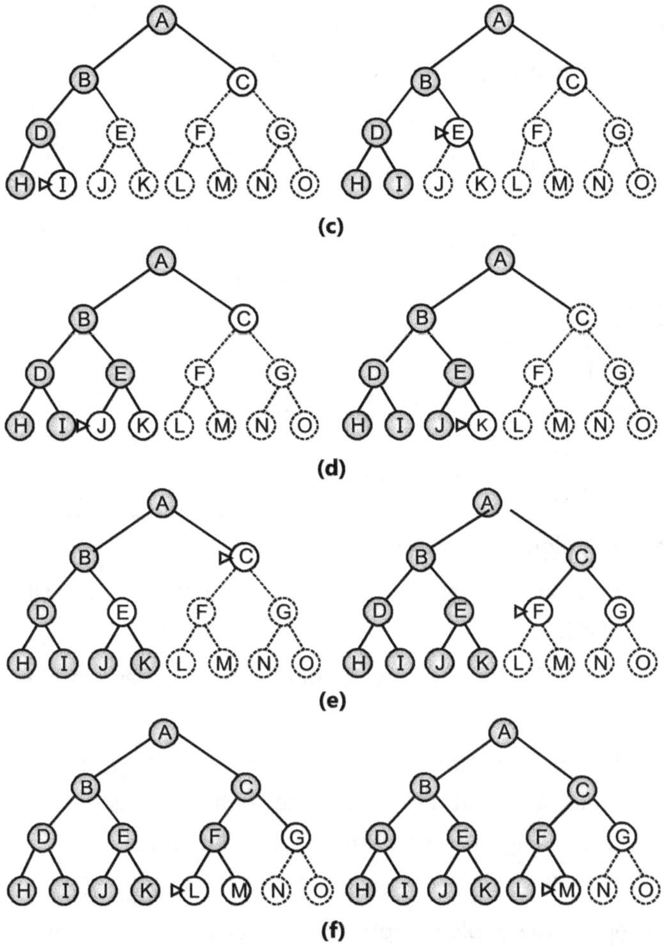

Fig. 2.9 : Depth-first search on a binary tree. Nodes that have been expanded and have no descendants in the fringe can be removed from memory; these are shown in black. Nodes at depth 3 are assumed to have no successors and M is the only goal node

- Depth-first search has very modest memory requirements.
- It needs to store only a single node on the path.
- Once a node has been expanded, it can be removed from memory as soon as all its descendants have been fully explored, as shown in Fig. 2.9.
- For a state space with branching factor 'b' and maximum depth 'm', depth-first search requires storage of only bm + 1 nodes.
- A variant of depth-first search called backtracking search uses still less memory. In backtracking only one successor is generated at a time rather than all successors.
- Each partially expanded node remembers which successor to generate next.
- In this way, only 0(m) memory is needed rather than 0(bm).

Drawbacks:

- The DFS can make a wrong choice and get stuck going down a very long (or even infinite) path when a different choice would lead to a solution near the root of the search tree.

  For example, in Fig. 2.9, DFS will explore the entire left subtree even if node C is a goal node. Hence, DFS search is not optimal.
- If the left subtree were of unbounded depth contain no solutions, DFS would never terminate. Hence, it is not complete.
- In the worst case, DFS will generates all the $0(b^m)$ nodes in the search tree, where m is the maximum depth of any node.
- If tree is unbounded m can be much larger than d (the depth of the shallowest solution) and is infinite.

2.5.4 Depth-Limited Search

- The problem of unbounded tree can be alleviated by supplying depth-first search with a predetermined depth limit *l*. That is, nodes at depth *l* are treated as if they have no successors. This approach is called depth-limited search.
- The depth limit solves the infinite-path problem.

Drawbacks:

- This method introduces an additional source of incompleteness if we choose $l < d$, that is, the shallowest goal is beyond the depth limit.
- Depth-limited search will also be non-optimal, if we choose $l > d$.
- Time complexity of depth-limited search is $0(b^l)$.
- Space complexity is $0(bl)$.
- DFS can be viewed as a special case depth-limited search with $l = \infty$.
- Depth-limited search can be implemented as a simple modification to the general tree-search algorithm or to the recursive DFS algorithm.
- Program 2.4 shows the pseudocode for recursive depth-limited search.
- Depth-limited search can terminate with two kinds of failure:
  1. The standard failure value indicates no solution.
  2. The cut-off value indicates no solution within the depth limit.

Program 2.4 : A recursive implementation of depth-limited search

```
function DEPTH-LIMITED-SEARCH (problem, limit) returns a solution, or failure/cut-off
    return RECURSIVE-DLS(MAKE-NODE(INITIAL-STATE[problem]), problem, limit)
function RECURSIVE-DLS (node, problem, limit) returns a solution, or failure/cut-off
    cut-off-occurred? ← false
    if GOAL-TEST[problem] (STATE[node]) then return SOLUTION(node)
    else if DEPTH[node] = limit then return cut-off
    else for each successor in EXPAND (node, problem) do
        result ← RECURSIVE-DLS (successor, problem, limit)
        if result = cut-off then cut-off occurred ? ← true
        else if result ≠ failure then return result
    if cut-off-occurred? then return cut-off else return failure
```

2.5.5 Iterative Deepening Depth-First Search

- Iterative deepening search (or iterative deepening depth-first search) is a strategy, often used in combination with depth-first search, that finds the best depth limit.
- It does this by gradually increasing the limit first 0, then 1, then 2 and so on until a goal is found.
- The goal is found when the depth limit reaches d, the depth of the shallowest goal node.
- The algorithm is shown in Program 2.5.
- Iterative deepening combines the benefits and DFS and BFS.
- Like DFS, its memory requirements are very modest 0(bd).
- Like BFS, it is complete when the branching factor is finite and optimal when the path cost is a non-decreasing function of the depth of the node.

Program 2.5 : The iterative deepening search algorithm, which repeatedly applies depth limited search with increasing limits. It terminates when a solution is found or if the depth limited search returns failure, meaning that no solution exists

```
function ITERATIVE-DEEPENING-SEARCH (problem) returns a solution or failure
    inputs: problem, a problem
    for depth ← 0 to ∞ do
        result ← DEPTH-LIMITED-SEARCH (problem, depth)
        if result ≠ cut-off then return result
```

- Fig. 2.10 shows four iterations of iterative deepening search on a binary search tree, where the solution s found on the fourth iteration.

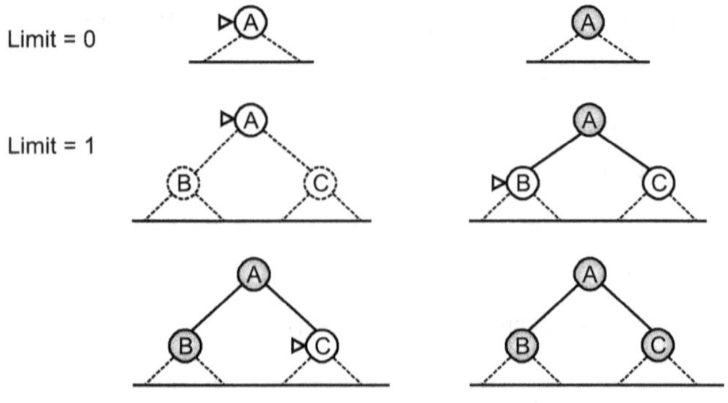

(a)

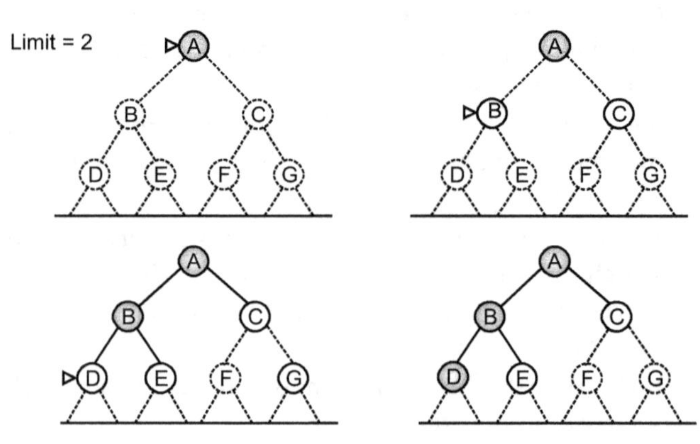

(b)

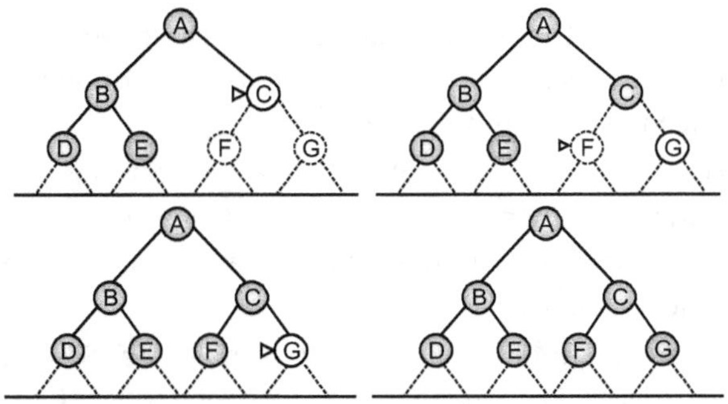

(c)

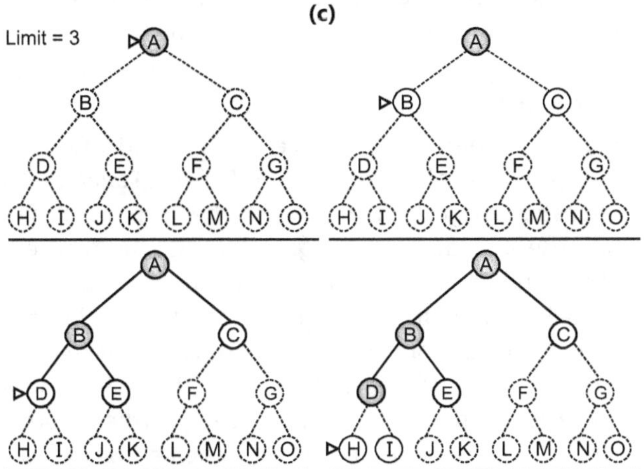

(d)

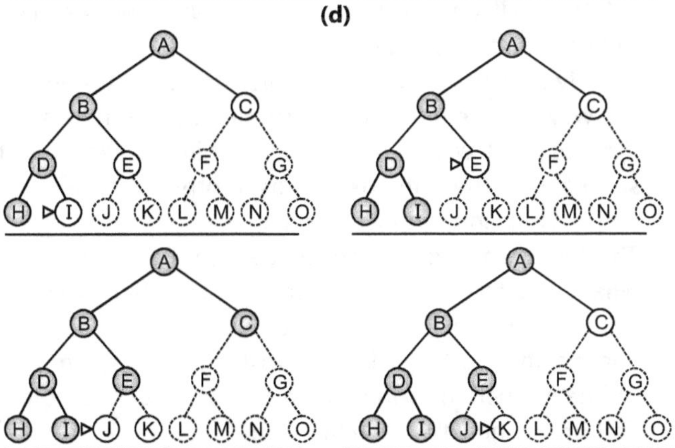

(e)

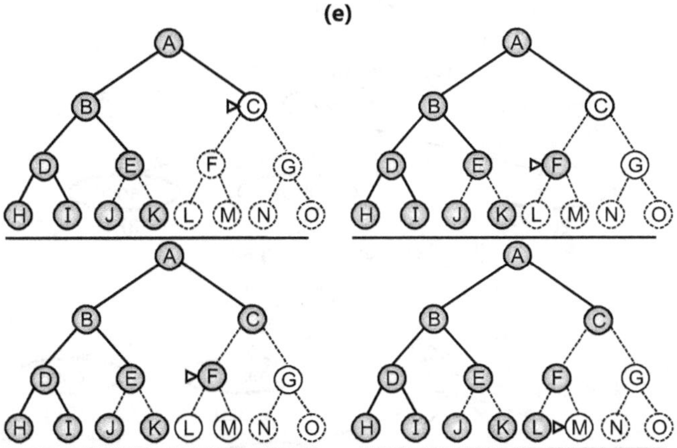

(f)

Fig. 2.10 : Four Iterations of Iterative Deepening Search on a Binary Tree

2.5.6 Bidirectional Search

The idea behind bidirectional search is to run two simultaneous searches:

1. forward from the initial state and
2. backward from the goal state.

- Stopping when the two searches meet in the middle, shown in Fig. 2.11.

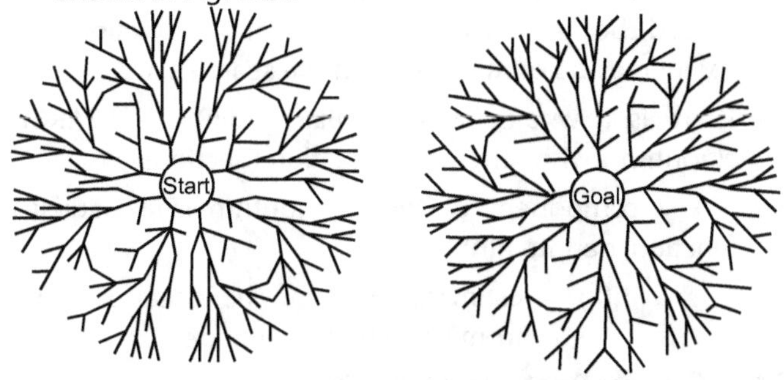

Fig. 2.11 : A Schematic View of a Bidirectional Search that is About to Succeed, when a Branch from the Start Node Meets a Branch From the Goal Node

- The motivation is that $b^{d/2} + b^{d/2}$ is much less than b^d, or in the Table 2.1 the area of the two small circles is less than the area of one big circle centered on the start and reaching to the goal.

Comparison of all uninformed search strategies.

Table 2.1 : Evaluation of Search Strategies, b is the Branching Factor; d is the Depth of the Shallowest Solution; m is the Maximum Depth of the Search Tree; *l* is the Depth Limit. Superscript Caveats are as Follows: [a]complete if b is Infinite, [b]complete if Step Costs ≥ ∈ for Positive ∈; [c]optimal if Step Costs are all Identical, [d]if Both Directions use Breadth-First Search

Criterion	Breadth-First	Uniform-Cost	Depth-First	Depth-Limited	Iterative Deepening	Bidirectional (If Applicable)
Complete?	Yes[a]	Yes[a, b]	No	No	Yes[a]	Yes[a, d]
Time	$O(b^{d+1})$	$O(b^{\lceil C^*/\epsilon \rceil})$	$O(b^m)$	$O(b^l)$	$O(b^d)$	$O(b^{b/2})$
Space	$O(b^{d+1})$	$O(b^{\lceil C^*/\epsilon \rceil})$	O(bm)	O(bl)	O(bd)	$O(b^{b/2})$
Optimal	Yec[c]	Yes	No	No	Yes[c]	Yes[c, d]

2.6 INFORMED (HEURISTIC) SEARCH STRATEGIES

- Informed search strategy uses problem. Specific knowledge beyond the definition of the problem itself can find solutions more efficiently than an uninformed strategy.

2.6.1 Best-First Search

- Best-first search is an instance of the general TREE - SEARCH or GRAPH - SEARCH algorithm in which a node is selected for expansion based on an evaluation function f(n). The node with the lowest evaluation is selected for expansion, because the evaluation measures distance to the goal.

- Best-first search can be implemented within general search framework via a priority queue. A priority queue is a data structure that will maintain the fringe in ascending order of f-values.
- The Best-first search choose the node that appears to be best according to the evaluation function. If the evaluation function is exactly accurate, then this will indeed be the best node. Evaluation function will sometimes be off and can lead the search astray.
- There is a whole family of BEST - FIRST - SEARCH algorithms with different evaluation functions.
- A key component of these algorithm is a heuristic function, denote h(n).

h(n) = Estimated cost of the cheapest path from node n to goal node

2.6.2 Greedy Best-First Search

- Greedy best-first search tries to expand the node that is closest to the goal, on the grounds that is likely to lead to a solution quickly.

  Thus, it evaluates nodes by using just the heuristic function:

  f(n) = h(n)
- Working of Greedy best-first search for route-finding problem in Romania, using the straight-line distance heuristic function : h_{SLD}.
- If the goal is Bucharest, we will need to know the straight-line distances to Bucharest, shown in Table 2.2.

For Example: h_{SLD} (In (Arad)) = 366, the values of h_{SLD} can not be computed from the problem description itself. Moreover, it takes a certain amount of experience to know that h_{SLD} is correlated with actual road distances and is therefore, a useful heuristic.

Table 2.2 : Values of h_{SLD} - Straight Line Distance to Bucharest

Arad	366	Mehadia	241
Bucharest	0	Neamt	234
Craiova	160	Oradea	380
Dobreta	242	Pitesti	100
Eforie	161	Rimnicu Vilcea	193
Fagaras	176	Sibiu	253
Glurgiu	77	Timi soara	329
Hirsova	151	Urziceni	80
Iasi	226	Vaslui	199
Lugoj	244	Zerind	374

- Table 2.2 shows the progress of a greedy best first search using h_{SLD} to find a path from Arad to Bucharest.
- The first node to be expanded from Arad will Sibiu, because it is closer to Bucharest than either Zerind or Timisora. The next node to be expanded will be Fagaras, because it is closest Fagaras in turn generates Bucharest, which is the goal.
- For this particular problem, greedy best-first search using h_{SLD} finds a solution without ever expanding a node that is not on the solution path, hence its search cost is minimal.
- It is not optimal, however the path via Sibiu and Fagaras to Bucharest is 32 kilometres longer than the path through Rimnicu Vilcea and Pitesti. This shows why the algorithm is called "greedy" - at each step it tries to get as close to goal as it can.
- Minimizing h(n) is susceptible to false starts. Consider the problem of getting from Iasi to Fagaras. The heuristic suggests that Neamt be expanded first, because it is closest to Fagaras, but it is a dead end. The solution is to go first to Vaslui, a step that is actually farther from the goal according to heuristic and then to continue to Urziceni, Bucharest and Fagaras. In this case, then, the heuristic causes unnecessary nodes to be expanded. Further more, if we are not careful to detect repeated states, the solution will be never found the search will oscillate between Neamt and Iasi.
- Greedy best-first search resembles depth-first search in the way it prefers to follow a single path all the way to the goal, but will back up when it hits a dead end. It suffers from the same defects as depth-first search it is not optimal and it is incomplete.
- The worst-case time and space complexity is $0(b^m)$, where m is the maximum depth of the search space.
- With a good heuristic function, however, the complexity can be reduced substantially. The amount of the reduction depends on the particular problem and on the quality of the heuristic.

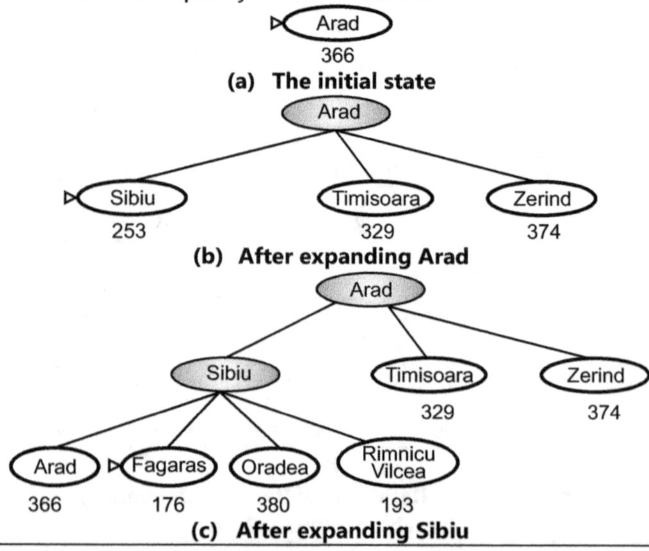

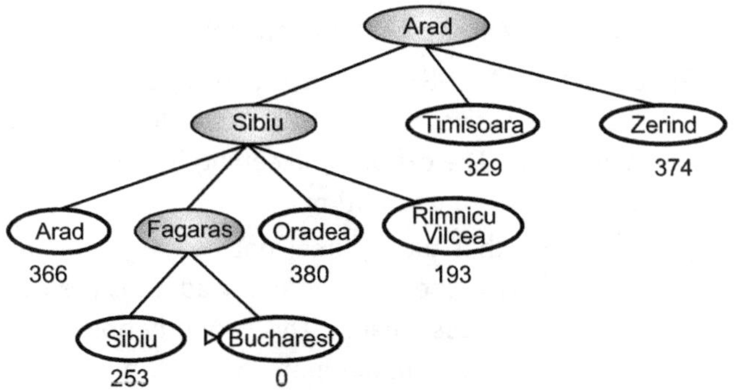

(d) After expanding Fagaras

Fig. 2.12 : Stages in a Greedy Best-first Search for Bucharest Using the Straight-line Distance Heuristic h_{SLD}. Nodes are labelled with their h-values

2.6.3 A* Search: Minimizing the Total Estimated Solution Cost

The most widely known form of the best-first search is called A* search. It evaluates nodes by combining g(n), the cost to reach the node and h(n), the cost to get from node to goal

$$f(n) = g(n) + h(n)$$

Since, g(n) – gives the path cost from the start node to node n

h(n) – is the estimated cost of the cheapest path from n to the goal

We have, f(n) – estimated cost of the cheapest solution through n

Thus, if we are trying to find the cheapest solution, a reasonable thing to try first is the node with the lowest value of g(n) + f(n).

Thus, this strategy is more than just reasonable provided that the heuristic function h(n) satisfies certain conditions. A* search is both complete and optimal.

Conditions for Optimality, Admissibility and Consistency

The optimality of A* is admissibility and consistency straight forward to analyze;

1. if it used with TREE-SEARCH algorithm, A* is optimal if h(n) holds property of admissibility,
2. if use the GRAPH-SEARCH algorithm, A* is optimal if h(n) holds property of consistency.

1. A* is Optimal if h(n) is an Admissible Heuristic:

- This means h(n) never overestimates the cost to reach the goal. Admissible heuristics are by nature optimistic, because they think the cost of solving the problem is less than it actually is. Since g(n) is the exact cost to reach n, we have as immediate consequence that f(n) never overestimates the true cost of solution through n.
- Example of an admissible heuristic is the straight-line distance h_{SLD} that used in getting the Bucharest. Straight-line distance is admissible because the shortest path between any two points is straight line, so the straight line cannot be an overestimate. Fig. 2.13 shows the progress of an A* tree search B for Bucharest. The values of g are computed from the step costs in and the values of h_{SLD} are given in Table 2.2.
- Bucharest first appears on the fringe at step (e), but it is not selected for expansion because its f-cost (450) is higher than that of Pitesti (417) that means there might be a solution through Pitesti whose cost is as low as 417, so the algorithm, will not settle for a solution that costs 450.
- From this example, we can extract a general proof, that A* using TREE-SEARCH is optimal if h(n) is admissible.
- Suppose a suboptimal goal node G2 appears on the fringe and let the cost of the optimal solution be C*. Then, because G2 is suboptimal and because h(G2) = 0

$$f(G2) = g(G2) + h(G2) = g(G2) > C^*$$

- Now consider a fringe node n that is on an optimal solution path. If h(n) does not overestimate the cost of completing the solution path, then

$$f(n) = g(n) + h(n) \leq C^*$$

$f(n) \leq C^* < f(G2)$, so G2 will not be expanded and A* must return an optimal solution.

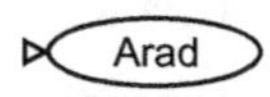

(a) The initial state

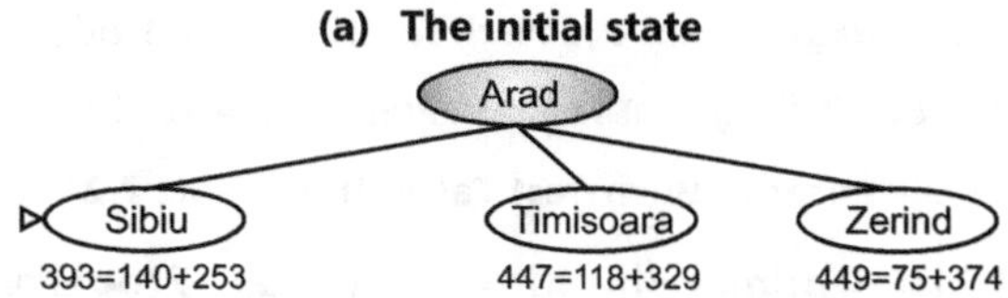

(b) After expanding Arad

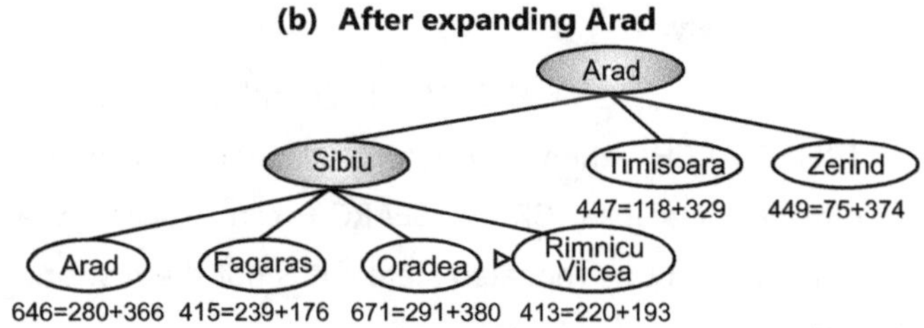

(c) After expanding Sibiu

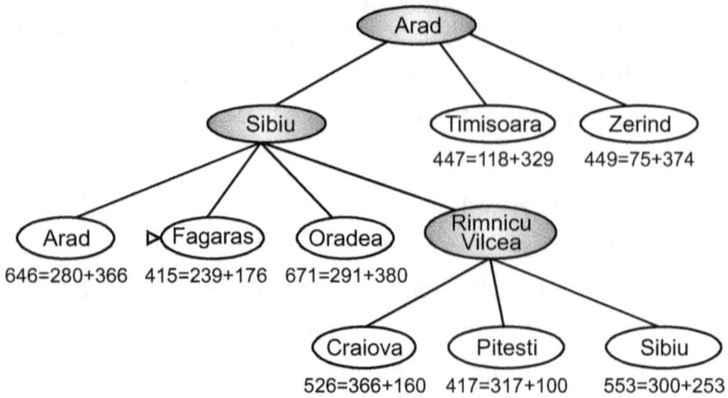

(d) After expanding Rimnicu Vilcea

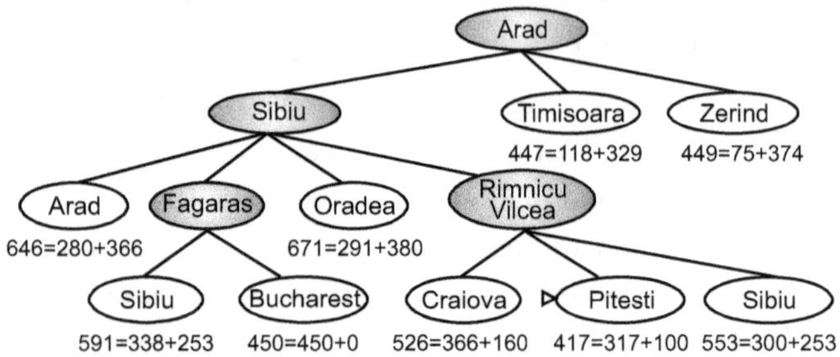

(e) After expanding Fagaras

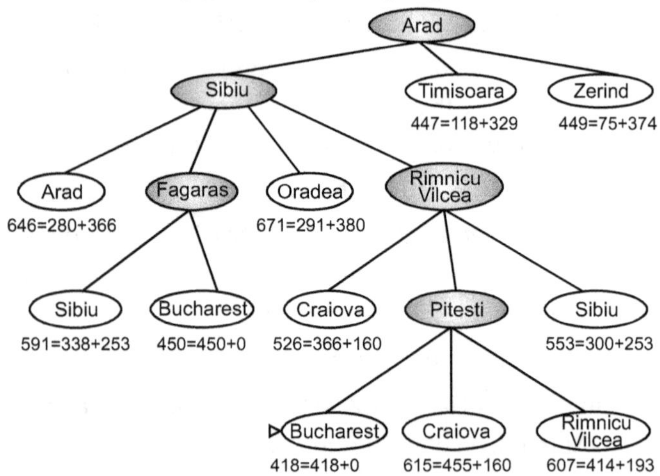

(f) After expanding Pitesti

Fig. 2.13: Stages in an A* Search for Bucharest. Nodes are Labelled with f = g + h. The h Values are the Straight-line Distances to Bucharest Taken from Table 2.2

2. A* is Optimal if h(n) is Holds Property of Consistency:

- If we use the GRAPH-SEARCH algorithm instead of TREE-SEARCH, then suboptimal solutions can be returned because GRAPH-SEARCH can discard the optimal path to a repeated state if it is not the first one generated.
- There are two ways to fix this problem:
  - **(i)** Extend GRAPH-SEARCH so that it discards the more expensive of any two paths found to the same node. The extra bookkeeping is messy, but it does not guarantee optimality.
  - **(ii)** To ensure that the optimal path to any repeated state is always the first one followed, as is the case with uniform cost search. This property holds if we impose an extra requirement on h(n), namely the requirement of **consistency** also called **monotonicity**.
- A heuristic h(n) is consistent if, for every node n and every successor n' of n generated by any action a, the estimated cost of reaching the goal from n is no greater than the step of cost getting to n' plus the estimated cost of reaching the goal from n'.

$$h(n) \leq C(n, a, n') + h(n')$$

- This is a form of the general triangle inequality, which stipulates that each side of a triangle cannot be longer than the sum of the other two sides. Here, the triangle is formed by n, n' and the goal closest to n.
- It is fairly easy to show that every consistent heuristic is also admissible. The most important consequence of consistency is the following:

  "A* using GRAPH-SEARCH is optimal if h(n) is consistent".
- Although consistency is a stricter requirement than admissibility one has to work quite hard to concoct heuristics that are admissible but not consistent. All the admissible heuristics are also consistent.
- Example, h_{SLD}, the general triangle inequality is satisfied when each side is measured by the straight-line distance and that the straight-line distance between n and n' is not greater than C(n, a, n'). Hence, h_{SLD} is a consistent heuristic.
- Another important consequence of consistency is the following:

  "If h(n) is consistent, then the values of f(n) along any path are non-decreasing".
- The proof follows directly from the definition of consistency. Suppose n' is a successor of n, then g(n') = g(n) + C(n, a, n') for some a, and we have,

$$f(n') = g(n') + h(n') = g(n) + C(n, a, n') + h(n')$$
$$\geq g(n) + h(n) = f(n)$$

- It follows that the sequence of nodes expanded by A* using GRAPH-SEARCH is in non-decreasing order of f(n). Hence, the first goal node selected for expansion must be an optimal solution, since all later nodes will be at least as expensive.

- The fact that f-costs are non-decreasing along any path also means that we can draw contours in the state space, just like the contours in a topographic map.
- Fig. 2.14 shows an example. Inside the contour labelled 400, all nodes have f(n) less than or equal to 400 and so on. Then, because A* expands the fringe node of lowest f-cost, we can see that an A* search fans out from the start node, adding nodes in concentric bands of increasing f-cost.

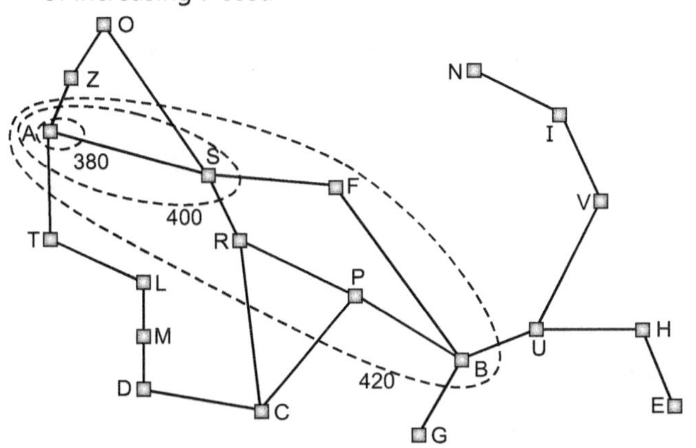

Fig. 2.14: Map of Romania Showing Contours at f = 380, f = 400 and f = 420, with Arad as the Start State. Nodes Inside a given Contour have f-costs less than or Equal to the Contour Value

Optimality of A*

- With uniform-cost search (A* search using h(n) = 0), the bands will be "circular" around the start state. With more accurate heuristics, the bands will stretch toward the goal optimal solution path, then we can say the followings:
  - ➢ A* expands all nodes with f(n) < C*.
  - ➢ A* might then expands some of the nodes right on the "goal contour", where f(n) = C*, before selecting a goal node.
- Intuitively, it is obvious that the first solution found must be an optimal one, because goal nodes in all subsequent contours will have higher f-cost and thus higher g-cost because all goal nodes have h(n) = 0. Intuitively, it is also obvious that A* search is complete.

As we add bands of increasing f, we must eventually reach a band where f is equal to the cost of the path to a goal state.

- A* expands no nodes with f(n) > C*. For example: Timisoara is not expanded in even though it is a child of the root. We say that the subtree below Timisoara is pruned, because h_{SLD} is admissible, the algorithm can safely ignore this subtree while still guaranteeing optimality. The concept of pruning - eliminating possibilities from consideration without having to examine them is important for many areas of AI.
- A* is optimally efficient for any given heuristic function. That is, no other optimal algorithm is guaranteed to expand fewer nodes than A*. This is because any algorithm that does not expand all nodes with f(n) < C* runs the risk of missing the optimal solution. Thus, A* search is complete optimal and optimally efficient among all such algorithms.

2.6.4 Memory-Bounded Heuristic Search

- A* keeps all generated nodes in memory. A* usually runs out of space long before it runs out of time. For this reason, A* is not practical for many large-scale problems.
- The simplest way to reduce memory requirements for A* is to adapt the idea of iterative deepening to the heuristic search context, resulting in the iterative-deepening A*(IDA*) algorithm.
- The main difference between IDA* and standard iterative deepening is that the cutoff used is the f-cost (g + h) rather than the depth. At each iteration, the cutoff value is the smallest f-cost of any node that exceeded the cutoff on the previous iteration.
- IDA* is practical for many problems with unit step costs and avoids the substantial. Overhead associated with keeping a sorted queue of nodes.

There are two more recent memory-bounded algorithms:

1. Recursive best-first search (RBFS).
2. Simplified Memory-bounded A* (SMA*).

1. Recursive Best-First Search (RBFS):

- Recursive best-first search (RBFS) is a simple recursive algorithm that attempts to mimic the operation of standard best-first search, but using linear space. The algorithm is shown in Program 2.6. Its structure is similar to that of a recursive depth-first search, but rather than continuing indefinitely down the current path, it keeps track of f-value of the best alternative path available from any ancestor of the current node. If the current node exceeds this limit, the recursion unwinds back to the alternative path.

- As the recursion unwinds, RBFS replaces the f-value of each node along the path with the best f-value of its children. In this way, RBFS remembers the f-value of the best leaf in the forgotten subtree and can therefore decide whether its worth re-expanding the subtree at some later time. Fig. 2.15 shows how RBFS reaches Bucharest.

Program 2.6 : The Algorithm for Recursive Best-first Search

```
function RECURSIVE-BEST-FIRST-SEARCH(problem) returns a solution, or failure
    RBFS(problem, MAKE-NODE(INITIAL-STATE[problem]), ∞)
function RBFS(problem, node, f_limit) returns a solution, or failure and a new f-cost limit
    if GOAL-TEST[problem](state) then return node
    successors ← EXPAND(node, problem)
    if successors is empty then return failure, ∞
    for each s in successors do
        f[s] ← max(g(s) + h(s), f[node])
    repeat
        best ← the lowest f-value node in successors
        if f[best] > f_limit then return failure, f[best]
        alternative ← the second-lowest f-value among successors
        result, f[best] ← RBFS(problem, best, min(f_limit, alternative))
        if result ≠ failure then return result
```

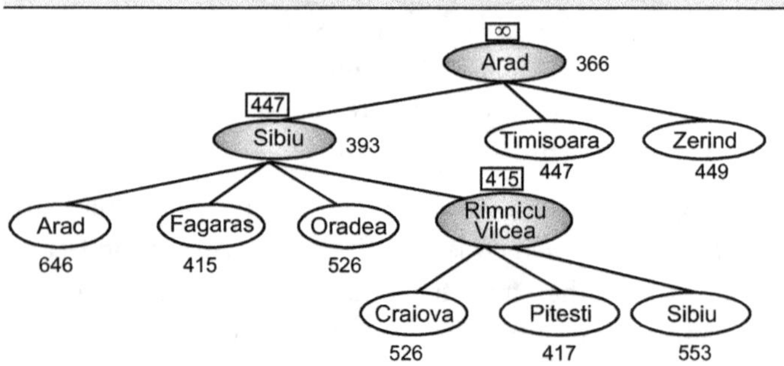

(a) After expanding Arad, Sibiu, and Rimnicu Vilcea

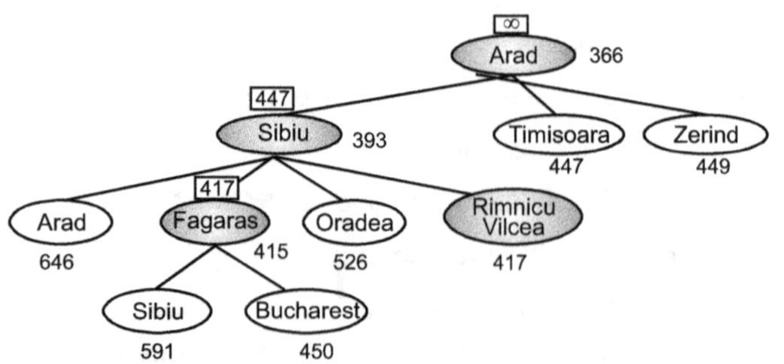

(b) After unwinding back to Sibiu and expanding Fagaras

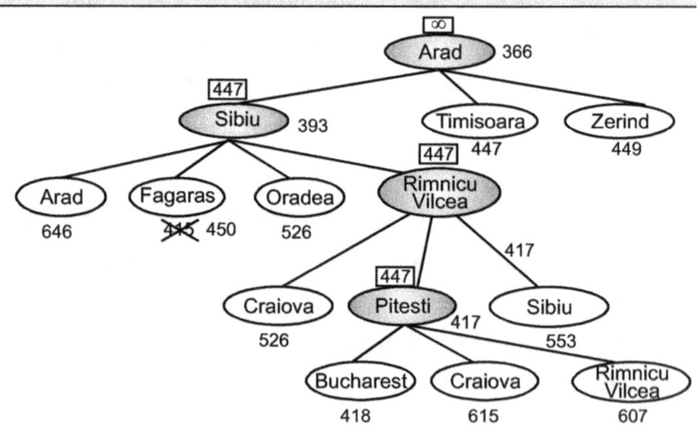

(c) After switching back to Riminicu Vilcea and expanding Pitesti

Fig. 2.15 : Stages in an RBFS for shorter Route to Bulcharest

- RBFS is somewhat more efficient than IDA*, but still suffers from excessive node regeneration. In example in Fig. 2.15, RBFS first follows the path via Rimnicu, Vilcea, then "changes its mind" and tries Fagaras and then changes its mind back again. These mind changes occur because every time the current best path is extended, there is a good chance that its f-value will increase h is usually less optimistic for nodes closer to the goal. When this happens, particularly in large search spaces, the second-best path might become the best path, so the search has to backtrack to follow it. Each mind change corresponds to an iteration of IDA* and could require many re-expansions of forgotten nodes to recreate the best path and extend it one more node.

- Like A*, RBFS is an optimal algorithm if the heuristic function h(n) is admissible. Its space complexity is 0(bd), but its time complexity is rather difficult to characterize, it depends both on the accuracy of the heuristic function and how often the best changes as nodes are expanded.
- Both IDA* and RBFS cannot check for repeated states other than those on the current path, exponentially increases complexity associated with searching on graph. They may explore same state many times.
- IDA* and RBFS suffer from using too little memory. Between iterations, IDA* retains only a single number i.e. the current f-cost limit. RBFS retains more information in memory, but it uses only 0(bd) memory. Even if more memory were available, RBFS has no way to make use of it.

2. Simplified Memory-Bounded A*(SMA*):

- Simplified memory-bounded A* algorithm is a simpler. SMA* proceeds just like A*, expanding the best leaf until memory is full. It cannot add a new node to the search tree without dropping an old one. SMA* always drops the worst leaf node, the one with the highest f-value. Like RBFS, SMA* then backs up the value of the forgotten node to its parent.
- In this way, the ancestor of a forgotten subtree knows the quality of the best path in that subtree. With this information, SMA* regenerates the subtree only when all other paths have been shown to look worse than the path it has forgotten. Another way of saying this is that, if all the descendants of a node n are forgotten, then we will not know which way to go from n, but we will still have an idea of how worthwhile it is to go anywhere from n.
- SMA* expands the best leaf and deletes the worst leaf. What if all the leaf nodes have the same f-values? Then the algorithm might select the same node for deleting and expansion. SMA* solves this problem by expanding the newest best leaf and deleting the oldest worst leaf. These can be a same node only if there is only one leaf. In that case, the current search tree must be a single path from the root to leaf that fills all of memory.
- If leaf is not a goal node then even if it is on an optimal solution path, that solution is not reachable with the available memory. Therefore, the node can be discarded exactly as if it had no successors.
- SMA* is complete if there is any reachable solution, that is, if d, the depth shallowest goal node, is less than the memory size (expressed in nodes). It is optimal if any optimal solution is reachable, otherwise it returns the best reachable solution. In practical terms, SMA* might well be the best general purpose algorithm for finding optimal solutions, particularly when the state space is a graph, step cost are not uniform and node generation is expensive compared to the additional overhead of maintaining the open and closed lists.
- SMA* is forced to switch back and forth continually between a set of candidate solution paths, only a small subset of which can fit in memory. (This resembles the problem of thrashing in disk paging systems). Then the extra time required for repeated regeneration of the same nodes means that problems that would be practically solvable by A*, given unlimited memory, become intractable for SMA*. That is to say, memory limitations can make a problem intractable from the point of view of computation time.

2.7 HEURISTIC FUNCTIONS

- Consider the 8-puzzle as a heuristic search problems. The object of the 8-puzzle is to side the tiles horizontally or vertically into the empty space until the configuration matches the goal configuration as shown in Fig. 2.16.

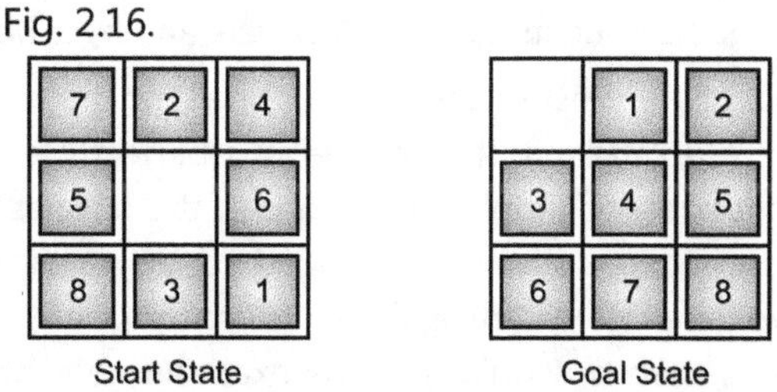

Fig. 2.16: A Typical Instance of the 8-puzzle. The Solution is 26 Steps Long

- The average solution cost for a randomly generated instance is about 22 steps. The branching factor is about 3. (When the tile is in the middle, there are four possible moves, when it is in a corner there are two and when it is along an edge there are three). This means that an exhaustive search to depth 22 would look at about $3^{22} \approx 3.1 \times 10^{10}$ states. By keeping track of repeated states, we would cut this down by a factor of about 170,000 because there are only 9!/2 = 181,440 distinct states that are reachable. This is manageable number, but corresponding number for the 15-puzzle is roughly 10^{13}, so the next order of business is to find a good heuristic function. If we want to find shortest solutions by using A*, we need a heuristic function that never overestimates the number of steps to the goal. Following are two commonly used candidates.

  1. h_1 = the number of misplaced tiles. For, Fig. 2.16, all the eight tiles are out of position, so the start state would have $h_1 = 8$. h_1 is an admissible heuristic, because it is clear that any tile that is out of place must be moved atleast once.
  2. h_2 = the sum of the distance of the tiles from goal positions. Because tiles cannot move along diagonals, the distance we will count is the sum of the horizontal and vertical distances. This is sometimes called the city block distance or Manhattan distance. h_2 is also admissible, because all any move can do is move on tile one step closer to the goal. Tiles 1 to 8 in the start state give a Manhattan distance of

$$h_2 = 3 + 1 + 2 + 2 + 2 + 3 + 3 + 2 = 18$$

  Neither of these overestimates the true solution cost, which is 26.

2.7.1 Generating Admissible Heuristics from Subproblems: Pattern Databases

- h_2 (misplaced tiles) and h_2 (Manhattan distance) are fairly good heuristics for the 8-puzzle and h_2 is better.
- h_1 and h_2 are estimates of the remaining path length for the 8-puzzle, but they are also perfectly accurate path length for simplified versions of the puzzles. If the rules of the puzzle were changed so that a tile could move any where, instead of just to adjacent empty square, then h_1 would give the exact number of steps in the shortest solution. Similarly, if tile could move one square in any direction, even onto an occupied square, then h_2 would give the exact number of steps in the shortest solution. A problem fewer restrictions on the actions is called a relaxed problem. The cost of an optimal solution to a relaxed problem. The heuristic is admissible because the optimal solution in the original problem is, by definition, also a solution in the relaxed problem and therefore must be at least as expensive as the optimal solution in the relaxed problem. Because the derived heuristic is an exact cost for the relaxed problem, it must obey the triangle inequality and is therefore consistent.
- If a problem definition is written down in a formal language, it is possible to construct relaxed problems automatically. For example, if the 8-puzzle actions are described as;

  A title can move from square A to square B if
  A is horizontally or vertically adjacent
  to B and B is blank
- We can generate three relaxed problems by removing one or both of the conditions:
  (a) A tile can move from square A to square B if A is adjacent to B.
  (b) A tile can move from square A to square B if B is blank.
  (c) A tile can move from square A to square B.
- From (a), we can derive h_2 (Manhattan distance). The reasoning is that h_2 would be the proper score if we moved each tile in turn to its destination.
- From (b), we can derive Gaschnig's heuristic, which is the exact solution of this problem.
- From (c), we can derive h_1 (misplaced tiles), because it would be the proper score if tiles could move to their intended destination in one step. It is crucial that the relaxed problems generated by this technique can be solved essentially without search, because the relaxed rules allow the problem to be decomposed into eight independent subproblems. If the relaxed problem is hard to solve, then the values of the corresponding heuristic will be expensive to obtain.
- A program called ABSOLVER can generate heuristics automatically from problem definitions, using the "relaxed problem" method and various other techniques. ABSOLVER generated a new heuristic for the 8-puzzle better than any pre-existing heuristic and found the first useful heuristic for the famous Rubik's cube puzzle.

- One problem with generating new heuristic functions is that one often fails to get one "clearly best" heuristic. If a collection of admissible heuristics $h_1 \dots h_m$ is available for a problem and none of them dominates any of the others, which should we choose? As it turns out, we need not make a choice. We can have the best of all worlds, by defining.

$$h(n) = \max\{h_1(n), \dots, h_m(n)\}.$$

- This composite heuristic uses whichever function is most accurate on the node in question. Because the component heuristics are admissible, h is admissible, it is also easy to prove that h is consistent. Furthermore, h dominates all of its component heuristics.
- Admissible heuristics can also be derived from the solution cost of a subproblem of a given problem. For example, Fig. 2.17 shows a subproblem of the 8-puzzle instance in Fig. 2.18. The subproblem involves getting tiles 1, 2, 3, 4 into their correct positions. Clearly, the cost of the optimal solution of this subproblem is a lower bound on the cost of the complete problem. It turns out to be substantially more accurate than Manhattan distance in some cases.
- The idea behind **pattern databases** is to store these exact solution costs for every possible subproblem instance - "in our example, every possible configuration of the four tiles and the blank. Then we compute an admissible heuristic h_{DB} for each complete state encountered during a search simply by looking up the corresponding subproblem configuration in the database. The database itself is constructed by searching backwards from the goal state and recording the cost of each new pattern encountered, the expense of this search is amortized over many subsequent problem instances.

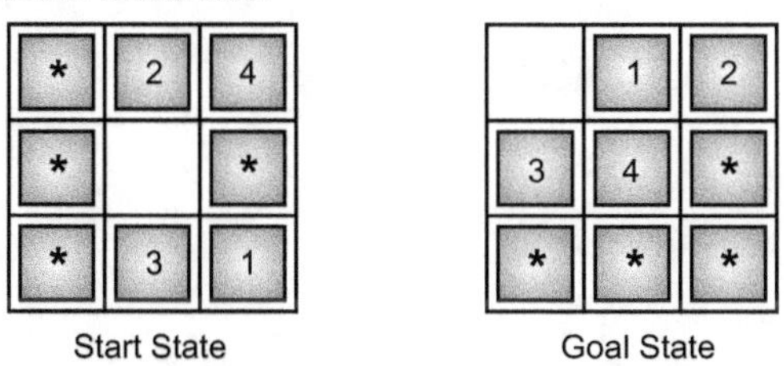

Fig. 2.17 : A Subproblem of the 8-puzzle Instance given in Fig. 2.16. The Task is to Get Tiles, 1, 2, 3 and 4 onto their Correct Positions, without Worrying About what Happens to the Other Tiles

- The choice of 1 – 2 – 3 – 4 is fairly arbitrary, we could also construct databases for 5 – 6 – 7 – 8 and for 2 – 4 – 6 – 8 and so on. Each database yields an admissible heuristic and these heuristics can be combined by taking the maximum value. A combined heuristic of this kind is much more accurate than the Manhattan distance, the number of nodes generated when solving random 15-puzzles can be reduced by a factor of 1000.
- One might wonder whether the heuristics obtained from the 1 – 2 – 3 – 4 database and the 5 – 6 – 7 – 8 could added. Since the two subproblems seem not to overlap. Would this still give an admissible heuristic? The answer is no, because the solutions of the 1 – 2 – 3 – 4 subproblem and the 5 – 6 – 7 – 8 subproblem for a given state will almost certainly share some moves, it is unlikely that 1 – 2 – 3 – 4 can be moved into place without touching 5 – 6 – 7 – 8 and vice-versa. But what if we don't count those moves? That is, we record not the total cost of solving the 1 – 2 – 3 – 4 subproblem, but just the number of moves involving 1 – 2 – 3 – 4. Then it is easy to see that the sum of the two costs is still a lower bound on the cost of solving the entire problem. This is the idea behind disjoint pattern databases. Using such databases, it is possible to solve random 15-puzzles in a few milliseconds - the number of nodes generated is reduced by factor of 10,000 compared with using Manhattan distance. For 24-puzzles, a speedup of roughly a million can be obtained.
- Disjoint pattern databases work for sliding - tile puzzle because the problem can be divided up in such a way that each move affects only one subproblem because only one tile is moved at a time. For a problem such as Rubik's cube, this kind of subdivision cannot be done because each move affects 8 or 9 of the 26 cubies.

2.7.2 Learning Heuristics from Experience

- A heuristic function h(n) is supposed to estimate the cost of a solution beginning from the state at node n. An agent construct such a function by:
  - ➢ Relaxed problems for which an optimal solution can be found easily.
  - ➢ Learn from experience.

- "Experience" here means solving lots of 8-puzzles, for instance. Each optimal solution to an 8-puzzle problem provides examples from which h(n) can be learned. Each example consists of a state from the solution path and the actual cost of the solution from that point. For these examples, an **inductive learning** algorithm can be used to construct a function h(n) and can predict solution costs for other states that arise during search.
- Inductive learning methods work best when supplied with features of a state that are relevant to its evaluation, rather than with just the raw state description. For example, the feature "number of misplaced tiles" might be helpful in predicting the actual distance of a state from the goal. Let's call this feature $x_1(n)$. We could take 100 randomly generated 8-puzzle configurations and gather statistics on their actual solution costs. We might find that when $x_1(n)$ is 5, the average solution cost is around 14, and so on. Given these data, the value of x_1 can be used to predict h(n). Of course, we can use several features. A second feature $x_2(n)$ might be "number of pairs of adjacent tiles that are also adjacent in the goal state". How should $x_1(n)$ and $x_2(n)$ be combined to predict h(n)? A common approach is to use a linear combination:

$$h(n) = c_1x_1(n) + c_2x_2(n)$$

- The constants c_1 and c_2 are adjusted to give the best fit to the actual data on solution costs. Presumably, c_1 should be positive and c_2 should be negative.

EXERCISE

1. What is problem? What are basic elements needed fir solving single-state problem.
2. Explain Breath-first search with example.
3. Explain Depth-first search with example.
4. What is the difference between nodes and states.
5. Explain Informed (Heuristic) search strategies.
6. Define Heuristic functions.
7. Explain problem solving agents.
8. Explain 8-Puzzle problem.

✠ ✠ ✠

CONSTRAINT SATISFACTION PROBLEMS

3.1 DEFINING CONSTRAINTS SATISFACTION PROBLEMS

- CSPs are mathematical problems where one must find states or objects that satisfy a number of constraints or criteria. A constraint restriction of the feasible solutions is an optimization problem.
- A CSP is defined by a set of variables $V_1, V_2, V_3, \ldots V_n$ and a set of constraints $C_1, C_2, C_3, \ldots C_n$.
- Each variable V_i has non-empty domain D_i of possible values. Each constraint C_i involves some subset of the variables.
- The goal test checks that all variables have been assigned and no constraints are violated.

Examples:

1. Sudoku
2. N-Queen Problem
3. Cryptarithmetic Problem
4. Map Colouring Problem.

Example : 4-Queen Problems

Place 4 queens on a 4 × 4 chess board such that no queen can take another.

Assume that one queen in each column.

Variables: Q_i (i is the column)

Domains D_i = (1, 2, 3, 4) (row) constraints

– $Q_i \neq Q_j$ (cannot be in same row).

– $|Q_i - Q_j| \neq |i - j|$ (or same diagonal)

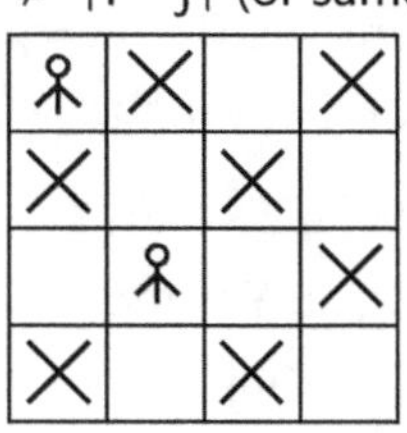

$Q_1 = 1$
$Q_2 = 3$

Fig. 3.1

- Translate each constraint into set of allowable values for its variables.
- For example, values for (Q_1, Q_2) are (1, 3), (1, 4), (2, 4), (3, 1), (4, 1), (4, 2).

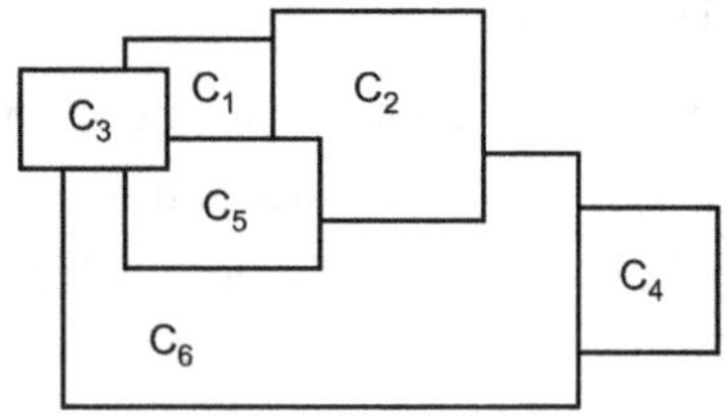

Fig. 3.2

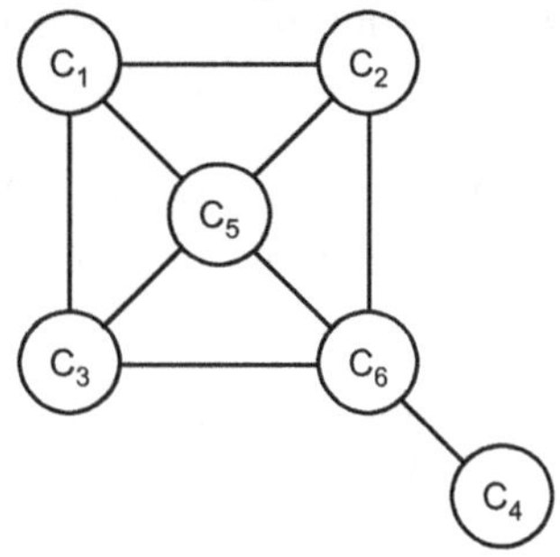

Fig. 3.3

Example: Map Colouring:

Colour a map so that no adjacent countries have the same colour.

Variables: Countries C_i

Domains: {Red, Blue, Green}

Constraints: $C_1 \neq C_2$, $C_1 \neq C_5$ etc.

- In CSP, the goal state satisfies a given set of constraints. CSP problems can be solved by using any of the search strategy. The general form of CSP is as follows.
- Until a complete solution is found or until all paths have led to lead ends do:
  1. Select an unexpected node of the search graph.
  2. Apply the constraint interface rules to the selected node to generate all possible new constraints.
  3. If the set of constraints contains a contradiction, then that path is a dead end.
  4. If the set of constraints describe a complete solution then it is a success.
  5. It neither a constraint nor a solution has been found then apply the rules to generate new partial solutions. Insert these partial solutions into the search graph.

3.2 CONSTRAINT PROPAGATION: INFERENCE IN CSPs

- In regular state space search, an algorithm can do only one thing i.e. search.
- In CSPs there is a choice, an algorithm can search (choose a new variable assignment from several possibilities) or do a specific type of interference called constraint propagation.
- Constraints use to reduce the number of legal values for a variable, which in turn can reduce the legal values for another variable, and so on.
- Constraints propagation may be intertwined with search, or it may be done as a preprocessing step, before search starts.
- Sometimes this preprocessing solved the whole problem, so no search is required at all.

Local Consistency :

If we treat each variable as a node in a graph and each binary constraints as an arc, then the process of enforcing local consistency in each part of the graph causes inconsistent values to be eliminated throughout the graph.

There are Four Types of Local Consistency :

1. Node Consistency :

- A single variable (corresponding to a node in the CSP network) is node-consistent if all the values in the variables domain satisfy the variables unary constraints. For example

(a) The principal states and territories of Australia. Coloring this map can be viewed as a constraint satisfaction (CSP). The goal is assign colors to each region so that no neighboring regions have the same color

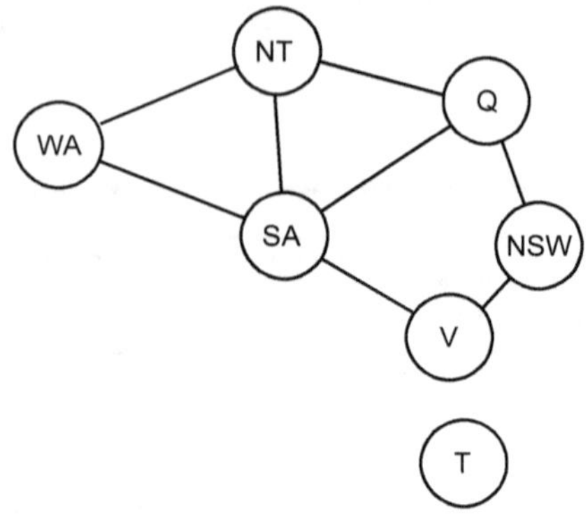

(b) The map-coloring problem represented as a constraint graph

Fig. 3.4

- In the variant of the Australia map-coloring problem. (Fig. 3.4) where South Australians dislike green the variable SA starts with domain {red, green, blue}, and we can make it node consistent by eliminating green, leaving SA with the reduced domain {red, blue} We say that a network is a node consistent if every variable in the network is node-consistent.
- It is always possible to eliminate all the unary constraints in a CSP by running node consistency. It is also possible to transform all n-ary constraints into binary ones.

2. Arc Consistency :

- A variable in a CSP is arc-consistent if every value in its domain satisfies the variable's binary constraints.

More formally,

- X_i is arc-consistent with respect to another variable X_j if for every value in the current domain D_i there is some value in the domain D_j that satisfies the binary constraint on the arc (X_i, Xj).
- A network is arc-consistent if every variable is arc-consistent with every other variable.

  e.g. consider the constraint $1 = X^2$

  where the domain X and Y is the set of digits. We can write this constraint explicitly as

  <(X, 1), {(0, 0), (1, 1), (2, 4), (3, 9)}>

  To make X arc-consistent with respect to 1, we reduce X' s domain to {0, 1, 2, 3}.
- If we also make 1 arc-consistent with respect to X, then Y's domain becomes {0, 1, 4, 9} and the whole CSP is arc-consistent.

3. Path Consistency :

- Arc consistency reduces the domains of variables, sometimes finding a solution (by reducing every domain to size 1) and sometimes finding that the CSP can not be solved (by reducing some domain to size 0). But for networks, arc consistency fails to make enough inferences.

  Consider the map-coloring problem on Australia, but with only two colors allowed; red and blue. Arc consistency can do nothing because every variable is already arc consistent : each can be red with blue at the other end of arc (or vice versa). But clearly there is no solution to the problem : because Western Australia, Northern Territory and South Australia all touches each other.
- Arc consistency tightens down the domains using arc. To make progress on problem like map coloring, we need a strong notion of consistency.
- Path consistency tightens the binary constraints by using implicit. Constraints that are inferred by looking at triples of variables.
- A two-variable set $\{X_i, X_j\}$ is path consistent with respect to third variable X_m if, for every assignment $\{X_i = a, X_j = b\}$ consistent with the constraint on $\{X_i, X_j\}$, there is an assignment to X_m that satisfies the constraint on $\{X_i, X_m\}$ and $\{X_m, X_j\}$. This is called as a path consistency because one can think of it as looking at a path from X_i to X_j with X_m in the middle.

  Example : Consider Australia map with two colors. We will make set {WA, SA} path consistent with NT.
- We start by enumerating the consistent assignments to the set. In this case there are only two : {WA = red, SA = blue} and {WA = blue SA = red}.
- With both of these assignments NT can be neither red nor blue. As there is no valid choice for NT, we eliminates both assignments, and end up with no valid assignments for {WA, SA}.

4. K-Consistency :

- A stronger forms of propagation can be defined with the notion of K-consistency.
- A CSP is K-consistent if, for any set of K-1 variables and for any consistent assignment to those variables, a consistent value can always be assigned to any K^{th} variable.
- 1 – consistency says that, given the empty set, we can make any set of one variable consistent, is called node consistency.
- 2 – Consistency is same as arc-consistency. For binary constraint networks, 3-consistency is sane as path-consistency.
- A CSP is strongly K-consistent if it is K-consistent and is also (K-1) – Consistent, (K-2) – Consistent, ... all the way down to 1-consistent.
- Consider CSP with n nodes and make it strongly n-consistent i.e. K = n. The problem can be solve as follows :
  (i) Chose the consistent value for X_1.
  (ii) Then guaranteed to be able to choose a value for X_2 because the graph is 2-consistent.
  (iii) For X_3 it is 3-consistent and so on.
- For each variable X_i, only search through the d values in the domain to find a value consistent with $X_1, \ldots X_{i-1}$.
- We are guaranteed to find a solution in time $O(n^2d)$.
- Any algorithm for establishing n-consistency take time exponential in n in the worst case, this also requires space that is exponential in n. The memory issue is even more severe than time.
- In practice determining appropriate level of consistency checking is mostly an empirical science. Practitioners commonly compute 2-consistency and less commonly 3-consistency.

Global Constraint :

- Global constraint involves an arbitrary number of variables (but not necessarily cell variables).
- Global constrains occur frequently in real problems and can be handled by special-purpose algorithms that are more efficient than the general purpose methods describe so far e.g. All diff constraint says that all the variables involved must have distinct values.

3.3 BACKTRACKING SEARCH FOR CSPs

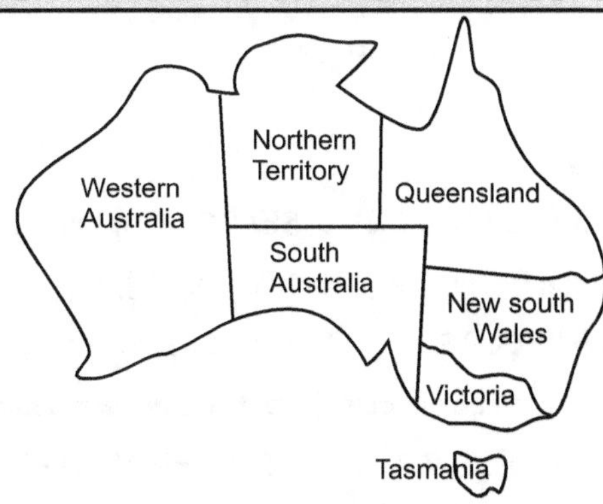

Fig. 3.5

Variables: WA, NT, Q, NSW, V, SA, T

Domains: D_i = {red, green, blue}

Constraints: adjacent regions must have different colours

Example: WA ≠ NT (if the language allows this), or

(WA, NT) ∈ {(red, green), (red, blue), (green, red), (green, blue), ...}

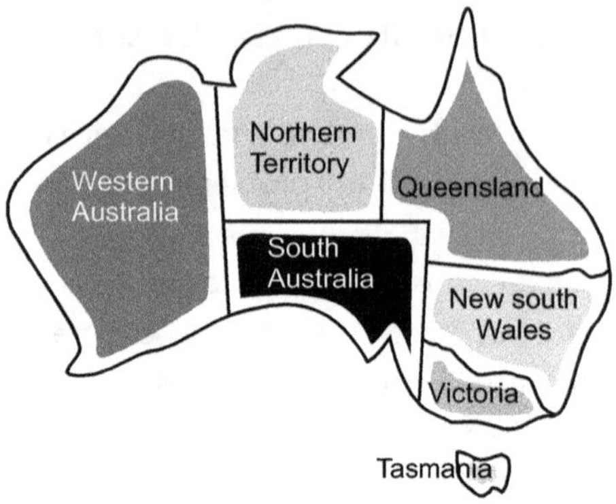

Fig. 3.6

Solutions are assignments satisfying all constraints, for example,

{WA – red, NT – green, Q – red, NSW – green, V – red, 3A – blue, T – green}

Constraint graph is as below:

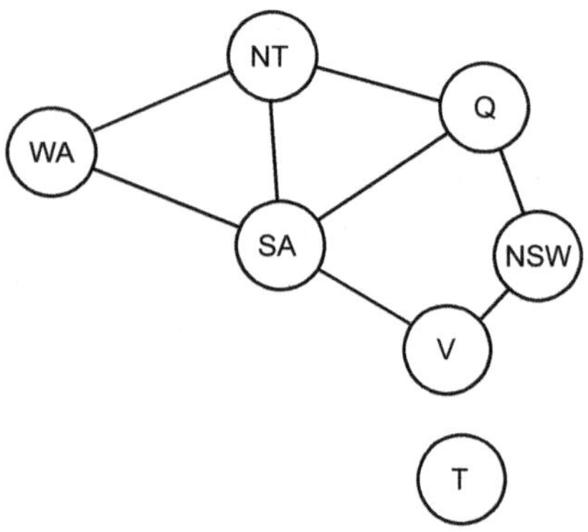

Fig. 3.7

Binary CSP: Each constraint relates at most two variables

Constraint Graph: Nodes are variables, arcs show constraints

Varieties of constraints are:

Unary constraints involve a single variable,

for example, SA ≠ green

Binary constraints involve pairs of variables,

for example, SA ≠ WA

Higher-order constraints involve 3 or more variables,

for example, cryptarithmetic column constraints

Preferences (soft constraints), for example, red is better than green often representable by a cost for each variable assignment → constrained optimization problems

Backtracking search is as below:

Variable assignments are commutative i.e.,

[WA = red then NT = green] same as [NT = green then WA = red]

Only need to consider assignments to a single variable at each node

⇒ b = d and there are d^n leaves

Depth-first search for CSPs with single-variable assignments is called backtracking search.

Backtracking search is the basic uninformed algorithm for CSPs.

The algorithm for backtracking search is as below:

Program 3.1

```
function BACKTRACKING-SEARCH (csp) returns solution/failure
    return Recursive_Backtracking ({ }, csp)
function RECURSIVE_BACKTRACKING (assignment, csp) returns soln/failure
    if assignment is complete then return assignment
    var ← SELECT ← UNASSIGNED-VARIABLE (VARIABLES[csp], assignment, csp)
    for each value in ORDER-DOMAIN-VALUES (var, assignment, csp) do
        if value is consistent with assignment given CONSTRAINTS[csp] then
            add {var = value} to assignment
            result ← RECURSIVE-BACKTRACKING (assignment, csp)
            if result ≠ failure then return result
            remove {var = value} from assignment
    return failure
```

Backtracking Example:

Step 1:

Fig. 3.8 (a)

Step 2:

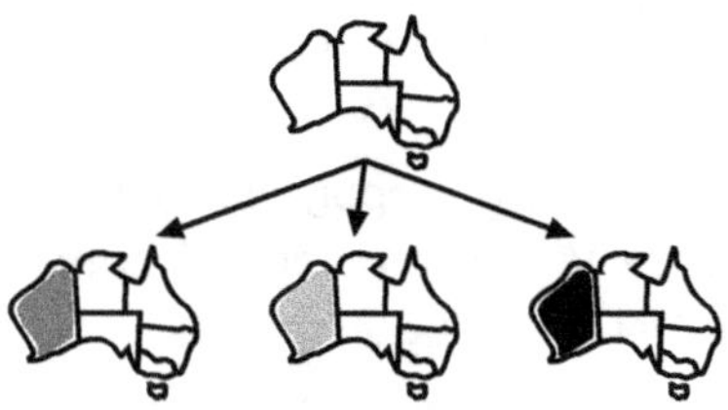

Fig. 3.8 (b)

Step 3:

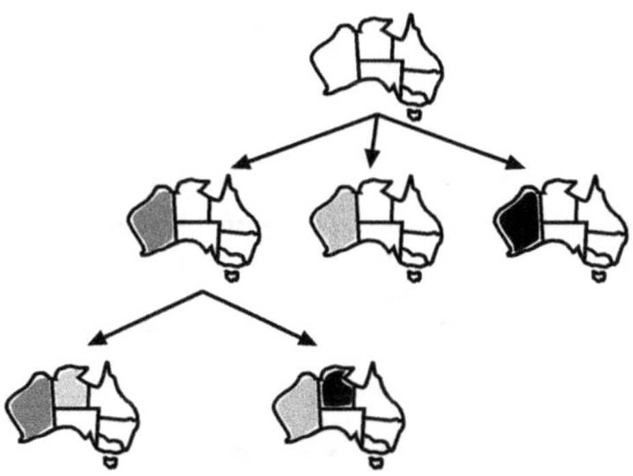

Fig. 3.8 (c)

Step 4:

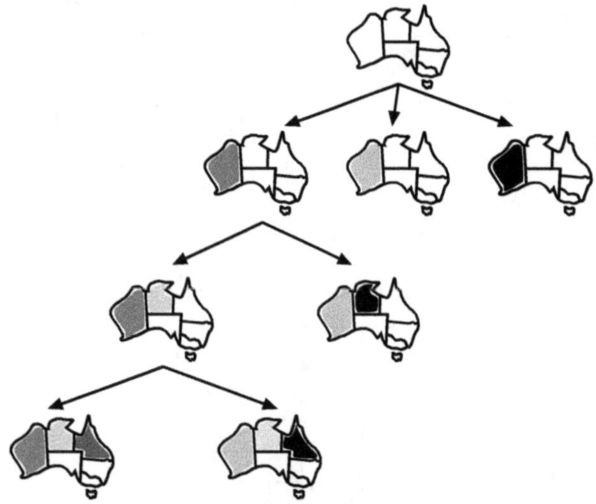

Fig. 3.8 (d)

3.4 LOCAL SEARCH FOR CSPs

- Local search algorithms are very efficient in solving many CSPs.
- They use a complete-state formulation: the initial state assigns a value to every variable, and the successor function usually works by changing the value of one variable at a time. For example, in the 8-queens problem, the initial state might be a random configuration of 8 queens in 8 columns and the successor function picks one queen and considers moving it elsewhere in its column. Another possibility would be start with the 8 queens, one per column in a permutation of the 8 rows and to generate a successor by having two queens swap rows.
- The algorithm for CSP is shown in Program 3.2 below. The two step solution for the 8 queens problem using CSP algorithm is shown in Program 3.2 below:

Program 3.2 : The MIN-CONFLICTS algorithm for solving CSPs by local search. The initial state may be chosen randomly or by a greedy assignment process that chooses a minimal-conflict value for each variable in turn. The CONFLICTS function counts the number of constraints violated by a particular value, given the rest of the current assignment

```
functions MIN-CONFLICTS(csp, max_steps) returns a solution or failure
    inputs: csp, a constraint satisfaction problem
        max_steps, the number of steps allowed before giving up
    current ← an initial complete assignment for csp
    for i = 1 to max_steps do
        if current is a solution for csp then return current
        var ← a randomly chosen, conflicted variable from VARIABLES[csp]
        value ← the value v for var that minimizes CONFLICTS (var, v, current, csp)
        set var = value in current
    return failure
```

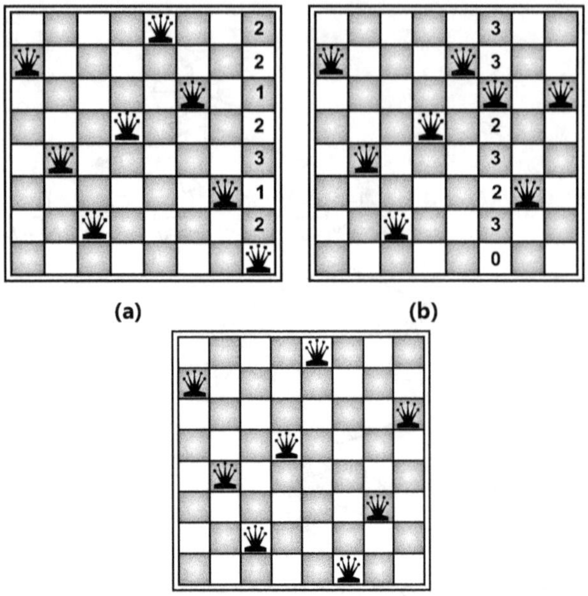

(a) (b) (c)

Fig. 3.9: A two-step solution for an 8-queens problem using min-conflicts. At each stage, a queen is chosen for reassignment in its column. The number of conflicts (in this case, the number of attacking queens) is shown in each square. The algorithm moves the queen to the min-conflict square, breaking ties randomly

- The advantage of local search is that it can be used in an online setting when the problem changes. This is important in scheduling problems.
- A week's airline schedule may involve thousands of flights and tens of thousands of personnel assignments, but bad weather at one airport can render the schedule infeasible. We would like to repair the schedule with a minimum number of changes. This can be easily done with a local search algorithm starting from the current schedule. A backtracking search with the new set of constraints usually requires much more time and might find a solution with many changes from the current schedule.

3.5 THE STRUCTURE OF PROBLEMS

Fig. 3.10 shows the example. We can show that any tree-structured CSP can be solved in time linear in the number of variables.

The algorithm has the following steps:

1. Choose any variable as the root of the tree and order the variables from the root to the leave in such a way that every node's parent in the tree precedes it in the ordering. (Fig. 3.11) label the variables V_1, V_2, ... V_n in order.

   Every variable except the root has exactly one parent variable.
2. For j from n down to 2, apply arc consistency to the arc (V_i, V_j), where V_i is the parent of X_j removing values from DOMAIN [V_i] as necessary.
3. For j from 1 to n, assign any values for X_j consistent with the values assigned for V_i, where V_i is the parent of V_j.

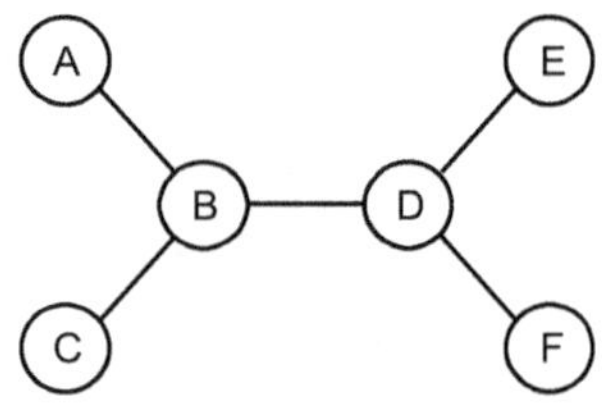

Fig. 3.10 : The constrained graph of a tree structured CSP

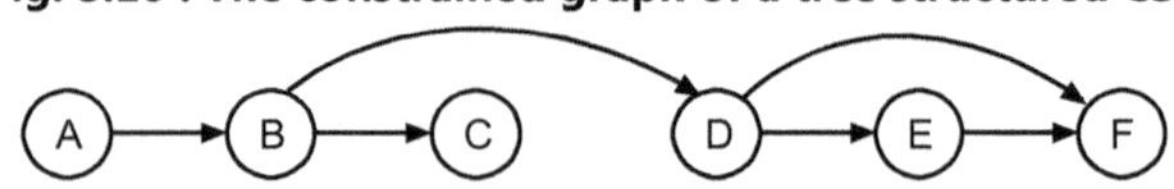

Fig. 3.11

EXERCISE

1. What is CSP? Explain with example.
2. Explain backtracking search for CSPs.
3. Explain local search for CSPs with example.
4. Define in brief local consistency and its types.
5. What is the structure of problem.

✠ ✠ ✠

UNIT IV

GAME PLAYING

4.1 ADVERSARIAL SEARCH

Adversarial search is a search, where we examine the problem which arises when we try to plan ahead of the world and other agents are planning against us.

- In previous topics, we have studied the search strategies which are only associated with a single agent that aims to find the solution which often expressed in the form of a sequence of actions.
- But, there might be some situations where more than one agent is searching for the solution in the same search space, and this situation usually occurs in game playing.
- The environment with more than one agent is termed as **Multi-Agent Environment**, in which each agent is an opponent of other agent and playing against each other. Each agent needs to consider the action of other agent and effect of that action on their performance.
- So, Searches in which two or more players with conflicting goals are trying to explore the same search space for the solution, are called adversarial searches, often known as Games.
- Games are modeled as a Search problem and heuristic evaluation function, and these are the two main factors which help to model and solve games in AI.

Types of Games in AI:

	Deterministic	Chance Moves
Perfect information	Chess, Checkers, go, Othello	Backgammon, monopoly
Imperfect information	Battleships, blind, tic-tac-toe	Bridge, poker, scrabble, nuclear war

- **Perfect Information:** A game with the perfect information is that in which agents can look into the complete board. Agents have all the information about the game, and they can see each other moves also. Examples are Chess, Checkers, Go, etc.
- **Imperfect Information:** If in a game agents do not have all information about the game and not aware with what's going on, such type of games are called the game with imperfect information, such as tic-tac-toe, Battleship, blind, Bridge, etc.
- **Deterministic Games:** Deterministic games are those games which follow a strict pattern and set of rules for the games, and there is no randomness associated with them. Examples are chess, Checkers, Go, tic-tac-toe, etc.
- **Non-Deterministic Games:** Non-deterministic are those games which have various unpredictable events and has a factor of chance or luck. This factor of chance or luck is introduced by either dice or cards. These are random, and each action response is not fixed. Such games are also called as stochastic games.

  Example: Backgammon, Monopoly, Poker, etc.

Zero-Sum Game

- Zero-sum games are adversarial search which involves pure competition.
- In Zero-sum game each agent's gain or loss of utility is exactly balanced by the losses or gains of utility of another agent.
- One player of the game try to maximize one single value, while other player tries to minimize it.
- Each move by one player in the game is called as ply.
- Chess and tic-tac-toe are examples of a Zero-sum game.

Zero-Sum Game: Embedded Thinking

- The Zero-sum game involved embedded thinking in which one agent or player is trying to figure out:
  - What to do.
  - How to decide the move
  - Needs to think about his opponent as well
  - The opponent also thinks what to do
- Each of the players is trying to find out the response of his opponent to their actions. This requires embedded thinking or backward reasoning to solve the game problems in AI.

Formalization of the Problem:

- A game can be defined as a type of search in AI which can be formalized of the following elements:
  - **Initial State:** It specifies how the game is set up at the start.
  - **Player(s):** It specifies which player has moved in the state space.

- **Action(s):** It returns the set of legal moves in state space.
- **Result(s, a):** It is the transition model, which specifies the result of moves in the state space.
- **Terminal-Test(s):** Terminal test is true if the game is over, else it is false at any case. The state where the game ends is called terminal states.
- **Utility(s, p):** A utility function gives the final numeric value for a game that ends in terminal states s for player p. It is also called payoff function. For Chess, the outcomes are a win, loss, or draw and its payoff values are +1, 0, ½. And for tic-tac-toe, utility values are +1, -1, and 0.

Game Tree:

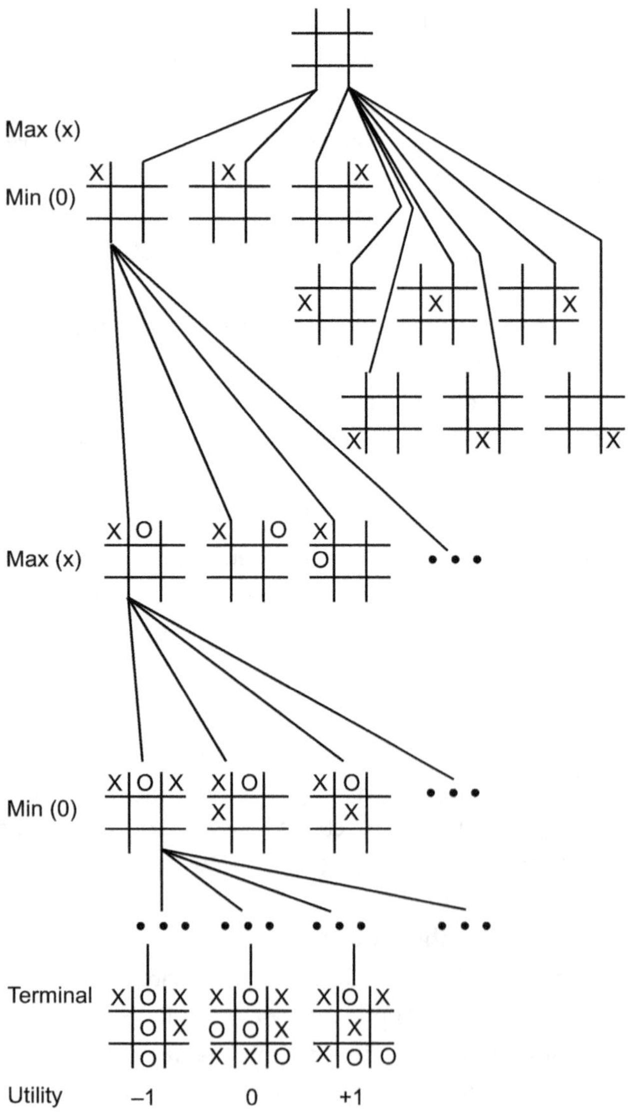

Fig. 4.1

A game tree is a tree where nodes of the tree are the game states and Edges of the tree are the moves by players. Game tree involves initial state, actions function, and result Function.

Example: Tic-Tac-Toe Game Tree:

The following Fig. 4.1 is showing part of the game-tree for tic-tac-toe game. Following are some key points of the game:

- There are two players MAX and MIN.
- Players have an alternate turn and start with MAX.
- MAX maximizes the result of the game tree
- MIN minimizes the result.

Example Explanation:

- From the initial state, MAX has 9 possible moves as he starts first. MAX place x and MIN place o, and both player plays alternatively until we reach a leaf node where one player has three in a row or all squares are filled.
- Both players will compute each node, minimax, the minimax value which is the best achievable utility against an optimal adversary.
- Suppose both the players are well aware of the tic-tac-toe and playing the best play. Each player is doing his best to prevent another one from winning. MIN is acting against Max in the game.
- So in the game tree, we have a layer of Max, a layer of MIN, and each layer is called as **Ply**. Max place x, then MIN puts o to prevent Max from winning, and this game continues until the terminal node.
- In this either MIN wins, MAX wins, or it's a draw. This game-tree is the whole search space of possibilities that MIN and MAX are playing tic-tac-toe and taking turns alternately.

Hence adversarial Search for the minimax procedure works as follows:

- It aims to find the optimal strategy for MAX to win the game.
- It follows the approach of Depth-first search.
- In the game tree, optimal leaf node could appear at any depth of the tree.
- Propagate the minimax values up to the tree until the terminal node discovered.

In a given game tree, the optimal strategy can be determined from the minimax value of each node, which can be written as MINIMAX(n). MAX prefer to move to a state of maximum value and MIN prefer to move to a state of minimum value then:

For a state S MINIMAX(s) =

$$\begin{cases} \text{UTILITY}(s) & \text{If terminal-test}(s) \\ \max_{a \in \text{Actions}(s)} \text{MINIMAX}(\text{RESULT}(s, a)) & \text{If PLAYER}(s) = \text{MAX} \\ \min_{a \in \text{Actions}(s)} \text{MINIMAX}(\text{RESULT}(s, a)) & \text{If PLAYER}(s) = \text{MIN.} \end{cases}$$

4.2 GAMES

Games are the good domains to explore the machine intelligence. The reasons for this are:

1. Games provide structured task. (we can easily measure success or failure)
2. It requires less amount of knowledge. They are solvable by straight forward search from the starting state to winning state.

   But the above point (2) is not true for chess.

Formalizing Game (For Example, Tic-Tac-Toe):

- **Consider Two Person, Zero Sum, Perfect Information :**
  - ➢ Both players have access to complete information about the state of the game.
  - ➢ No information is hidden from either player.
  - ➢ Players alternately move.
- **Apply Iterative Methods:**
  - ➢ Required because search space may be large for the games to search for a solution.
  - ➢ Do search before each move to select the next best move.
- **Adversary Method:**

  Required because alternate moves are made by an opponent who is trying to win and these moves are not controllable.
- **Static Evaluation Functions:**
  - ➢ Used to evaluate the "goodness" of a configuration of the game.
  - ➢ It estimates board quality leading to win for one player.

  Example: Let a board be associated with node n, then

  If f(n) = large positive value

  that means board is good for me and bad for opponent.

  If f(n) = large negative value

  that means board is bad for me and good for opponent.

  If f(n) near 0

  means board is in neutral position

  If f(n) = + infinity

  means winning position for me

  If f(n) = – infinity

  means winning position for opponent

Zero-Sum Assumption:

- If one player is in loss, the other one will have gain.
- Do not know how your opponent plays? So use a single evaluation function to describe the goodness of a board with respect to both the players.

Example: Evaluation function for the game Tic-Tac-Toe.

f(n) = [number of 3 lengths open for me] – [number of 3 lengths open for opponent] 3 length - complete row, column or diagonal.

Game Tree:

- Root node: Represents board configuration and decision required as to what is the best single next move.

  My turn - Root is labelled as MAX node.

  Opponents turn - MIN node.
- Arcs: Represents possible legal moves for the player.
- At each level: The tree has nodes that are all MAX or all MIN.
- Alternate moves: So, nodes at level i are opposite from nodes at level (i + 1)

  (MAX V/s. MIN).

4.3 OPTIMAL DECISIONS IN GAMES

If we consider two player games, we can call it MAX and MIN. A game can be defined as a kind of search problem having the following components:

- The initial state: It includes the board positions and identifies the player to move.
- A successor function: which returns a list of (move, state) pairs, each indicating a legal move and the resulting state.

- A terminal state: where the game has ended are called terminal states.
- A utility function: It gives a numeric value for terminal state. In this case, outcome can be win(0), loss(−1) or draw(0).

4.3.1 Mini-Max Algorithm

The mini-max search procedure is a depth-first, depth limited search procedure:

- Searching game tree using the mini-max algorithm.
- Steps used in picking the next move:
  - ➢ Since its my turn to move, the start node in MAX node with current board configuration.
  - ➢ Expand nodes down to some depth of look-ahead in the game.
  - ➢ Apply evaluate function at each of the leaf node.
  - ➢ "back-up" values for each non-leaf nodes until computed for the root node.
  - ➢ At MIN node, the backed-up value is the minimum of the values associated with its children.
  - ➢ At MAX node, the backed-up value is the maximum of the values associated with its children.

Example:

It assumes that the static evaluation function that returns values ranging from −10 to 10.

10 – indicates win for us

– 10 – indicates win for opponent

0 – even match.

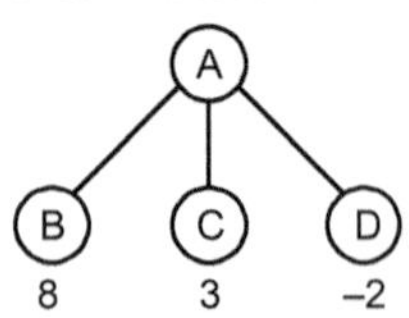

Fig. 4.2 : One-ply Search

As our goal is to maximize the value of the heuristic function, we will choose B. (A to B). Backing-up the value to A, A's values is 8. Static evaluation function is not completely accurate, we should carry search ahead.

Example: In chess game, after our move, the situation is good, but if we look one move ahead, one of our piece gets captured. So before taking any action, we should look ahead, what our opponent will play.

So, instead of applying the static evaluation function to each of the position, we have generated (B, C, D), we can apply the possible move generator, generating a set of successor positions for each position. If we wanted to stop at two-ply, then evaluate the static evaluation function for each node.

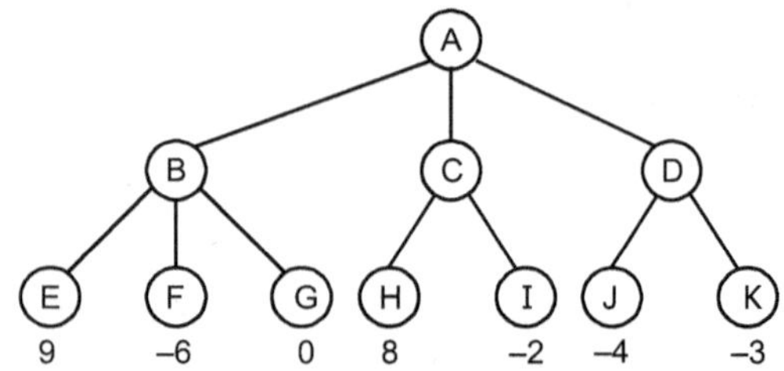

Fig. 4.3

Suppose we make move B, then the opponent must choose among E, F and G. He want to minimize it, so he will choose F. So the actual position in which we send-up is very bad for us.

Following Fig. 4.4 shows the values from second ply backed-up.

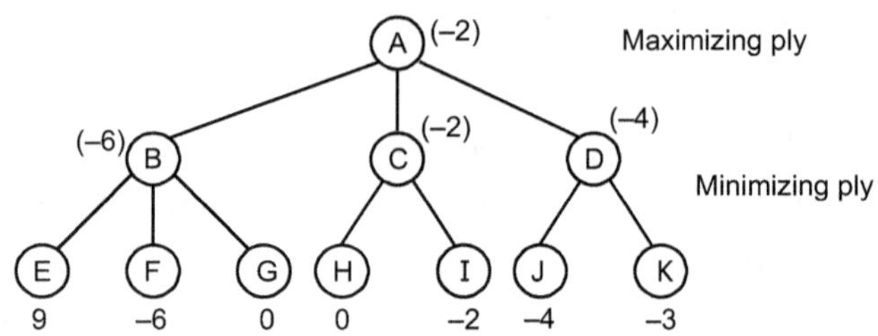

Fig. 4.4

So, the correct move for us to make at the first level is C.

Since there is nothing the opponent can do from there to produce a value worse than – 2.

Tic-Tac-Toe:

(Game playing with Mini-Max)

Mini-max Game Tree can program computers to play games. There are two players taking turns to play move.

Moves are as below:

1. Start: X's Moves

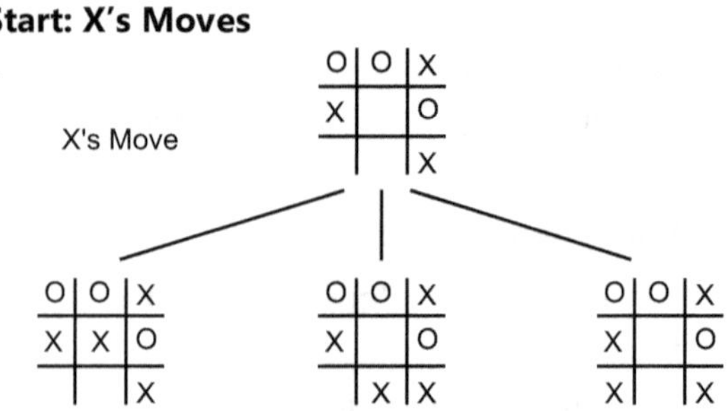

Fig. 4.5

2. **Next: O's Moves**

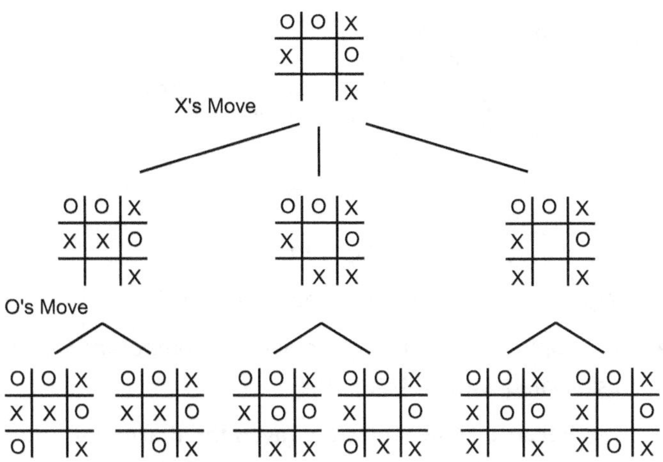

Fig. 4.6

3. **X's Moves:**

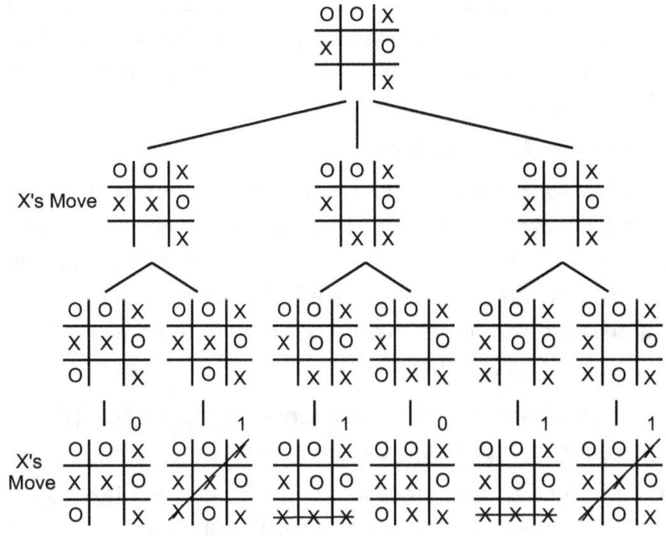

Fig. 4.7

Back-up Evaluation:

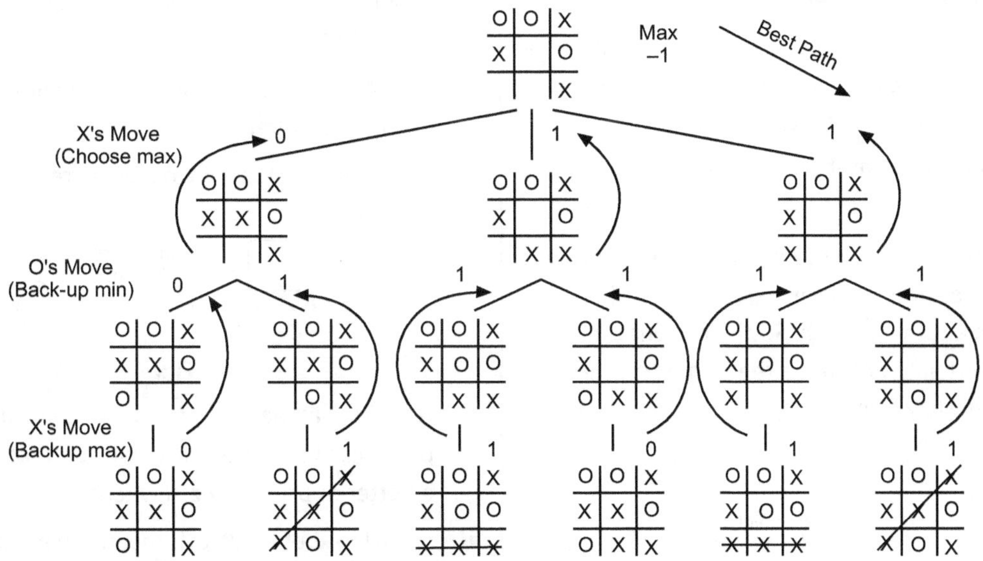

Fig. 4.8

4.3.2 Optimal Decisions in Multiplayer Games

- Some types of game allows more than two players. How the idea of minimax is extending to multiplayer games.
- For that, we need to replace the single value for each node with a vector of values.

  Example: there is a game with three players A, B, C, a vector (vA, vB, vC) is associated with each node
- For terminal states, this vector gives the utility of the state from each players view point.
- Now considering non-terminal states, Consider the node marked X in the game tree, shown in Fig below.
- In that state, player C chooses what to do. The two choices lead to terminal states with utility verctor (vA = 1, vB = 2, vC = 6) and (vA = 4, vB = 2, vC = 3). Since 6 is bigger than 3, C should the first move. This means that if state X is reached, subsequent play will lead to a terminal state with utilities (vA = 1, vB = 2, vC = 6), Hence the backed-up value of X is this vector.
- The backed-up values of a node n is the utility vector of whichever successor has the highest value for the player choosing at n.

4.4 ALPHA- BETA PRUNING

The problem with mini-max algorithm is that the number of game states it has to examine is exponential in the number of moves.

The Alpha-Beta Pruning:

It helps to arrive at correct mini-max algorithm decision without looking at every node of a tree. While using mini-max, some situations may arise when search of a particular branch can be safely terminated. So, while doing search, figure out those nodes that do not require to be expanded.

The procedure is as below:

- Max-player cuts-off search when he knows Min-player can force a probably bad outcome.
- Min-player cuts-off search when he knows Max-player can force probably good (for max) outcome.
- Apply an alpha cut-off means we stop search of a particular branch because, we see that we already have a better opportunity elsewhere.
- Apply a beta-cut-off means we stop search of a particular branch because we see that the opponent already has a better opportunity elsewhere.
- Apply both forms in alpha-beta pruning.

Alpha Cut-Off:

It may be found that, in the current branch, an opponent can achieve a state with a lower value for us than our achievable state in another branch. So the current branch is the one that we certainly not move the game to search of this branch can be safely terminated.

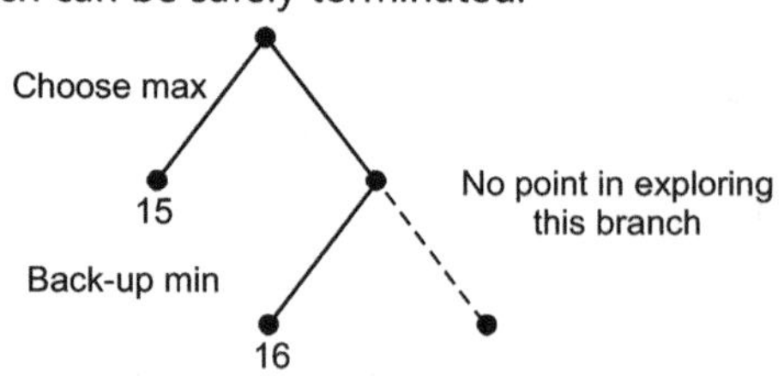

Fig. 4.9

Beta Cut-Off:

- It is the reverse process of alpha-cut-off.
- It may be found that, in the current branch, we would be able to achieve a state which has a higher value for us than one of the opponent can hold as to in another branch.
- The current branch can be identified as one that the opponent will certainly not move the game to search in this branch can be safely terminated.

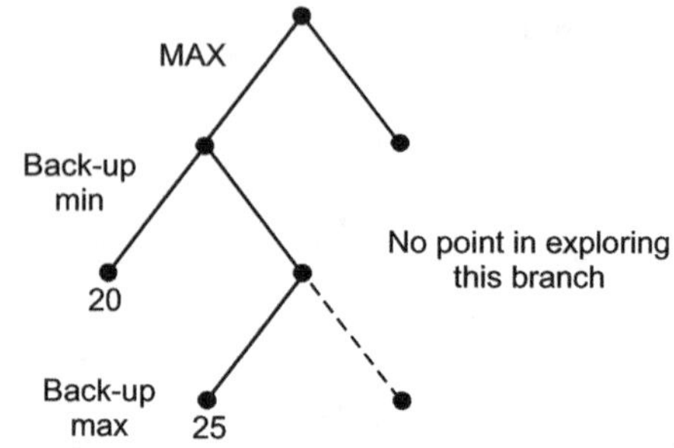

Fig. 4.10

- Alpha-beta procedes in a depth-first fashion.
- An alpha value is an initial or temporary value associated with a MAX node:
  - ➢ Because MAX nodes are given the maximum value among their children.
  - ➢ An alpha value can never decrease, it can only go up.
- A beta value is an initial or temporary value associated with a MIN node:
  - ➢ MIN nodes are given the minimum value among their children.
  - ➢ A beta value can never increases, it can only go down.

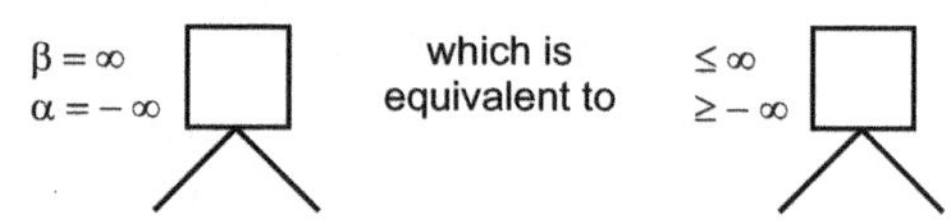

Fig. 4.11

- Applying alpha cut-off means, we stop search of a particular branch because we see that we already have a better opportunity elsewhere.
- Applying beta cut-off means, we stop search of a particular branch because we see that opponent already has a better opportunity elsewhere.

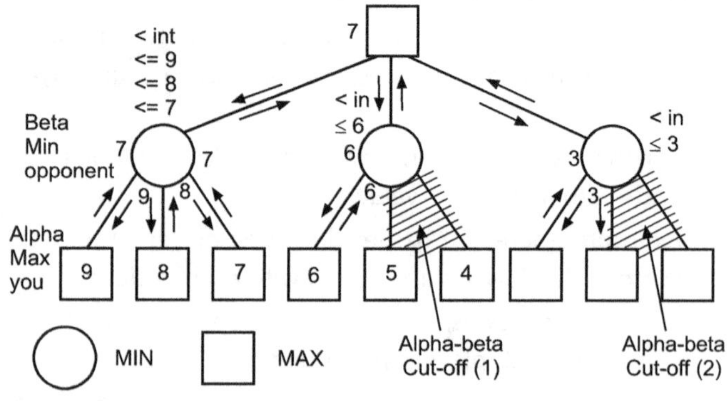

Fig. 4.12

Example: A left to right alpha-beta prune of mini-max search space.

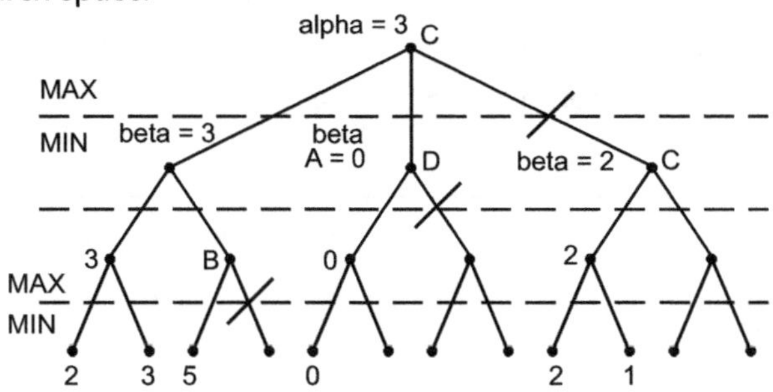

Fig. 4.13

- Start at C. Descend to full-ply depth and assign the heuristic to a state and all siblings (MIN 2, 3). Back-up these values to their parent node (MAX, 3).
- Offer this value to the grandparent (A), as its beta value, so A has beta = 3, A will be not larger than 3.
- Descend to A's other grandchildren. Terminate the search of their present if any grandchild is >= A's beta. Node B is beta-pruned, as shown, because its value must be at least 5.
- Once A's value is known, offer it to its parent (C) as its alpha value. So C has alpha = 3. C will be no smaller than 3.
- Repeat this process, descending to C's great grandchildren (0) in a depth first fashion. D is alpha pruned, because no matter what happens to its right branch, it can not be greater than 0.
- Repeating on E, E is alpha - pruned because its beta value (2) is less than its parent's alpha value (3). So no matter what happens on its right branch, E cannot have a value greater than 2.
- Therefore, C is 3.

Program 4.1 : The Alpha Beta Search Algorithm

```
function MIN-VALUE(state, α, β) returns a utility value
    inputs: state, current, state in game
        α, the value of the best alternative for MAX along the path to state
        β, the value of the best alternative for MIN along the path to state
    if TERMINAL-TEST(state) then return UTILITY(state)
    v ← + ∞
    for a, s, in SUCCESSORS(state) do
        v ← MIN(v, MAX-VALUE(s, α, β))
        if v ≤ α then return v
        β ← MIN(β, v)
    return
function ALPHA-BETA-SEARCH(state) returns an action
    inputs: state, current state in game
    v ← MAX-VALUE(state, −∞, +∞)
    return the action in SUCCESSORS(state) with value v
```

```
function MAX-VALUE(state, α, β) returns a utility value
    inputs: state, current state in game
        α, the value of the best alternative for MAX along the path to state
        β, the value of the best alternative for MIN along the path to state
    if TERMINAL-TEST(state) then return UTILITY(state)
    v ← − ∞
    for a, s, in SUCCESSORS(state) do
        v ← β(v, MIN-VALUE(s, α, β))
        if v ≤ α then return v
        α ← MAX(α, v)
    return v
```

EXERCISE

1. Write a note on : Adversarial search.
2. Explain Mini-Max algorithm with example.
3. What is Alpha-Beta pruning?
4. Explain Alpha cut-off and Beta-cut–off.
5. Explain Mini-Max with Tic-Toc-Toe.
6. Explain Game three.
7. Write a short note on games.

✠ ✠ ✠

UNIT V

LOGICAL AGENTS AND FIRST ORDER LOGIC

A : LOGICAL AGENTS

5.1 KNOWLEDGE-BASED AGENTS

5.1.1 Representation and Mapping

Problem solving requires large amount of knowledge and some mechanism for manipulating that knowledge. The knowledge and the representation plays a central role in an intelligent system. Knowledge is a description of the world and the representation is the way knowledge is encoded.

In simple words, we

- Need to know about things we want to represent.
- Need some means by which we can manipulate things.

Knowledge representation can be considered at two levels:

1. Knowledge level (at which facts are described).
2. Symbol level (at which the representation of the objects, defined in terms of symbols, can be manipulated in the programs).

Mapping between Facts and Representation:

Knowledge is a collection of facts from some domain. We need a representation of "facts" that can be manipulated by a program. Normal English is insufficient, and too hard for computer program to draw inferences in natural languages. Thus, some symbolic representation is necessary.

Therefore, we must be able to map "facts to symbols" and "symbols to facts".

Example: Consider an English Sentence.

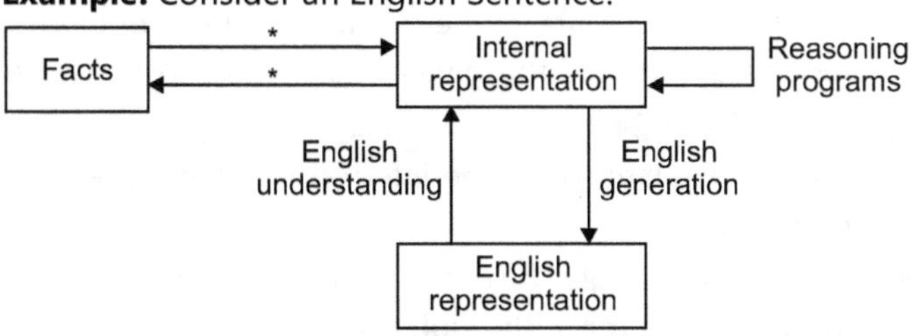

Fig. 5.1

Facts	Representation
Judy is a cat	A fact represented in English sentence.
cat (Judy)	Using forward mapping (maps facts to representation)
∀x: cat (x) → hastail (x)	A logical representation of the fact that "All cats have tails".

Now, using deductive mechanism, we can generate a new representation of object.

hastail (Judy)	A new object representation.
Judy has a tail	Using backward mapping function (maps representation to facts) to generate English sentence.

Judy has a tail is a new knowledge.

Forward and Backward Representation:

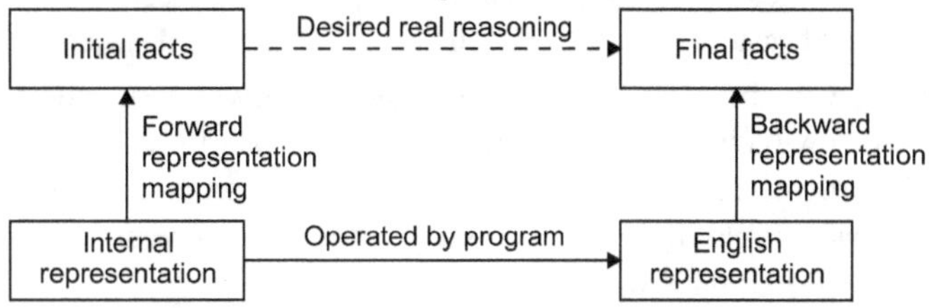

Fig. 5.2

- The dotted line on top indicates the abstract reasoning process that a program is intended to model.
- The solid lines on bottom indicates the concrete reasoning process that the program performs.

Approach in Knowledge Representation:

A knowledge representation system should have the following properties:

- **Representational Adequacy:** The ability to represent all kinds of knowledge that are needed in that domain.
- **Inferential Adequacy:** The ability to manipulate the representational structures to derive new structure corresponding to new knowledge inferred from old.
- **Inferential Efficiency:** The ability to incorporate additional information into the knowledge structure that can be used to focus the attention at the inference mechanisms in the most promising direction.
- **Acquisitional Efficiency:** The ability to acquire new knowledge using automatic methods whenever possible rather than relying on human intervention.

To date, no single system can optimizes all of the above properties.

5.1.2 Types of Knowledge Representation

There are four types of knowledge representations:

1. Relational knowledge
2. Inheritable knowledge
3. Inferential knowledge
4. Declarative/Procedural knowledge

1. Relational Knowledge:

- Relational knowledge provides a framework to compare two objects based on equivalent attributes.
- This knowledge associates elements of one domain with another domain.
  - ➢ Relational knowledge consists of objects with their attributes and values.
  - ➢ The result of this knowledge type is a mapping of element among different domains.

Example: Simple Relational Knowledge.

Employee Name	Salary	Designation
Akshay	50,000	Associate Manager
Roshani	60,000	Manager
Yogesh	70,000	Manager
Shamal	55,000	Assistant Manager

- Given the facts, it is not possible to answer a question like which employee is having highest salary? But, if the procedure is provided for the same, then these facts will enable that procedure to compute an answer.

2. Inheritable Knowledge:

- The knowledge elements inherit attributes from their parents. Inheritance is a powerful form of inference, but not adequate. The basic KR (Knowledge Representation) needs to be augmented with inference mechanism.
- The KR in hierarchical structure is called 'semantic network' as a collection of "frames" or "slot and filler structure". The structure shows property inheritance and way for insertion of additional knowledge.
- **Property Inheritance:** The objects or elements of specific classes inherit attributes and values from more general classes. The classes are organized in a generalized hierarchy.

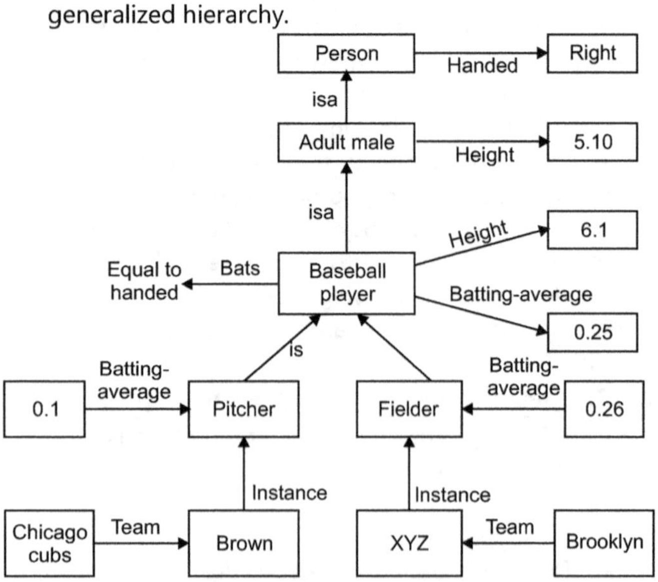

Fig. 5.3: Inheritable Knowledge Representation (KR)

- The directed arrow represents attributes (isa, instance, team), originates at object being described and terminates at object or its value.
- The box nodes represent objects and values of the attributes.
- Viewing a node as a frame.

Example: Baseball player

isa – Adult - Male

Bats – EQUAL Handed

Height – 6.1

Batting avg. – 0.25

Algorithm: Property inheritance

Retrieve a value V for an attribute A of an instance object O Steps to follow :

- Find object O in the knowledge base.
- If there is a value for the attribute A then report that value.
- Else, if there is a value for the attribute instance, If not, then fail.
- Else, move to the node corresponding to that value and look for a value for the attribute A. If one is found, report it.
- Else, do until there is no value for the "isa" attribute or until an answer is found:
  - ➢ Get the value of a "isa" attribute and move to that node.
  - ➢ See if there is a value for the attribute A, If yes, report it.

3. Inferential Knowledge:

- This knowledge generates new information from the given information. The new information does not require further data gathering from source but does require analysis of the given information to generate new knowledge.
- Values or relations can be inferred from the given set of relations.
- A predicate logic is used to infer from a set of attributes. Inference through predicate logic uses a set of logical operations to relate individual data. The symbols used for the logical operations are: $\neg$ (not), $\wedge$ (and), $\vee$ (or), $\neg$ (negation), $\forall$ (for all), $\exists$ (there exists), $\Rightarrow$ (implication), $\Leftrightarrow$ (equivalence).

For Example:

(i) "Moti" is a name of dog, dog (Moti).

(ii) All dogs belong to the class of animals $\forall x$: dog (x) $\Rightarrow$ animal(x).

(iii) All animals either live on land or in water.

$\forall x$: animal (x) $\Rightarrow$ live (x, land), $\vee$ live (x, water)

- From above three, we can infer that "Moti lives either on land or in water".
- If more information is available about these objects and their relations, then more knowledge can be inferred.

4. Declarative/Procedural Knowledge:

Declarative Knowledge:

The knowledge is based on declarative facts about axioms and domains.

- Axioms are assumed to be true unless a counter example is found to invalidate them.
- Domain represents the physical world and the perceived functionality.
- Axions and domains thus simply exist and serve as declarative statements that can stand alone.

Procedural Knowledge:

- The procedural knowledge is a mapping between domains that specify "what to do when" and the representation is of "how to make it" rather than "what it is".
- The procedural knowledge may have inferential efficiency, but no inferential adequacy and acquisitional efficiency. This knowledge is represented as small programs that know how to do specific things, and how to proceed.

  Example: A parser in a natural language has the knowledge that a noun phrase may contain articles, adjectives and nouns. It thus call routines that know how to process articles, adjectives and nouns.

5.1.3 Issues in Knowledge Representation

Many issues arise while using KR techniques. Some of them are:

1. **Important Attributes:** Any attributes of objects, it is so basic that they occur in almost every problem domain.
2. **Relationship among Attributes:** Any relationship that exists among attributes.
3. **Choosing Granularity:** At what level of details should the knowledge be represented?
4. **Set of Objects:** How sets of objects be represented?
5. **Finding Right Structure:** How can relevant parts be accessed, when a large amount of knowledge is given.

1. Important Attributes:

- There are attributes that are of general significance. There are two attributes "instance" and "isa", that are of general importance. These attributes are important as they support property inheritance.

2. Relationship among Attributes:

- The attributes to describe objects are themselves entities they represent. The relationship between the attributes of an object, independent of specific knowledge they encode, may hold properties like inverses, existence in an 'isa' hierarchy, techniques for reasoning about values and single valued attributes.
- **Inverses:** The Fig. 5.3 shows attributes (isa, instance, team) each with a directed arrow, originating at the object being described and terminating either at the object or its value.
- There are two ways of realizing this:
  (i) Represent two relationships in a single representation e.g. a logical representation team (XYZ, Brooklyn), that can be interpreted as a statement about XYZ or Brooklyn.
  (ii) Use attributes that focus on a single entity but use them in pairs, one the inverse of the other. For example: One team = Brooklyn and the other team = XYZ.
- The second approach is followed in semantic net and frame-based systems, accomplished by a knowledge acquisition tool that guarantees the consistency of inverse slot by checking. Each time a value is added to one attribute then the corresponding value is added to the inverse.
- **Existence in an 'isa' Hierarchy:** This is about generalization-specialization, like classes of objects and specialized subsets of those classes. These are attributes and specialization of attributes. These generalization-specialization relationships for attribute support inheritance.
- **Techniques for Reasoning about Values:** This is about reasoning values of attributes not given explicitly.

  Several kinds of information are used in reasoning, like

  Age - Of a person cannot be greater than the age of person's parents.

  Height - It must be in a unit of length, cannot be in kg.

  These values are often specified when a knowledge base is created.
- **Single Valued Attributes:** These are attributes which take unique values.

Example: A base ball player can at a time have only a single height and be a member of only one team.

In an employee database, employee id is a unique value assigned to each employee.

3. Choosing Granularity:

- At what level should the knowledge be represented and what are the primitives?
- Should there be a large number or a small number of low level primitives or high level facts.
- High level facts may be adequate for inference while low level primitives may require a lot of storage.

For Example: Suppose, we are interested in the fact.

John spotted Merry, can be represented as, spotted (agent (John), object (Merry)).

Such a representation is easy to answer.

Who spotted Merry?

Suppose we want to know.

Did John see Merry?

- Given only one fact, we cannot discover that answer, we can add other facts.

spotted (X, Y) $\rightarrow$ saw (X, Y)

- We can now infer the answer to the question.

4. Set of Objects:

- Certain properties of objects that are true as member of a set but not as individual.

Example: Consider the assertion made in the sentences below.

"There are more girls than boys in India", and

"English speaker can be found all over the world".

- To describe these facts, the only way is to attach assertion to the sets representing girls, boys and English.
- The reason to represent sets of object is,
  - ➢ If property is true for all or most elements of a set, then it is more efficient to associate it once with the set rather than to associate it explicitly with every element of the set.
  - ➢ This can be done by:
    1. In logical representation by using universal quantities and
    2. In hierarchical structure, where node represents sets, the inheritance propagates the set level assertion down to individual.

  Example: assert large (elephant)

- Make clear distinction between:
  (i) The set of elephants is large or
  (ii) Anything that is an elephant is large.
- Sets can be represented by three ways:
  (i) Name, In Fig. 5.3, the node Baseball player and the predicates as Ball and Batter in logical representation.
  (ii) Extensional definition is to list the numbers.
  (iii) Intensional definition is to provide a rule, that returns true or false depending on whether the object is in the set or not.

5. Finding Right Structure:

- What is a right structure, for describing particular situation?
- It requires, selecting an initial structure and then revising the choice. For this, it is necessary to solve the following problems.
  - ➢ How to perform an initial selection of the most appropriate structure.
  - ➢ How to fill appropriate details from the current situations.
  - ➢ How to find a better structure if the one chosen initially turns out not to be appropriate.
  - ➢ What to do if no structure is appropriate.
  - ➢ When to create a structure and when to remember a new structure.
- There is no good general purpose method for solving all these problems. Some knowledge representation techniques solve some of them.

5.2 THE WUMPUS WORLD PROBLEM

- We know the syntax and semantics for propositional logic. Now, we can construct a Knowledge Base (KB) for the wumpus world problem.

What is Wumpus World Problem?

- A wumpus world is a cave consisting of rooms connected by passageways.
- Lurking somewhere in the cave is wumpus, wumpus is an animal that eats anyone who enters its room.
- An agent can shoot the wumpus, but agent is having only one arrow.
- Some room contains pits, that will trap anyone in the room except wumpus.
- The only mitigating feature of lining in the environment is the possibility of finding the heap of gold.

The PEAS for the Problem is Performance Measure:

+ 1000 for picking up the gold.

– 1000 for falling into the pit or being eaten by wumpus.

– 1 for each action taken.

– 10 for using up the arrow.

Environment:

A 4 × 4 grid of rooms.

- The agent always starts in the square labelled [1, 1], facing to the right.
- The location of the gold and the wumpus are chosen randomly, with a uniform distribution, from the squares other than start square.
- Each square other than the start can be a pit with probability 0.2.

Actuators:

- The agent can move forward, turn left by 90°, turn right by 90°.
- The agent does a miserable death if it enters a square containing a pit or a live wumpus.
  - ➢ Moving forward has no effect, if there is a wall in front of the agent.
  - ➢ Action **Grab** is used to pick up the object.
  - ➢ **Shoot** is used to fire an arrow.

Sensors:

The agent has five sensors, each of which gives a single bit of information:

1. In the square containing the wumpus and in the directly (not diagonally) adjacent squares the agent will perceive a strench.
2. In the squares directly adjacent to a pit, the agent will perceive a breeze.
3. In the square, where the gold is, the agent will perceive a glitter.
4. When an agent walks into a wall, it will perceive a bump.
5. When the wumpus is killed, it emits a woeful scream that can be perceived anywhere in the cave.

Example: If there is a strench and a breeze, but no glitter, bump or scream the agent will perceive the percept.

[Strench, Breeze, None, None, None]

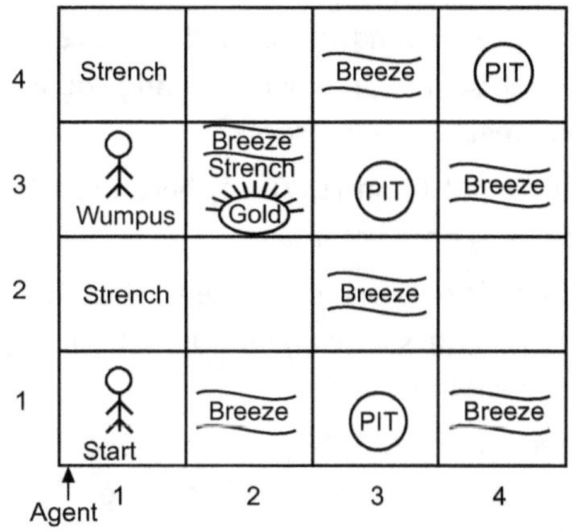

Fig. 5.4: A wumpus world

- The first percept is [None, None, None, None, None] from which the agent can conclude that its neighbouring squares are safe.

1, 4	2, 4	3, 4	4, 4
1, 3	2, 3	3, 3	4, 3
1, 2	2, 2	3, 2	4, 2
1,1	2, 1	3, 1	4, 1

Fig. 5.5: Initial state

1, 4	2, 4	3, 4	4, 4
1, 3	2, 3	3, 3	4, 3
1, 2 OK	2, 2 P ?	3, 2	4, 2
1,1 V OK	2, 1 B [A] OK	3, 1 P ?	4, 1

[A] - Agent
B - Breeze
G - Glitter
OK - Safe
P - Pit
S - Strench
W - Wumpus
V - Visited

Fig. 5.6: After one move, with percept

[None, Breeze, None, None, None]

Fig. 5.6 shows agents state of knowledge.

- As there was no strench or breeze in [1, 1], the agent can infer that [1, 2] and [2, 1] are safe (OK).
- The agent will move only into a square that is safe (OK).

- As shown Fig. 5.6, agent decided to move in [2, 1], so there must be a pit in a neighbouring square, as [2, 1] contain breeze from (sensors (2)).
- The pit cannot be in [1, 1], so there must be a pit in [2, 2] or [3, 1] or in both.
- Now, there is only one square left (which is not visited and OK) is [1, 2], so the agent will go back at [1, 1] and then proceed to [1, 2].
- Now percept in [1, 2] is [Strench, None, None, None, None], resulting in state of knowledge as shown in Fig. 5.7 below.

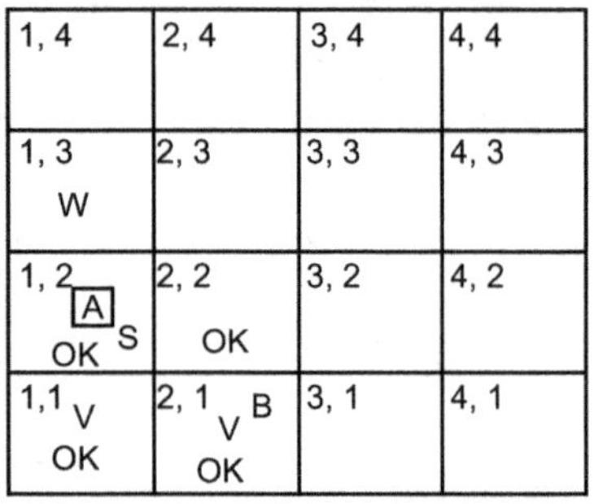

Fig. 5.7: [Strench, None, None, None, None]

- The strench in [1, 2] means, there is a wumpus nearby.
- But wumpus cannot be in [2, 2] and in [1, 1] so the agent can infer that, wumpus must be in [1, 3].
- The lack of breeze in [1, 2] implies that there is no pit in [2, 2]. Yet we already inferred that, there must be a pit in either [2, 2] or [3, 1], so this means it must be in [3, 1].
- The agent now proved to itself that there is neither a pit nor a wumpus in [2, 2], so it is OK to move there.
- So, we will not show the agents state of knowledge at [2, 2], we will assume that the agent turns and moves to [2, 3], as shown in Fig. 5.8 below.

In this, agent detect a glitter, so it will grab the gold and thereby end the game.

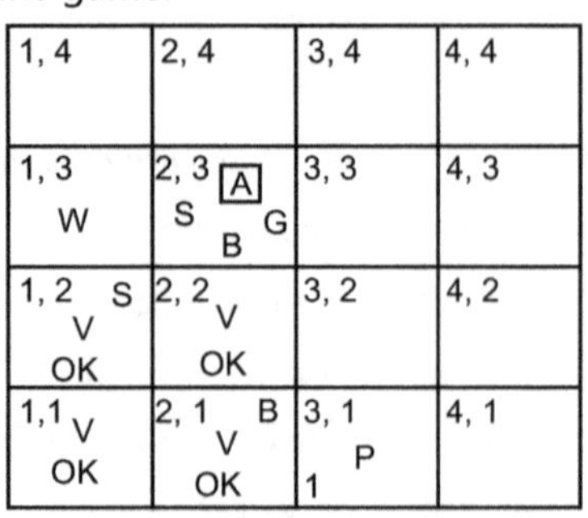

Fig. 5.8: [Strench, Breeze, Glitter, None, None]

5.3 LOGIC

- The knowledge bases consist of many sentences. It is represented according to the syntax of the presentation languages that are well formed. E.g. 'x + y = 4' is a well formed sentence where as 'x4y+ = ' is not.
- The logic should not contain only syntax but also define semantics or meaning of sentences. It tells the facts of the real world. E.g. $x \times y = 6$ is true if $x = 2$ and $y = 3$ but becomes false if $x = 2$ and $y = 2$. Hence logic can have only two possible value true or false. It doesn't contain any intermediate state.
- 'Model' is representing the possible world. If a sentence α is true in model m, we say that m satisfies α and can be represented as a m (α).
- Logical reasoning involves the relation of logical entailment between sentences and mathematically can be written as

$$\alpha \neq \beta$$

- The entailment means in every model in which α is true β is also true. Most of the time the sentences do not show only entailment but are applied to device conclusions that is to find logical inference.
- An inference algorithm that derives only entailed sentences is called sound/truth preserving. The inference algorithm is complete if it can derive any sentence that is entailed. Grounding is the connection between the logical reasoning and the real environment in which agent exists.

5.4 PROPOSITIONAL LOGIC : A VERY SIMPLE LOGIC

- The central component of a knowledge based agent is Knowledge Base (KB).
- Each sentence in the KB is expressed in knowledge representation language.
- Adding new sentences to the KB (By using TELL) and way to query KB (using ASK). Both tasks may involve inference (Deriving new sentences from old).
- The following program is a generic knowledge based agent program.

```
Function KB-AGENT (percept) returns an action
Static: KB, t (counter), initially 0, indicating time
TELL (KB, make-percept-sentence (percept,t))
action ← ASK (KB, make-action-query (t))
TELL (KB, make-action-sentence (action,t))
t ← t + 1
return action
```

Agent takes percept as input and returns an action. KB, maintained by agent contains some background knowledge.

Each time when agent program is called:

1. It tells the knowledge base what it perceives.
2. It asks the knowledge base what action it should perform.

- Once the action is chosen, the agent records its choice and executes the action.
- By using second TELL, the KB knows the actions are actually been executed.
- MAKE-PERCEPT-SENTENCE takes a percept and a time and returns a sentence asserting that the agent perceived the percept at the given time.
- MAKE-ACTION-QUERY takes time as input and returns a sentence that asks what action should be performed at that time as output.

Propositional Logic – Example

- We can easily represent real world facts as logical propositions.
- Prepositions are elementary atomic sentences written as formula or Well Formed Formula (WFF). Every preposition is either true or false.
  e.g. Snow is White, Sky is Blue.
- If the proposition is true, then the truth value is true. If the proposition is false, then the truth value is false.
  e.g. Sky is blue - truth value is TRUE.
  4 + 4 = 9 - truth value is FALSE.
  In prepositional Logic (PL) a user defines a set of propositional symbols, like P and Q. User defines the semantics of each of these symbols.

Example: P means "It is hot"
Q means "It is humid"
R means "It is raining"

A sentence also called formula or WFF is defined as,

1. A symbol.
2. If S is a sentence then ~S is a sentence where "~" is the "not" logical operator.
3. If S and T are sentences, then (S∨T), (S∧T), (S⇒T), (S⇔T) are sentences where, form logical connectives correspond to "or", "and", "implies" and "if and only if" respectively.
4. A finite number of applications of (1) – (3)
   ➢ (P∧Q) ⇒ R (If it is humid, then it is raining)
   ➢ Q ⇒ P (If it is humid, then it is hot)
   ➢ Q (It is humid)

Syntax and Semantics of PL

Syntax:

- It defines allowable sentences.
- Automic sentences: These are simple sentences, consisting of a single proposition symbol.
- We will use uppercase letters for symbols – P, Q, R and so on.
- Complex sentences are constructed from Simple sentences + Logical connectives.

Table 5.1

Sr. No.	Connective	Symbol	Read as
(1)	Assertion	P	"P is true".
(2)	Negation	¬ P	"P is false".
(3)	Conjunction	P ∧ Q	"Both P and Q are true".
(4)	Disjunction	P ∨ Q	"Either P is true or Q is true or both".
(5)	Implication	P ⇒ Q	"If P is true, then Q is true "P implies Q".
(6)	Equivalence	⇔	"P and Q are either both true or both false".

- The order of precedence in propositional logic is (from highest to lowest)
  ¬, ∧, ∨, ⇒ and ⇔
  For example: ¬ P ∧ Q ∨ R ⇒ S is equivalent to (¬P) ∨ (Q∧R) ⇒ S
- A ∧ B ∧ C which could be read as ((A ∧ B) ∧ C) or as (A ∧ (B ∧ C))
  Allowed sentences: A ∨ B ∨ C, A ⇔ B ⇔ C
  Not allowed sentences: A ⇒ B ⇒ C. Because two readings have different meanings.

A BNF (Backup-Name Form) grammar of sentences in propositional logic:

$$\begin{aligned} \mathit{Sentence} &\rightarrow \mathit{AtomicSentence} \mid \mathit{ComplexSentence} \\ \mathit{AutomicSentence} &\rightarrow \mathit{True} \mid \mathit{False} \mid \mathit{Symbol} \\ \mathit{ComplexSentence} &\rightarrow \neg\ \mathit{Sentence} \\ &\mid (\mathit{Sentence} \wedge \mathit{Sentence}) \\ &\mid (\mathit{Sentence} \vee \mathit{Sentence}) \\ &\mid (\mathit{Sentence} \Rightarrow \mathit{Sentence}) \\ &\mid (\mathit{Sentence} \Leftrightarrow \mathit{Sentence}) \end{aligned}$$

Semantics:

- It defines the rules for determining the truth of a sentence with respect to a particular model.

- All sentences are constructed from automic sentences and five connectives. Therefore, we need to specify how to compute the truth of automic sentences and how to compute the truth of sentences formed with each of the five connectives.
- In automic sentences
  - ➢ Truth is true in every model and false is false in every model.
  - ➢ The truth value of every other proposition symbol must be specified directly in the model.
- For complex sentences
  - ➢ For any sentence S and any model M, the sentence $\neg$ S is true in M if and only if S is false in M.
- Truth table defining the basic connectives:

Table 5.2

P	Q	$\neg$P	$\neg$Q	$P \wedge Q$	$P \vee Q$	$P \Rightarrow Q$	$P \Leftrightarrow Q$	$Q \Rightarrow P$
T	T	F	F	T	T	T	T	T
T	F	F	T	F	T	F	F	T
F	T	T	F	F	T	T	F	F
F	F	T	T	F	F	T	T	T

$P \Rightarrow Q$: If P is true, then I am claiming that Q is true. Otherwise no claim.

The only way for this sentence to be false is if P is true but Q is false.

$P \Leftrightarrow Q$: It is true, whenever both $P \Rightarrow Q$ and $Q \Rightarrow P$ are true.

"P iff Q" or "Q iff Q".

Tautologies:

- A proposition that is always true is called "Tautology".
- For example: ($P \vee \neg$ P) is always true regardless of the truth value of the proposition P.

Contradictions:

- A proposition that is always false is called a "contradiction".
- For example: ($P \wedge \neg P$) is always false regardless of the truth value of the proposition P.

Contingencies:

- A proposition is called a "contingency", if that proposition is neither a tautology nor a contradiction.

Antecedent, Consequent:

- These two are parts of conditional statements.

  For example: $p \rightarrow q$.

  1st statement or if clause (here p) is called antecedent.

  2nd statement or then clause (here q) is called consequent.

Argument:

- An argument is a demonstration as a proof of some statement.
- For example: "That bird is a crow, therefore, its black". Any argument can be expressed as a compound statement. In logic, an argument is a set of one or more meaningful declarative sentences (or "propositions") known as the premises alongwith another meaningful declarative sentence (or "proposition") known as the conclusion.
  - ➢ **Premise** is a proposition which gives reasons, grounds or evidence for accepting some other proposition, called the conclusion.
  - ➢ **Conclusion** is a proposition, which is purported to be established on the basis of other propositions.

Knowledge-Based Agents - The Wumpus World Example

- We know the syntax and semantics for propositional logic. Now, we can construct a Knowledge Base (KB) for the wumpus world problem.

What is Wumpus World Problem?

- A wumpus world is a cave consisting of rooms connected by passageways.
- Lurking somewhere in the cave is wumpus, wumpus is an animal that eats anyone who enters its room.
- An agent can shoot the wumpus, but agent is having only one arrow.
- Some room contains pits, that will trap anyone in the room except wumpus.
- The only mitigating feature of lining in the environment is the possibility of finding the heap of gold.

The PEAS for the Problem is Performance Measure:

+ 1000 for picking up the gold.

– 1000 for falling into the pit or being eaten by wumpus.

– 1 for each action taken.

– 10 for using up the arrow.

Environment:

A 4×4 grid of rooms.

- The agent always starts in the square labelled [1, 1], facing to the right.
- The location of the gold and the wumpus are chosen randomly, with a uniform distribution, from the squares other than start square.

- Each square other than the start can be a pit with probability 0.2.

Actuators:

- The agent can move forward, turn left by 90°, turn right by 90°.
- The agent does a miserable death if it enters a square containing a pit or a live wumpus.
  - ➢ Moving forward has no effect, if there is a wall in front of the agent.
  - ➢ Action **Grab** is used to pick up the object.
  - ➢ **Shoot** is used to fire an arrow.

Sensors:

The agent has five sensors, each of which gives a single bit of information:

1. In the square containing the wumpus and in the directly (not diagonally) adjacent squares the agent will perceive a strench.
2. In the squares directly adjacent to a pit, the agent will perceive a breeze.
3. In the square, where the gold is, the agent will perceive a glitter.
4. When an agent walks into a wall, it will perceive a bump.
5. When the wumpus is killed, it emits a woeful scream that can be perceived anywhere in the cave.

Example: If there is a strench and a breeze, but no glitter, bump or scream the agent will perceive the percept.

[Strench, Breeze, None, None, None]

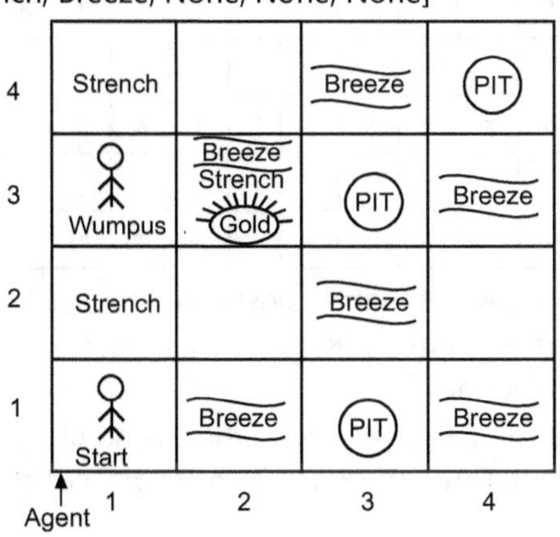

Fig. 5.9: A wumpus world

- The first percept is [None, None, None, None, None] from which the agent can conclude that its neighbouring squares are safe.

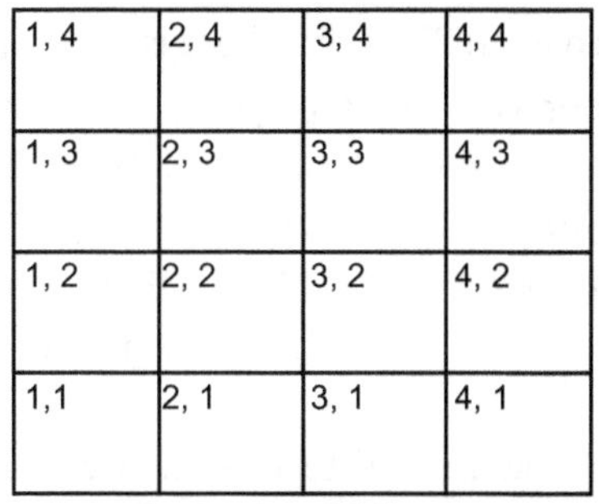

Fig. 5.10: Initial state

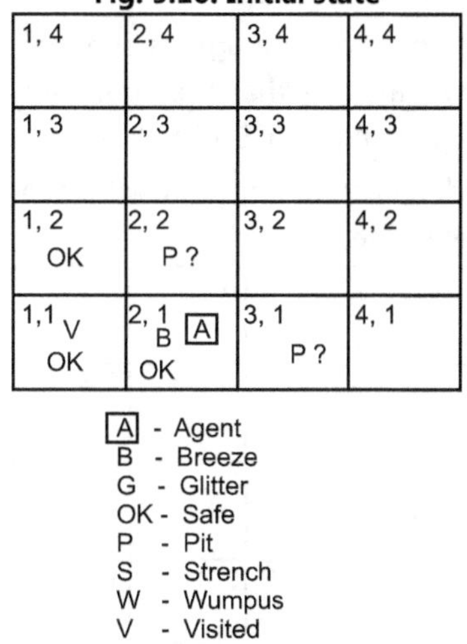

Fig. 5.11: After one move, with percept

[None, Breeze, None, None, None]

Fig. 5.11 shows agents state of knowledge.

- As there was no strench or breeze in [1, 1], the agent can infer that [1, 2] and [2, 1] are safe (OK).
- The agent will move only into a square that is safe (OK).
- As shown Fig. 5.11, agent decided to move in [2, 1], so there must be a pit in a neighbouring square, as [2, 1] contain breeze from (sensors (2)).
- The pit cannot be in [1, 1], so there must be a pit in [2, 2] or [3, 1] or in both.
- Now, there is only one square left (which is not visited and OK) is [1, 2], so the agent will go back at [1, 1] and then proceed to [1, 2].
- Now percept in [1, 2] is [Strench, None, None, None, None], resulting in state of knowledge as shown in Fig. 5.12 below.

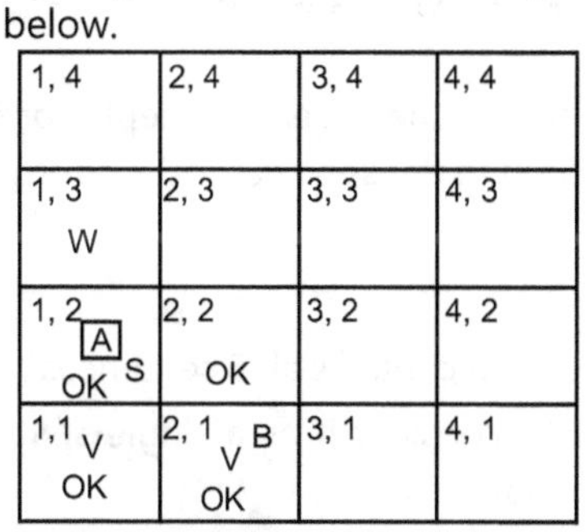

Fig. 5.12: [Strench, None, None, None, None]

- The strench in [1, 2] means, there is a wumpus nearby.
- But wumpus cannot be in [2, 2] and in [1, 1] so the agent can infer that, wumpus must be in [1, 3].
- The lack of breeze in [1, 2] implies that there is no pit in [2, 2]. Yet we already inferred that, there must be a pit in either [2, 2] or [3, 1], so this means it must be in [3, 1].
- The agent now proved to itself that there is neither a pit nor a wumpus in [2, 2], so it is OK to move there.
- So, we will not show the agents state of knowledge at [2, 2], we will assume that the agent turns and moves to [2, 3], as shown in Fig. 5.13 below.

In this, agent detect a glitter, so it will grab the gold and thereby end the game.

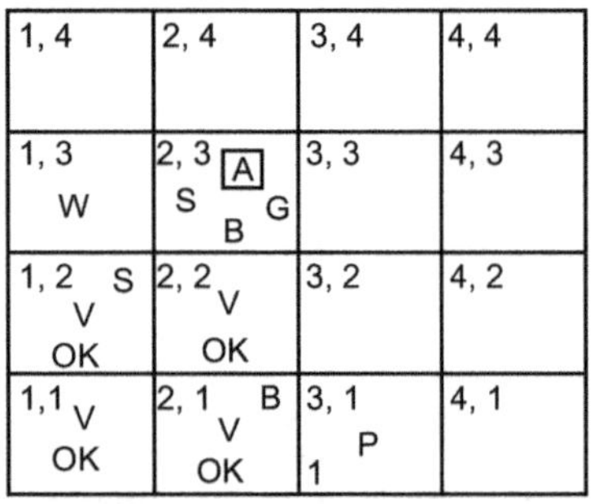

Fig. 5.13 : [Strench, Breeze, Glitter, None, None]

5.4.1 Propositional Theorem Proving

Consider a Simple Knowledge Base

- Choose the vocabulary for proposition symbols for x, y.
- Let $P_{x, y}$ be true, if there is pit in [x, y].
- Let $B_{x, y}$ be true, if there is breeze in [x, y].

The KB includes:

- There is no pit in [1, 1].

  $R_1 : \neg P_{1, 1}$
- The square is breezy, iff there is a pit in a neighbouring square.

  $R_2 : B_{1, 1} \Leftrightarrow (P_{1, 2} \vee P_{2, 1})$

  $R_3 : B_{2, 1} \Leftrightarrow (P_{1, 1} \vee P_{2, 2} \vee P_{3, 1})$
- The preceding sentences are true for all wumpus world.
- Now, we include the breeze percepts for the first two squares visited in the specific world the agent is in.

  $R_4 : \neg B_{1, 1}$

  $R_5 : B_{2, 1}$
- Knowledge base contains all 5 sentences (R_1 to R_5).
- If we want to consider it as a single sentence, we can use conjunction.

  $R_1 \wedge R_2 \wedge R_3 \wedge R_4 \wedge R_5$.

5.4.2 Inference and Proofs

- The aim of logical inference is to decide whether KB $\neq$ α for some sentence α.
- Inference algo, is a direct implementation of the definition of entailment. (Enumerate the model, and check that α is true in every model in which KB is true).
- For PL, models are assignment of true or false to every proposition symbol.
- For example, wumpus world problem.

  The relevant proposition symbols are

  $B_{1, 1}$, $B_{2, 1}$, $P_{1, 1}$, $P_{1, 2}$, $P_{2, 1}$, $P_{2, 2}$ and $P_{3, 1}$ all are used in KB.
- Therefore, 2^7 = 128 possible models. For only three of these, KB is true (shown in Table 5.3 below).
- In those three models, $\neg P_{1, 2}$ is true, hence there is no pit in [1, 2], on the other hand, $P_{2, 2}$ is true in two of the three models and false in one, so we cannot yet tell, there is a pit in [2, 2].

Table 5.3 : Truth Table for KB

$B_{1,1}$	$B_{2,1}$	$P_{1,1}$	$P_{1,2}$	$P_{2,1}$	$P_{2,2}$	$P_{3,1}$		R_1	R_2	R_3	R_4	R_5	KB
F	F	F	F	F	F	F		T	T	T	T	F	F
F	F	F	F	F	F	T		T	T	F	T	F	F
:	:	:	:	:	:	:		:	:	:	:	:	:
F	T	F	F	F	F	F		T	T	F	T	T	F
F	T	F	F	F	F	T		T	T	T	T	T	T
F	T	F	F	F	T	F		T	T	T	T	T	T
F	T	F	F	F	T	T		T	T	T	T	T	T
F	T	F	F	T	F	F		T	F	F	T	T	F
:	:	:	:	:	:	:		:	:	:	:	:	:
T	T	T	T	T	T	T		F	T	T	F	T	F

- Table 5.3, A truth table constructed for the KB given in the text, KB is true if R_1 to R_5 are true, it occurs in only 3 rows (out of 128 rows).
- In all 3 rows, $P_{1, 2}$ is false, so there is no pit in (1, 2). On the other hand, there might or might not be a pit in [2, 2].

5.4.3 Proof by Resolution

- Even if the inference rules covered so far are sound, there is a question of completeness for the inference algorithms that use them.

- The idea of resolution is simple: if we know that
  - p is true or q is true
  - and we also know that p is false or r is true
  - then it must be the case that q is true or r is true.
- This line of reasoning is formalized in the Resolution Tautology:

(p OR q) AND (NOT p OR r) -> q OR r

- In order to apply resolution in a proof:
  - We express our hypotheses and conclusion as a product of sums (conjunctive normal form), such as those that appear in the Resolution Tautology.
  - Each maxterm in the CNF of the hypothesis becomes a clause in the proof.
  - We apply the resolution tautology to pairs of clauses, producing new clauses.
  - If we produce all the clauses of the conclusion, we have proven it.

Proof with Resolution

- Given the following hypotheses:
  - If it rains, Joe brings his umbrella (r -> u)
  - If Joe has an umbrella, he doesn't get wet (u -> NOT w)
  - If it doesn't rain, Joe doesn't get wet (NOT r -> NOT w) prove that Joes doesn't get wet (NOT w)
- We first put each hypothesis in CNF:
  - r -> u == (NOT r OR u)
  - u -> NOT w == (NOT u OR NOT w)
  - NOT r -> NOT w == (r OR NOT w)
- We then use resolution on the hypotheses to derive the conclusion (NOT w):

1. NOT r OR u	Premise
2. NOT u OR NOT w	Premise
3. r OR NOT w	Premise
4. NOT r OR NOT w	L1, L2, resolution
5. NOT w OR NOT w	L3, L4, resolution
6. NOT w	L5, idempotence
7. QED	

Proofs by Contradiction using Resolution

- We can combine resolution with proof by contradiction (where we assert the negation of what we wish to prove, and from that premise derive FALSE) to direct our search towards smaller and smaller clauses, with the goal of producing FALSE.

  Proof by contradiction:

  (NOT p -> 0) == p

- We use proof by contradiction to drive our search for a proof; we are looking for the smallest possible goal clause (false), so any use of equivalences or resolution that brings us to simpler expressions is working towards that goal.
- We can redo the previous proof (about Joe and his umbrella) using proof by contradiction with resolution:

1. NOT r OR u	Premise
2. NOT u OR NOT w	Premise
3. r OR NOT w	Premise
4. w	Negation of conclusion
5. NOT r OR NOT w	L1, L2, resolution
6. NOT w OR NOT w	L3, L5, resolution
7. NOT w	L6, idempotence
8. FALSE	L4, L7, resolution

5.4.4 Conjuctive Normal Form (CNF)

There is another kind of normal form called conjunctive normal form which is sometimes useful.

We had like to prove:

$KB \models \alpha$
equivalent to: $KB \wedge \neg \alpha$ unsatifiable

We first rewrite $KB \wedge \neg \alpha$ to conjuctive normal form (CNF)

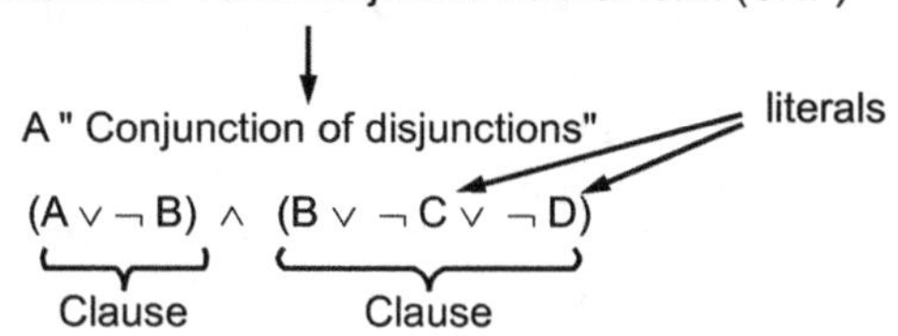

Any KB can be converted into CNF.

In fact, any KB can be converted into CNF-3 using clauses with a most 3 literals.

Example: Conversion to CNF:

$B_{1,1} \Leftrightarrow (P_{1,2} \vee P_{2,1})$

1. Eliminate $\Leftrightarrow$, replacing $\alpha \Leftrightarrow \beta$ with $(\alpha \Rightarrow \beta) \wedge (\beta \Rightarrow \alpha)$.

   $(B_{1,1} \Rightarrow (P_{1,2} \vee P_{2,1})) \wedge ((P_{1,2} \vee P_{2,1}) \Rightarrow B_{1,1})$

2. Eliminate $\Rightarrow$, replacing $\alpha \Rightarrow \beta$ with $\neg\alpha \vee \beta$.

   $(\neg B_{1,1} \vee P_{1,2} \vee P_{2,1}) \wedge (\neg(P_{1,2} \vee P_{2,1}) \vee (B_{1,1})$

3. Move $\neg$ inwards using de Morgan's rules and double-negation: $\neg(\alpha \vee \beta) = \neg\alpha \vee \neg\beta$

   $(\neg B_{1,1} \vee P_{1,2} \vee P_{2,1}) \wedge ((\neg P_{1,2} \wedge \neg P_{2,1}) \vee B_{1,1})$

4. Apply distributive law ($\wedge$ over $\vee$) and flatten:

   $(\neg B_{1,1} \vee P_{1,2} \vee P_{2,1}) \wedge (\neg P_{1,2} \vee B_{1,1}) \wedge (\neg P_{2,1} \vee B_{1,1})$

   $B_{1,1} \Leftrightarrow (P_{1,2} \vee P_{2,1})$

5. KB is the conjunction of all of its sentences (all are true), so write each clause (disjunct) as a sentence in KB:

   ...

   $(\neg B_{1,1} \vee P_{1,2} \vee P_{2,1})$

   $(\neg P_{1,2} \vee B_{1,1})$

   $(\neg P_{2,1} \vee B_{1,1})$

   ...

5.4.5 Horn Clauses and Definite Clauses

- A Horn clause is a clause containing at most one positive literal. A definite clause contains exactly one positive literal.
- Clauses are used two ways:
  1. as disjunctions: (rain ∨ sleet)
  2. as implications: (¬child ∨ ¬male ∨ boy)
- Here focus on second use
- Horn clause = at most one +ve literal in clause
  - ➢ Positive / definite clause = exactly one +ve literal
    e.g. [¬p1, ¬p2, ..., ¬pn, q]
  - ➢ Negative clause = no +ve literals
    e.g. [¬p1, ¬p2, ..., ¬pn] and also [ ]
    Note: [¬p1, ¬p2, ..., ¬pn, q] is a representation for (¬p1 ∨ ¬p2 ... ∨ ¬pn ∨ q) or [(p1 ∨ p2 ∨ ... ∨ pn) q]
    so can read as: If p1 and p2 and ... and pn then q
    and write as: p1 ∧ p2 ∧ ... ∧ pn p q or q ∧ p1 ∧ p2 ∧ , ..., ∧ pn

Resolution with Horn Clause

Only two possibilities:

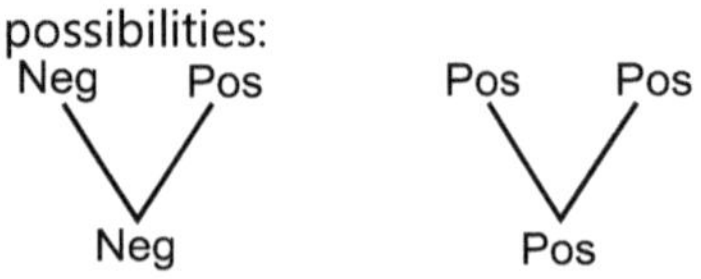

- It is possible to rearrange derivations of negative clauses so that all new derived clauses are negative.

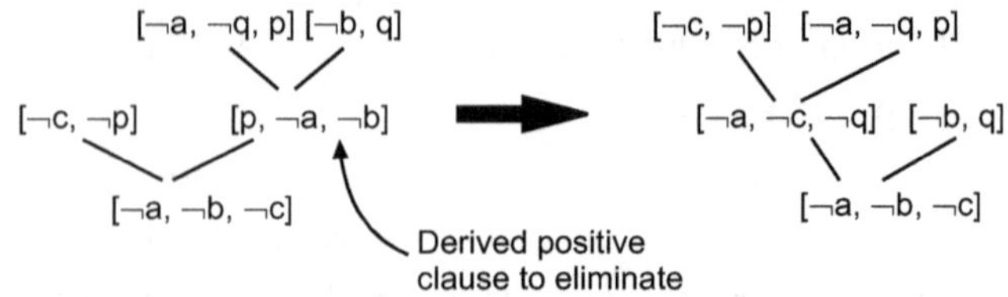

5.4.6 Forward and Backward Chaining

- The completeness of resolution makes it a very important inference model.
- Real-world knowledge only requires a restricted form of clauses:
  - ➢ Horn clauses = disjunction of literals with at most one positive literal.
  - ➢ Three important properties:
    - (i) Can be written as an implication
      $(\neg L_{1,1} \vee \neg \text{Breeze} \vee B_{1,1}) \rightarrow (L_{1,1} \vee \text{Breeze}) \Rightarrow B_{1,1}$
    - (ii) Inference through forward chaining and backward chaining.
    - (iii) Deciding entailment can be done in a time linear size of the knowledge base.
- Idea: fire any rule whose premises are satisfied in the KB.
  - ➢ Add its conclusion to the KB, until query is found.

$P \Rightarrow Q$

$L \wedge M \Rightarrow P$

$B \wedge L \Rightarrow M$

$A \wedge P \Rightarrow L$

$A \wedge B \Rightarrow L$

A

B

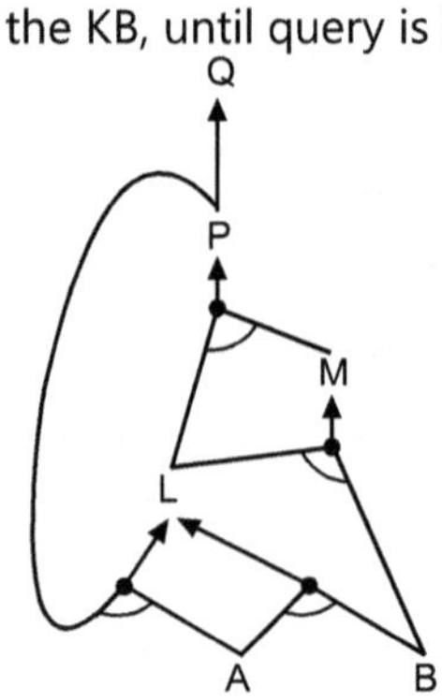

Fig. 5.14

Program 5.1 : Forward Chaining is Sound and Complete for Horn KB

```
function PL-FC-ENTAILS? (KB, q) returns true or false
    local variables: count, a table, indexed by clause, initially the number of premises inferred, a table, indexed by
                     symbol, each entry initially false agenda, a list of symbols, initially the symbols known to be true
    while agenda is not empty do
        p ← POP(agenda)
        unless inferred[p] do
            inferred[p] ← true
            for each Horn clause c in whose premise p appears do
                decrement count[c]
                if count[c] = 0 then do
                    if HEAD[c] = q then return true
                    PUSH(HEAD[c], agenda)
    return false
```

Forward Chaining Example

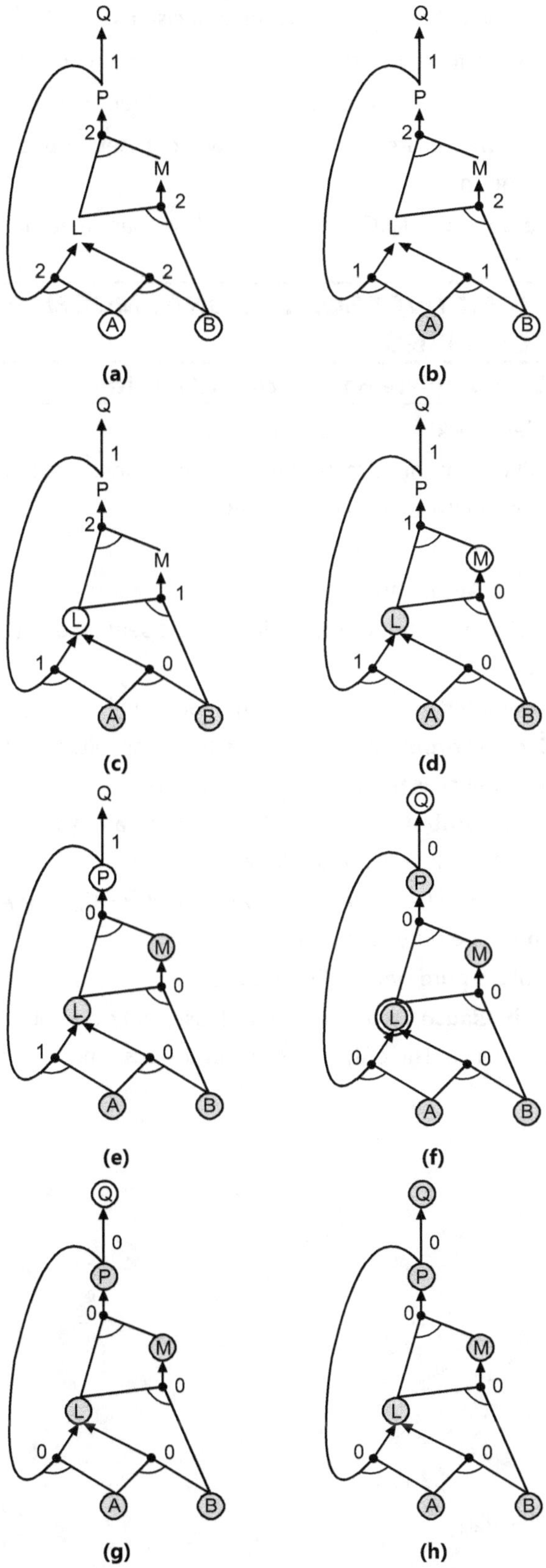

Fig. 5.15

Proof of Completeness

FC derives every atomic sentence that is entailed by KB

- FC reaches a fixed point where no new atomic sentences are derived.
- Consider the final state as a model m, assigning true/false to symbols.
- Every clause in the original KB is true in m

  $a_1 \wedge \ldots \wedge a_k \Rightarrow b$
- Hence m is a model of KB.
- If KB $\models$ q, q is true in every model of KB, including m.

Backward Chaining

Idea: work backwards from the query q:

to prove q by BC,

check if q is known already, or

prove by BC all premises of some rule concluding q

Avoid loops: check if new subgoal is already on the goal stack.

Avoid repeated work: check if new subgoal

1. has already been proved true, or
2. has already failed.

Backward Chaining Example:

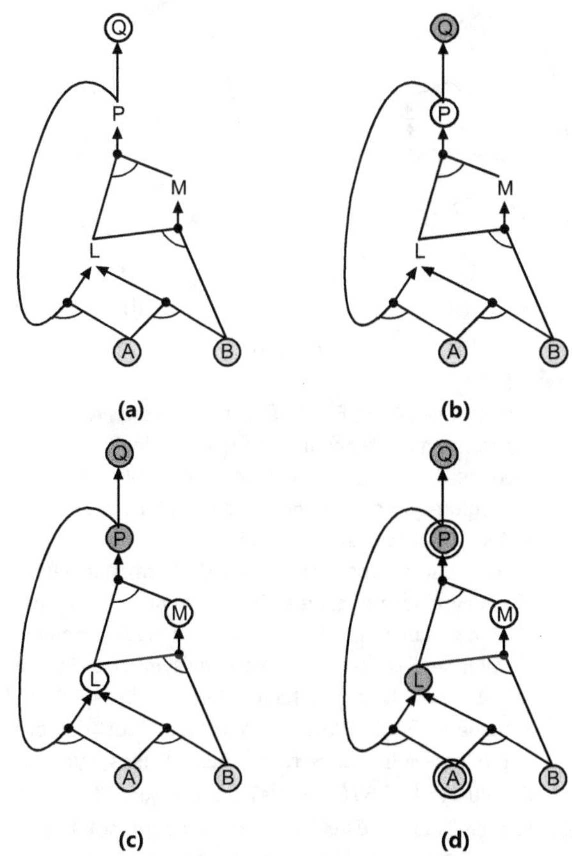

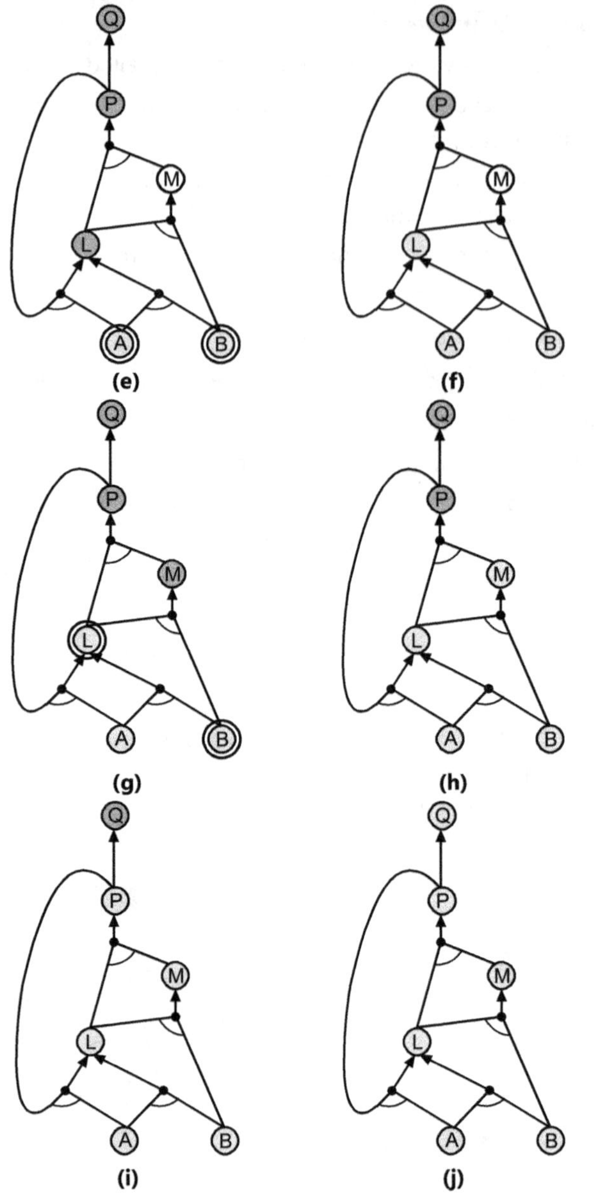

Fig. 5.16

- FC is data-driven, automatic, unconscious processing, e.g., object recognition, routine decisions.
- May do lots of work that is irrelevant to the goal.
  BC is goal-driven, appropriate for problem-solving,
  e.g., where are my keys? How do I get into a PhD program ?
- Complexity of BC can be much less than linear in size of KB.

5.5 EFFECTIVE PROPOSITIONAL MODEL CHECKING

5.5.1 A Complete Backtracking Algorithm

Complete backtracking search algorithms:

- DPLL algorithm (Davis, Putnam, Logemann, Loveland).
- Incomplete local search algorithms
  - ➢ WalkSAT algorithm.

The DPLL Algorithm

Determine if an input propositional logic sentence in (CNF) is satisfiable.

Improvements over truth table enumeration:

1. **Early Termination:** A clause is true if any literal is true. A sentence is false if any clause is false.
2. **Pure Symbol Heuristic:** Pure symbol: always appears with the same "sign" in all clauses.
   e.g., In the three clauses (A ∨ ¬B), (¬B ∨ ¬C), (C ∨ A), A and B are pure, C is impure.
   Make a pure symbol literal true.
3. **Unit Clause Heuristic:** Unit clause: only one literal in the clause. The only literal in a unit clause must be true.

Program 5.2 :

```
function DPLL-SATISFIABLE?(s) returns true or false
    inputs; s, a sentence in propositional logic
    clauses ← the set of clauses in the CNF representation of s
    symbols ← a list of proposition symbols in s
    return DPLL(clauses, symbols, [ ])
function DPLL(clauses, symbols, model) returns true or false
    if every clause in clauses is true in model then return true
    if some clause in clauses is false in model then return false
    P, value ← FIND-PURE-SYMBOL(symbols, clauses, model)
    if P is non-null then return DPLL(clauses, symbols-P, P = value|model)
    P, value ← Find - UNIT-CLAUSE (clauses, model)
    if P is non-null then return DPLL (clauses, symbols - P,|P = value|model|)
    P, value ← FIRST(symbols); rest ← REST(symbols)
    return DPLL(clauses, rest, [P = true|model]) or
            DPLL(clauses, rest, [P - false|model])
```

The WalkSAT Algorithm:

- Incomplete, local search algorithm.
- Evaluation function: The min-conflict heuristic of minimizing the number of unsatisfied clauses.
- Steps are taken in the space of complete assignments, flipping the truth value of one variable at a time.
- Balance between greediness and randomness.
  - To avoid local minima

Program 5.3 :

```
function WALKSAT(clauses, p, max-flips) returns a satisfying model or failure
    inputs: clauses, a set of clauses in propositional logic
        p, the probability of choosing to do a "random walk" move
        max-flips, number of flips allowed before giving up
    model ← a random assignment of true/false to the symbols in clauses
    for i - 1 to max-flips do
        if model satisfies clauses then return model
        clause ← a randomly selected clause from clause that is false in model
        with probability p flip the value in model of a randomly selected symbol from clause
        else flip whichever symbol in clause maximizes the number of satisfied clauses
    return failure
```

Local Search Algorithm

- Hill climbing and simulated annealing are the example of the local search algorithm. By choosing right evaluation function, these algorithm are applied to satisfiability problem. All these algorithms take the space of complete assignments, flipping the truth value of one symbol at a time. This space contains many local minimax, to escape from it various forms of randomness is required. Simplest example of this is walk sat algorithm. In recent research the good balance is obtained between the greediness and randomness.

The Landscape of Random SAT Problem :

- Easy problem can be solved by on of algorithms but to solve SAT problem, at landscape
- Some problem instances must require exponential run time as SAT is NP-complete problem.
- When we look at satisfiability problem in conjunctive normal form an under constrained problem is one with relatively few clauses constraining the variables For example, a randomly generated 3 CNF sentence with five symbols and five clauses.

  $(\neg D \vee \neg B \vee C) \wedge (B \vee \neg A \vee \neg C) \wedge (\neg C \vee \neg B \vee E) \wedge (E \vee \neg D \vee B) \wedge (B \vee E \vee \neg C)$
- Sixteen of the 32 possible assignments are models of this sentence, so an average, it would take just two random guesses to find a model. This is an easy satisfiability problem on the other hand, an oven constrained problems has many clauses relative to the number of variables and is likely to have no solutions.
- To go beyond these basic intuition we must define exactly how random sentences are generated.

5.6 AGENTS BASED ON PROPOSITIONAL LOGIC

Steps for to construct wumpus world agents that use propositional logic are :

- Enable the agent to deduce, to extent possible, the state of the world given its percent history. This requires writing down a complete logical model of the effects of actions.
- Keep track of the world efficiently without going back into the percept history for each inference.
- Agent can use logical inference to construct plans that are guaranteed to achieve its goal.

The Current State of the World

- A logical agent operates by deducing what to do from a knowledge base of sentences about the world.
- The knowledge base is composed of
  - Axioms : General knowledge about how the world works
  - Percept : Sentences obtained from the agent's experience in a particular world.
- Problems for deducing the current state of world are as follows :
  - We began collecting axioms : The agent knows that the starting square contains no pit ($\neg P_1$, 1) and no wumpus ($\neg W_1$, 1). We gradually needs to add wumpus.

- Adding new assertion would also result in a contradiction.
- So to need to add stench to the knowledge base.
- We need axioms that allow the agent to keep track of fluents.
- These fluents change as the result of actions taken by the agent.
- So, need to write down the transition model at the wumpus world as a set of logical sentences.
- To describe how the world changes needs to write effect axioms that specify the outcome of an action at the next time step.
- If the effect axiom fails to state, information may has been lost this gives rise to the frame problem.
- One possible solution to the frame problem would be to add frame axioms explicitly asserting all propositions that remains the same.
- The specific manifestation of the frame problem is called the representation frame problem.
- There is also inferential frame problem, the problem of projecting forward the result of at step plan of action in time O(Kt) rather than O(nt).
- The solution to the problem involves changing one's focus from writing axioms about actions to writing axioms about fluents. An axiom of this form is called as a successive – state axiom.

- Solving the representational and inferential frame problems is a big step forward but a pernicious problem remains.
- We need to confirm that all the necessary preconditions of an action hold for it to have its intended effect.
- Forward action moves the agent ahead unless there is a wall in the way, but there are many other unusual exceptions that could cause the action to fail : agent might trip and fall, be stricken with a heart attack be carried away by glants bats, etc.
- Specifying all these exceptions is called the qualification problem.
- There is no complete solution with logic system designers have to use good judgment in deciding how detailed they want to be in specifying their model, and what details they want to leave out.

A Hybrid Agent :

- The ability to deduce various aspects of the state of the world, can be combined fairly straight-forwardly with condition-action rules and with problem-solving algorithms to produce a hybrid agent for the wumpus world.

Program 5.4 : A hybrid agent program for the wumpus world. It uses a propositional knowledge base to infer the state of the world, and a combination of problem-solving search and domain-specific code to decide what actions to take

```
function HYBRID-WUMPUS-AGENT (percept) returns an action
    inputs: percept, a list, [stench, breeze, glitter, bump, scream]
    persistent: KB, a knowledge base, initially the atemporal "wumpus physics"
                t, a counter, initially 0, indicating time
                plan, an action sequence, initially empty
    TELL(KB, MAKE-PERCEPT-SENTENCE(percept, t))
    TELL the KB the temporal "physics" sentences for time t
    safe ← {[x, y] : ASK (KB, OK^t_x,y ) = true}
    if ASK (KB, glitter^t) = true then
        plan ← [Grab] + PLAN-ROUTE(current, {[1,1]},safe)+[Climb]
    if plan is empty then
        unvisited ← {[x, y] : ASK (KB, L^t'_x,y ) = false for all t' ≤ t}
        plan ← PLAN-ROUTE(current, unvisited ∩ safe, safe)
    if plan is empty and ASK(KB, HaveArrow^t) = true then
        possible_wumpus ← {[x, y] : ASK(KB, ¬ W_x,y) = false}
        plan ← PLAN-SHOT(current, possible_wumpus, safe)
    if plan is empty then  // no choice but to take a risk
```

```
        not_unsafe ← {[x, y] : ASK(KB, ¬ OK^t_x,y ) = false}
        plan ← PLAN-ROUTE(current, unvisited ∩ not_unsafe, safe)
    if plan is empty then
        plan ← PLAN-ROUTE(current, {[1,1]}, safe) + [Climb]
    action ← POP(plan)
    TELL(KB, MAKE-ACTION_SENTENCE(action,t))
    t ← t + 1
    return action
```

```
function PLAN-ROUTE(current,goals,allowed) returns an action sequence
    inputs: current, the agent's current position
            goals a set of squares; try to plan a route to one of them
            allowed, a set of squares that can form part of the route
    problem ← ROUTE-PROBLEM(current,goals,allowed)
    return A*-GRAPH-SEARCH(problem)
```

- Program 5.4 Shows one possible way to do this
- The main body of the agent program constructs a plan based on a decreasing priority of goals.
- First, if there is a glitter, the program constructs a plan to grab the gold, follow a route back to the initial location, and clim out of the wave.
- Otherwise, if there is no current plan the program plans a route of the closet safe square that it has not visited yet, making sure the route goes through only safe squares.
- Route planning is done with A* search, not with ASK.
- If there are no safe squares to explore.
- If the agent still has an arrow is to try to make a safe square by shooting at one of the possible wumpus locations. These are determined by asking where ASK(KB, ¬ $w_{x,y}$) is false, that is where it is not known that there is not a wumpus.

Logical State Estimation

The agent program Program 5.4 works well, but it has one major weakness

- As time goes by, the computation expense involved in the call to ASK goes up and up.
- This happens mainly because the required inferences have to go back further and further in time and involve more and more proposition symbols.
- We cannot have agent whose time to process each percent grows in proportion to the length of its life, So we need constant update time, that is independent of t.
- This can be achieve by saving the result interference, so that the interference process at the next time step can build on the results of earlier steps instead of having to start again from scrach.
- The past history of percepts and all their ramification can be replaced by the belief state, that is, some representation of the set of all possible current states of the world.
- The process of updating the belief state as new percepts arrive is called state estimation.
- Maintaining an exact belief state as a logical formula is not easy.
- If there are n fluent symbols for time t, then there are 2^n possible states, i.e. assignments of truth values to those symbols.
- There are 2^n physical states, hence 2^{2n} belief states i.e. exact state estimation may require logical formulas whose size is exponential in the number of symbols.
- One very common and natural scheme for approximate skate estimation is to represent belief states as conjunctions of literals is 1-CNF formulas.
- The conjunction of provable literals becomes the new belief state and the previous belief state is discarded.
- It is important to understand that this scheme may lose some information as time goes along.
- Thus, the set of possible states represented buy the 1-CNF belief includes all states that are in fact possible given the full percept history.
- As shown in Fig. 5.17, the 1 – CNF belief state acts as a simple outer envelope, or conservative appropriation around the exact belief state.

- This idea of conservative, approximations to complicated sets as a recurring, theme used in may areas of AI.

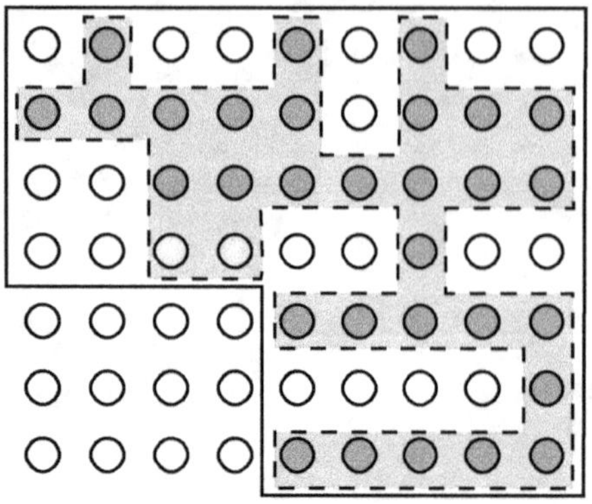

Fig. 5.17 : Depiction of a 1-CNF belief state (bold outline) as a simply representable, conservative approximation to the exact (wiggly) belief state (shaded region with dashed outline). Each possible world is shown as a circle; the shaded ones are consistent with all the percepts.

Making Plans by Propositional Inference

- The agent in Program 5.4 A uses logical inference to determine which squares are safe, but uses A* search to make plans.
- Making plans by proportional inference is very simple, following are the steps.
  1. Construct a sentence that includes
     (i) Init^{o}, a collection of assertions about the initial state.
     (ii) Tranistion^{1}, ..., transition^{t}, the successor – state axioms for all possible actions at each time yp to maximum time t.
     (iii) The assertion that the goal is achieved at time t.
     Have Gold^{t} $\cap$ Climbedout^{t}

Program 5.5 : The SATPLAN algorithm. The planning problem is translated into a CNF sentence in which the goal is asserted to hold at a fixed time step t and axioms are included for each time step up to t. If the satisfiability algorithm finds a model, then a plan is extracted by looking at those proposition symbols that refer to actions and are assigned true in the model. If no model exists, then the process is repeated with the goal moved one step later.

```
function SATPLAN(init, transition, goal, Tmax)returns solution or failure
  inputs: init, transition, goal, constitute a description of the problem
      Tmax, an upper limit for plan length
  for t = 0 to Tmax do
      cnf ← TRANSLATE-TO-SAT(init, transition, goal, t)
      model ← SAT-SOLVER(cnf)
      if model is not null then
          return EXTRACT-SOLUTION(model)
  return failure
```

2. Present the whole sentence to a SAT solver. If the solver finds a satisfying model, then the goal is achievable, if the sentence is unsatisfable, then the planning problem is impossible.
3. Assuming a model is found, extract from the model those variables that represent actions and are assigned true. Together they represent a plan to achieve the goals.

- A propositional planning procedure, SATPLAN, is shown in Program 5.5. It implements the basic idea just given, with one twist.
- Because the agent does not know how many steps it will take to search the goal, the algorithm tries each possible number of steps t, up to some maximum conceivable plan length T_{max}.
- In this way, it is guaranteed to find the shortest plan it one exists.
- Because of the way SATPLAN searches for a solution, this approach cannot be used in a partially observable environment. SATPLAN would just set the unobservable variables to the values it needs to create a solution.

B : FIRST-ORDER LOGIC

5.7 REPRESENTATION REVISITED

- Propositional logic assumes that the world or system being modelled can be described in terms of fixed, known set of proposition. This assumption is impossible for many pieces of knowledge.

  Example: Consider the general statement about people.
- "If a person is rich then they have a nice car".
- We could encode is knowledge in propositional knowledge by creating a large set of rules. One rule for each person.

  (Akshay) AkshayHasNiceCar

  (Julie) JulieHasNiceCar

  (Seema) SeemaHasNiceCar

  ⋮

This is completely impractical and unintuitive way to represent, reason about and communicate such knowledge.

Example:

"If n is a natural number, then n + 1 is also a natural number".

We could try to encode this statement in propositional logic (PL) as:

(Natural 1) Natural 2

(Natural 2) Natural 3

(Natural 3) Natural 4

⋮

We would need to have an infinite number of propositional formulae, one for each natural number.

Updating propositional logic with quantifiers:

- In both of these examples we need the ability to directly talk about objects (e.g. people and numbers) and to write down logical statements that generalize (or quantify) over these objects.
- FOL is a logic that gives us the ability to quantify over objects.
- You will often see FOL called first-order predicate logic or first order predicate calculus. These all are the names of the same thing.

These examples (car and natural numbers) can be encoded in FOL.

$$\forall_x (\text{Rich}(X) \Rightarrow \exists_y (\text{Owns}(X, Y) \wedge \text{Cars}(Y) \wedge \text{Nice}(Y)))$$

and $\forall_x (\text{Natural}(X) \Rightarrow \text{Natural}(X + 1))$

where, $\forall$, $\exists$ are universal and existential quantifiers respectively.

Table 5.4 : Formal Languages and Their Ontological and Epistemological Commitments

Language	Ontological Commitment (what exists in the world)	Epistemological commitments (what an agent believes about facts)
Propositional logic	Facts	True/False/Unknown
First order logic	Facts, objects, relations	True/False/Unknown
Temporal logic	Facts, objects, relations, times	True/False/Unknown
Probability theory	Facts	Degree of belief belongs [0, 1]
Fuzzy logic	Facts with degree of truth belongs [0, 1]	Known interval value.

Ontological commitment - what is assumed about the nature of reality.

Epistemological commitments: Possible state of knowledge that it allows with respect to each fact.

5.8 SYNTAX AND SEMANTICS OF FIRST-ORDER LOGIC

Models of FOL have objects in them.

Example: Model contains five objects, two binary relation, three unary-relations and one function.

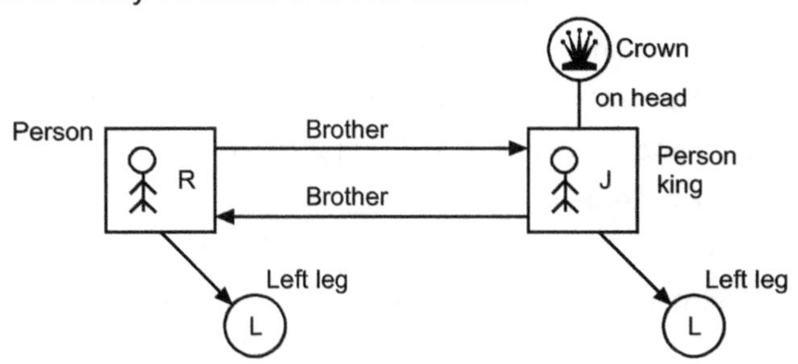

Fig. 5.18 : Example model of FOL

Model with Five Objects:

1. Richard the Lion heart (king from 1190 to 1195).
2. John (King from 1195 to 1200).
3. Left leg of Richard.
4. Left leg of John.
5. The crown.

Relation:

1. Richard and John are **brothers.**
   {<Richard, John>, <John, Richard>}
2. The crown is on King John's head, **on head**.
   {<the crown>, <John>}

Binary Relation: Relate pairs of objects.

Unary Relation: The 'person' property in true for both Richard and John.

Crown property is only true for crown.

Function: Each person has only one left leg.

Predicate:

Every complete sentence contains two parts (1) Subject, (2) Predicate.

The subject is what (or whom) the sentence is about.

The predicate tells something about the subject.

E.g. : A sentence "Akshay {runs}".
Subject - Akshay, Predicate - runs.

Predicate always include verb, which tells something about subject.

E.g.: "The car Sheela is driving is blue".
"The sky is blue".
"The cover of this book is blue".
Predicate - 'is blue'.

Predicate are given names. Let 'A' is name of predicate 'is blue'. Sentence is represented as "A(x)", read as "x is blue, symbol x is any object".

Symbols:

1. Constant (which stand for objects).
   E.g. Richard and John.
2. Predicate (which stand for relation).
   E.g. Brother, Onhead, Person, King and Crown.
3. Function (which stand for function).
   E.g. Leftleg.

The BNF for FOL is

Sentence $\rightarrow$ Atomic sentence
| (Sentence Connective Sentence)
| Quantifier variable, … sentence
| $\neg$ Sentence

Atomic Sentence $\rightarrow$ Predicate (Term, …) | Term = Term

Term $\rightarrow$ Function (Term, …)
| Constant
| Variable

Connective $\rightarrow \Rightarrow | \wedge | \vee | \Leftrightarrow$

Quantifier $\rightarrow \forall | \exists$

Constant $\rightarrow$ A | B | John | …

Variable $\rightarrow$ x | y | z …

Predicate $\rightarrow$ Return | Runing | Cooking | …

Function $\rightarrow$ Mother | Father | Left Leg | …

- The semantics must relate sentences to models in order to determine truth.
- For this, the interpretation is needed that specifies exactly which objects, relations and functions are referred to by the constants, predicates and function symbols.

Intended Interpretations:

- **Richard** refers to the Richard the Lion heart and **John** refers to the King John.
- **Brother** refers to the brotherhood relation. **Onhead** refers to the on head relation.
- **Person, King** and **Crown** refer to the sets of object that are persons, King and Crowns.
- **Leftleg** refers to the left leg function.

Terms:

- Term refers to an object. The term is either individual constant or a variable or a function applied to n terms $f(t_1, t_2, \dots t_n)$.

Atomic Sentences:

- The sentences are formed from a predicate symbol followed by a parenthesized list of term.
  E.g. brother (Richard, John).
- Atomic sentences can have complex term as arguments.
  Marrved (Mother (Richard), Father (John)).

Complex Sentences:

- It uses logical connectives.
  E.g. King (John) V King (Richard) is true as either John was a King or Richard was a King.

Quantifiers:

There are two quantifiers used in FOL, Universal Quantifier ($\forall$) and Exestential Quantifier ($\exists$).

1. **Universal Quantifier ($\forall$):**

- $\forall$ – "For all"
- $\forall_x$ Dog (x) $\Rightarrow$ Animal (x)
  For all x if x is a dog, then x is an animal.
- X is a variable.
- $\forall_x P$, where P is a logical expression, says that P is true, for every object x.

2. **Exestential Quantifier (∃):**

- It makes statement about some object in the universe.
- $\exists_x$ - "There exists x such that" or "For some x".
- $\exists_x P$ - says that P is true for at least one object x.
- King John has crown on his head $\exists_x$ Crown (x) ∧ Onhead (x, John)

Nested Quantifiers:

- We can use multiple quantifiers.

  E.g. Brothers are siblings.

  $\forall_x \forall_y$ Brothers (x, y) ⇒ Siblings (x, y)
- We can use one quantifier with several variables.

  $\forall_{x, y}$ Sibling (x, y) ⇔ Sibling (y, x)
- We can have a mixture of quantifiers.

  E.g. Everybody loves somebody (for every person there is someone that person loves)

  $\forall_x \exists_y$ Loves (x, y)

  $\forall_x$ ($\exists_y$ Loves (x, y)) - Everyone has a particular property, the property that somebody loves them.

  E.g. There is someone who is loved by everyone.

  $\exists_x \forall_y$ Loves (x, y)

  $\exists_x$ ($\forall_y$ Loves (x, y)), someone in the world has a particular property, the property of being loved by everybody.

Connection between ∀ and ∃:

We can connect ∀ and ∃ with the help of negation (¬).

- Everybody dislikes Judy is the same as asserting there does not exist someone who likes Judy.

  $\exists_x \neg$ Likes (x, Judy) is equivalent to $\neg \exists_x$ Likes (x, Judy)

  Everybody likes Roses

  $\forall_x$ likes (x, Roses) is equivalent to $\neg \exists_x \neg$ likes (x, Roses)

The de Morgan's Rule for quantified and unquantified sentences.

$$\forall_x \neg P \equiv \neg \exists_x P$$
$$\neg \forall_x P \equiv \exists_x \neg P$$
$$\forall_x P \equiv \neg \exists_x \neg P$$
$$\exists_x P \equiv \neg \forall_x \neg P$$
$$\neg (P \land \neg Q) \equiv \neg (P \lor Q)$$
$$\neg (P \land Q) \equiv \neg (\neg P \lor \neg Q)$$
$$P \land Q \equiv \neg (\neg P \lor \neg Q)$$
$$P \lor Q \equiv \neg (\neg P \land \neg Q)$$

Equality:

- To make statements to the effect that two terms refer to some object.
- Equality symbol can be used to state facts about a given function.

  Sister (John) = Julie
- Equality symbol can be used with negation to insist that two terms are not the same object.

5.9 USING FIRST-ORDER LOGIC

- In this, we study how we can use FOL, we can learn to use FOL with the help of examples. We will learn this at the domain of family relationships, number sets and lists.

The Kinship Domain (Family Relationships):

- Object in the domain are peoples, unary predicates used are Male and Female kinship relations - parenthood, brotherhood, marriage and so on.
- Kinship relations are represented by binary predicates - Parent, Sibling, Brother, Sister, Child, Daughter, Wife, Husband, Spouse, Grandparent, Grandchild, Cousin, Aunt, Uncle etc.
- **Functions Used:** Mother and Father (because every person has exactly one of each of these).

Examples:

1. One's mother is one's female parent.

   $\forall_{m, c}$ Mother (c) = m ⇔ Female (m) ∧ Parent (m, c)
2. One's husband is one's male spouse.

   $\forall_{w, h}$ Husband (h, w) ⇔ Male (h) ∧ Spouse (h, w).
3. Male and Female are disjoint categories.

   $\forall_x$ Male (x) ⇔ ¬ Female (x).
4. Parent and child are inverse relation.

   $\forall_{p, c}$ Parent (p, c) ⇔ Child (c, p)
5. A grandparent is a parent of one's parent.

   $\forall_{g, c}$ Grandparent (g, c) ⇔ $\exists_p$ Parent (g, p) ∧ Parent (p, c).
6. A sibling is a another child of one's parent.

   $\forall_{x, y}$ Sibling (x, y) ⇔ x ≠ y ∧ $\exists_p$ Parent (p, x) ∧ Parent (p, y)

Numbers, Sets and Lists:

The theory of natural numbers or non-negative integers are described here.

Predicate used - NatNum

Symbol constant - 0

One function symbol - S (successor)

Natural numbers are defined recursively NatNum (0) - 0 is a natural number.

$\forall_n$ NatNum (n) $\Rightarrow$ NatNum (S(n)).

For every of object of n, if n is a natural number, then s(n) is a natural number.

So, the natural numbers are 0, S(0), S(S(0)) and so on.

Axioms to constrain the successor function.

$\forall_n \; 0 \neq S(n)$

$\forall_{m,n} \; m \neq n \Rightarrow S(m) \neq S(n)$

Addition in terms of successor function:

1. $\forall_m$ NatNum (m) $\Rightarrow$ + (m, 0) = m
2. $\forall_{m,n}$ NatNum (m) $\wedge$ NatNum (n) $\Rightarrow$ + (S(m), n) = S(+ (m, n))

Explanation of 1: This axioms says that adding 0 to any natural number m gives m itself.

+ (m, 0) is equivalent to (m + 0) using infix notation.

+ (m, 0) - prefix (operator comes at first place)

(m + 0) - infix (operator comes in the middle)

FOL uses prefix notation.

We can also write axiom (2)

$\forall_{m,n}$ NatNum (m) $\wedge$ NatNum (n) $\Rightarrow$ (m + 1) + n = (m + n) + 1 because S(n) = n + 1.

Sets:

The empty set is written as { }

Unary predicate - Set

Binary predicates are

$x \in s$ – x is a member of set s.

$s_1 \subseteq s_2$ – s_1 is a subset of s_2 (not necessary proper subset).

$s_1 \cap s_2$ – Intersection of two sets.

$s_1 \cup s_2$ – Union of two sets.

$\{x|s_2\}$ – The set resulting from adjoining element x to set s.

One possible set of axioms is as below:

1. The only sets are the empty set and those made by adjoining something to set.

   $\forall_s$ set (s) $\Leftrightarrow$ (s = { }) $\vee$ ($\exists_{x}$, s_2 set (s_2) $\wedge$ s = $\{x|s_2\}$).

2. The empty set has no elements adjoined to it.

   (There is no way to decompose empty set into a smaller set).

   $\neg \exists_{x,s} \{x|s\} = \{\}$

   Lists: Lists are similar to sets.

   The differences are that lists which are ordered and the same element can appear more than once in a list.

3. Adjoining an element already in the set has no effect:

   $\forall_{x,s} \; x \in s \Leftrightarrow s = \{x|s\}$.

4. The only members of a set are the elements that were adjoined into it. We express this recursively, saying that x is a member of s if and only if s is equal to some set s_2 adjoined with some element y, where either y is the same as x or x is a member of s_2.

   $\forall_{x,s} \; x \in s \Leftrightarrow [\exists y_1 s_2 \; (s = \{y|s_2\} \wedge (x = y \wedge x \in s_2))]$

5. A set is subset of another set if and only if all of the first set's members are members of the second set.

   $\forall s_1 s_2 \; s_1 \subseteq s_2 \Leftrightarrow (\forall_x \; x \in s_1) \Leftrightarrow x \in s_2$.

6. Two sets are equal if and only if each is a subset of other.

   $\forall s_1, s_2 \; (s_1 = s_2) \Leftrightarrow (s_1 \subseteq s_2 \wedge s_2 \subseteq s_1)$.

7. An object is in the intersection of two sets if and only if it is a member of both sets.

   $\forall x, s_1, s_2 \; x \in (s_1 \cap s_2) \Leftrightarrow (x \in s_1 \wedge x \in s_2)$

8. An object is in the union of two set iff it is a member of either set.

   $\forall x, s_1, s_2 \; x \in (s_1 \cup s_2) \Leftrightarrow (x \in s_1 \vee x \in s_2)$

5.10 KNOWLEDGE ENGINEERING IN FIRST-ORDER LOGIC

General process of knowledge base construction called as knowledge engineering.

A knowledge Engineers:

- Investigates a particular domain.
- Learns what concepts are important in that domain.
- Creates a formal representation of the objects and relations in the domain.

The Knowledge Engineering Process:

It includes the following steps:

1. **Identify the Task:**

- The knowledge engineering must define the range of questions that the knowledge base will support.
- The task will determine what knowledge must be represented in order to connect problems to answers.

2. **Assemble the Relevant Knowledge:**

- If knowledge engineering is not an expert in a domain, then knowledge engineering need to work with real experts to extract what they know (called knowledge acquisition).
- There is a need to understand the scope of the knowledge base, as determined by the task and to understand how the domain actually works.

3. **Decide on a Vocabulary of Predicates, Functions and Constants:**

- Translate the important domain level concepts into logical level names. This involves the questions of knowledge engineering style. Like programming style, this can have a significant impact on the success of the project.

4. **Encode General Knowledge about the Domain:**

- The knowledge engineering has to write down the axioms for all vocabulary. This hold down the meaning of the terms, enabling the expert to check the content.

5. **Encode the Description of the Specific Problem Instance:**

- If the ontology (The ontology determines what kinds of things exist, but does not determine their specific properties and interrelationships) is well planned, then this step is easy.
- For a logical agent, problem instances are supplied by the sensors, whereas a "disembodies" knowledge base is supplied with additional sentences in the same way that traditional programs are supplied with input data.

6. **Pose Queries to the Inference Procedure and Get Answers:**

- We can let the inference procedure operate on the axioms and problem specific facts to derive the facts we are interested in knowing.

7. **Debug the Knowledge Base:**

- We can disturb the knowledge base in various ways to see what kind of wrong behaviour emerges.
- To understand these seven steps, we will apply all these steps to the domain of electronic circuit.
- The domain of electronic circuit.

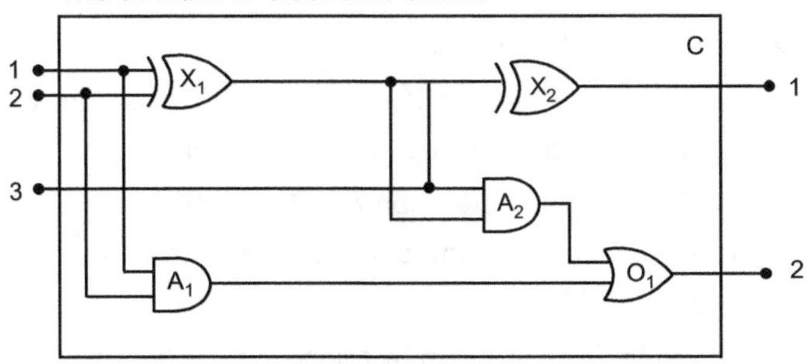

Fig. 5.19 : Electronic circuit

- Fig. 5.19 shows circuit C is a one bit adder, having 3 input signals and two output signals (1 - sum and 2 - for carry).
- Circuit contains two X-OR gates, 2-AND gates and one OR gate.

1. **Identify the Task:**

There can be many tasks associated with digital circuit.

- Analyzing circuits functionality.

  E.g. Does the circuit adds properly? If all the inputs are high, what will be the output of O_1 or X_2?

- Analyzing the circuit structure.

  E.g. Which gates are connected to first input terminal?, which are connected to second input terminal? Does the circuit contains feedback?

- Detailed level of analysis.

  E.g. Timing delays?, circuit area?, power consumption? production cost? etc.

2. **Assemble the Relevant Knowledge:**

- Assembling the knowledge about digital circuits like circuit is composed of wires and gates. Signal flows through the wire. How gate transforms the signals? Some gates have two terminals like AND, OR, XOR. But the NOT gate have only one terminal.
- There are many other factors of the domain that are irrelevant to our analysis, such as colour, shape, size and cost of various components.

3. **Decide on a Vocabulary:**

- Need to choose functions, predicates and constants to represent circuits, terminals, signals and gates.
- How we can distinguish the gates, by naming the gates with **constants** e.g. X_1, X_2, A_1, A_2, O_1.
- Functions are used to represent the type of a gate

  E.g. Type (X_1) = XOR

  Type (X_1, XOR)

  XOR (X_1)

- We can name input and output terminals with constant.

  Gate X_1 terminal name X_1In_1, X_1In_2 and X_1Out_1.

  E.g. In(1, X_1) - First input terminal for gate X_1.

- Connectivity between the gates are represented by predicates. Here predicate is **connected**.

  It takes two terminals as argument.

  E.g. Connected (Out (1, X_1), In(1, X_2)).

- Unary predicate on and off are used, because we need to know whether the signal is on or off.

Encode General Knowledge of the Domain:

Each rule can be stated clearly iff, we have a good vocabulary, we need only seven simple rules to describe everything, we need to know about circuits.

1. If two terminals are connected, then they have the same signal.

   $\forall_{t_1, t_2}$ connected $(t_1, t_2) \Rightarrow$ Signal (t_1) = Signal (t_2)

2. Connected is a commutative predicate.

   $\forall_{t_1, t_2}$ connected $(t_1, t_2) \Leftrightarrow$ Connected (t_2, t_1)

3. The signal at every terminal is either 1 or 0 (but not both).

   $\forall_1$ signal (t) = 1 $\vee$ signal (t) = 0

   $1 \neq 0$

4. An OR gates output is 1 iff any of its input is 1.

   $\forall_g$ Type (g) = OR $\Rightarrow$ Signal (Out (1, g)) = 1 $\Leftrightarrow \exists_n$ signal (In (n, g)) = 1

5. An AND gate's output is 0 iff any of its input is 0.

   $\forall_g$ Type (g) = AND $\Rightarrow$ Signal (Out (1, g)) = 0 $\Leftrightarrow \exists_n$ Signal (In(n, g)) = 0

6. An XOR gate's output is 1 iff its inputs are different.

   $\forall_g$ Type (g) = XOR $\Rightarrow$ Signal (Out (1, g)) = 1 $\Leftrightarrow$ Signal (In (1, g)) $\neq$ Signal (In (2, g))

7. A NOT gate's output is different from its input.

   $\forall_g$ (Type (g) = NOT) $\Rightarrow$ Signal (Out (1, g)) $\neq$ Signal (In (1, g))

Encode the Specific Problem Instance:

The circuit is encoded as circuit C with the following description:

1. Need to categorize the gates.

   Type (X_1) = XOR

   Type (X_2) = XOR

   Type (A_1) = AND

   Type (A_2) = AND

   Type (O_1) = OR

2. Connection between the gates are:

   Connected (Out $(1, X_1)$, In $(1, X_2)$)

   Connected (Out $(1, X_1)$, In $(2, A_2)$)

   Connected (Out $(1, A_2)$, In $(1, O_1)$)

   Connected (Out $(1, A_1)$, In $(2, O_1)$)

   Connected (Out $(1, X_2)$, Out $(1, C_1)$)

   Connected (Out $(1, O_1)$, Out $(2, C_1)$)

   Connected (In $(1, C_1)$, In $(1, X_1)$)

   Connected (In $(1, C_1)$, In $(1, A_1)$)

   Connected (In $(2, C_1)$, In $(2, X_1)$)

   Connected (In $(2, C_1)$, In $(2, A_1)$)

   Connected (In $(3, C_1)$, In $(2, X_2)$)

   Connected (In $(3, C_1)$, In $(1, A_2)$)

Pose Queries to the Inference Procedure:

What combinations of inputs would cause the first output of C (The sum bit) to be 0 and the second output of C_1 (carry bites) to be 1?

$\exists_{i_1, i_2, i_3}$ signal (In $(1, C_1)$) = $i_1 \wedge$ signal (In $(2, C_1)$) = i_2

$\wedge$ signal (In $(3, C_1)$) = $i_3 \wedge$ signal (Out $(1, C_1)$) = 0

$\wedge$ signal (Out $(2, C_1)$) = 1.

After substituting for the variables i_1, i_2 and i_3 the resulting sentence is entailed by the KB (Knowledge Base).

i_1	i_2	i_3	Sum	Carry	
0	0	0	0	0	
0	0	1	1	0	
0	1	0	1	0	
0	1	1	0	1	$\{i_1/0, i_2/1, i_3/1\}$
1	0	0	1	0	
1	0	1	0	1	$\{i_1/1, i_2/0, i_3/1\}$
1	1	0	0	1	$\{i_1/1, i_2/1, i_3/0\}$
1	1	1	1	1	

Another example is:

What are the possible sets of values of all the terminals for the adder circuit?

$\exists_{i_1, i_2, i_3, o_1, o_2,}$ signal (In $(1, C_1)$) = $i_1 \wedge$ signal (In $(2, C_1)$) = i_2

$\wedge$ signal (In $(3, C_1)$) = $i_3 \wedge$ signal (Out $(1, C_1)$) = O_1

$\wedge$ signal (Out $(2, C_1)$) = O_2.

This query returns a complete input output table for the device, which can be used to check that, does the circuit adds properly?

Debug the Knowledge Base:

- We can disturb the knowledge base in various ways to see what kind of erroneous behaviours comes out.
- E.g. If we omit the assertion that $1 \neq 0$, the system will be unable to prove any output for the circuit (except for 000 and 110).
- We can find the problem by asking the outputs of each gate, we can ask.

  $\exists_{i_1, i_2, o}$ signal (In $(1, C_1)$) = $i_1 \wedge$ signal (In $(2, C_1)$) = 12 $\wedge$ signal (Out $(1, X_1)$)

  which reveals that no outputs are known at X_1 for input cases 10 and 01.

5.11 INFERENCE IN FIRST-ORDER LOGIC

- Inference in first order logic define effective procedures for answering questions posed in first order logic. It has been already shown that for propositional logic how the complete inference can be achieved. Now in this section it is extended to obtain algorithms that can answer any answerable question stated in first-order logic. It contains the following point :
  - **Proportional V/s First Order Logic :** This subsection introduces inference rules for quantifiers and shows how to reduce first order inference to proportional inference.
  - **Unification :** It shows how it can be used to construct inference rules that work directly with first order sentences.
  - **The Major Families of First Order Algorithms Includes :** Forward chaining and backward chaining. Forward and backward chaining can be very efficient, but are applicable only to knowledge bases that can be expressed as set of floor chausses,
  - General first order sentence require resolution based theorem proving.

5.12 PROPOSITIONAL V/s FIRST-ORDER INFERENCE

- To do inference in FOL, you can always convert First Order Logic (FOL) sentences into propositional logic statements and perform propositional logic inference.

Example:

Suppose our KB has the first order logic sentence.

$\forall$x King (x) $\wedge$ Male (x) $\Rightarrow$ HasCrown (x)

Then we can replace the variable X with ground terms.

E.g. $\forall$x King (John) $\wedge$ Male (John) $\Rightarrow$ HasCrown (John)

$\forall$x King (Richard) $\wedge$ Male (Richard) $\Rightarrow$ HasCrown (Richard)

$\forall$ King (Robert) $\wedge$ Male (Robert) $\Rightarrow$ HasCrown (Robert)

$\forall$ King (Father (John)) $\wedge$ Male (Father (John)) $\Rightarrow$ HasCrown (Father (John)) and so on.

The Rule of Universal Instantiation (UI):

We can infer any sentence obtained by substituting ground term for the variable.

We can write the rule as

$$\frac{\forall v \alpha}{\text{SUBSET}(\{v|g\}, \alpha)}$$

Substitute ground term g for variable v in sentence α.

For example: In first order logic sentence.

$\forall$x King (x) $\wedge$ Male (x) $\Rightarrow$ HasCrown (x)

We applied the substitution

{x | John}, {x | Richard}, {x | Robert}

The Rule of Existential Instantiation (EI):

States that for any sentence α, variable v and constant k, that does not appear elsewhere in the knowledge base

$$\frac{\exists v \alpha}{\text{SUBSET}(\{v|k\}, \alpha)}$$

For example, in the FOL, sentence

$\exists$x Truck (x) $\wedge$ Drives (x, John)

We can infer the sentence

Truck (T_1) $\wedge$ Drives (T_1, John)

- T_1 is the name of the object that does not appear elsewhere in the KB. It is an assigning a unique propositional symbol.
- Universal instantiation can be applied many times to produce many different consequences.
- Existential instantiation can be applied once and then the existential qualified sentence can be discarded.
- Example: Once, we have added.

  Truck (T_1) $\wedge$ Drives (T_1, John)

  We can discard

  $\exists$x Truck (x) $\wedge$ Drives (x, John)
- Note that the new KB is not logically equivalent. But it is inferentially equivalent i.e. it is satisfiable when the original KB is satisfiable.
- To reduce the FOL inference to propositional inference.

1. Replace a universally quantified sentence by the set of all possible instantiations.

   Example: Suppose we have the KB.

   $\forall$x King (x) $\wedge$ Male (x) $\Rightarrow$ HasCrown (x)
   King (John)
   Male (John)
   HasCrown (John)

   We get, using the substitutions

   {x | John}, {x | Robert}

   King (John) $\wedge$ Male (John) $\Rightarrow$ HasCrown (John)

   King (Robert) $\wedge$ Male (Robert) $\Rightarrow$ HasCrown (Robert)
2. Replace an existential quantified sentence by one instantiation.
3. Treat the ground automic sentences as propositional symbols.
4. Apply any propositional logic inference algo.

5.13 UNIFICATION AND LIFTING

Suppose we have the KB.

$\forall x$ King (x) $\wedge$ Male (x) $\Rightarrow$ HasCrown (x)

King (John)

Male (John)

Brother (John, Robert)

Suppose we want to prove

HasCrown (John)

From inference, we get,

King (John) $\wedge$ Male (John) $\Rightarrow$ HasCrown (John)

king (Robert) $\wedge$ Male (Robert) $\Rightarrow$ HasCrown (Robert)

This last sentence has no use (unnecessary sentence).

As a human, we can conclude HasCrown (John) by the following thought:

- Find a person x who is a King and is Male.
- Then infer that x has a Crown.
- Do the substitution {x | John} and we have done the same.
- Note that are do not infer unnecessary sentences.

A more complicated example, given the KB.

$\forall x$ King (x) $\wedge$ Male (x) $\Rightarrow$ HasCrown (x)

$\forall y$ King (y)

Male (John)

Brother (John, Robert)

Prove:

HasCrown (John)

Requires us to find a substitution that makes the following identical.

King (X), Male (x)

King (Y), Male (John)

This can be done by

{x | John, y | John}

Generalized Modulus Pones:

- For atomic sentences P_i, P_i' and q where there is a substitution

  SUBSET (θ, P_i') = SUBSET (θ, P_i)

  For all;

$$\frac{P_1', P_2', \ldots, P_n', (P_1 \wedge P_2 \wedge \ldots \wedge P_n \Rightarrow q)}{\text{SUBSET } (\theta, q)}$$

Apply substitution θ to the consequent q

$$\frac{P_1', P_2', \ldots, P_n', (P_1 \wedge P_2 \wedge \ldots \wedge P_n \Rightarrow q)}{\text{SUBSET } (\theta, q)}$$

$$\frac{\text{King (y), Male (John), (King (x)} \wedge \text{Male (x)} \Rightarrow \text{HasCrown (x))}}{\text{SUBSET (\{x | John, y | John\}, HasCrown (x)) = HasCrown (John)}}$$

Proof that generalized modus pones is a sound inference rule.

- For any sequence P, whose variables are assumed to be universally quantified and for any substitution θ,

  P| = SUBSET (θ, P) – for the same reason that universal instantiation holds.

- From P_1', ..., P_n' we can infer

  SUBSET (θ, P_1') $\wedge$ ... $\wedge$ SUBSET (θ, P_n')

- From $P_1 \wedge \ldots \wedge P_n \Rightarrow q$, we can infer

  SUBSET (θ, P_1) $\wedge$ ... $\wedge$ SUBSET (θ, P_n) $\Rightarrow$ SUBSET (θ, q)

- In generalized modus pones, we define θ so that

  SUBSET (θ, P_i') = SUBSET (θ, P_i) for all i

  Hence, SUBSET (θ, q), follows by modus pones.

- Generalized modus pones is a lifted version of modus pones. Lifted means F.O. generalization of a propositional logic statement.
- Note that, generalized modulus pones is generalized in that it allows any number of P_i's.

5.14 FORWARD CHAINING

- It is also called as a data driven search, when we start form the starting state and we apply the rules one by one to reach to the goal state called as forward chaining.
- This is the one way to searching for a space.

Example:

	In fact base
Rule 1 – $a \wedge b \wedge c \Rightarrow e$	a
	b
Rule 2 – $e \wedge f \rightarrow g$	c
	f
Rule 3 – $g \wedge b \rightarrow x$	e
x is a goal	g

In the fact base, we already have a, b, c and f are true.

- As a, b, c are true, rule 1 fires, so e will also be true, e is also added in the fact base.
- As e and f are also true, rule 2 fires, and g is also added in the fact base.
- As g and b are true, rule 3 fires and x will be true. So, x is found.

Here, we started with the given facts and inferred the new fact, in this way, we can reach to the goal. Forward chaining may lead search to a dead-end. In this case, backtracking is needed. Backtracking strategies can be chronological or intelligent. Example of how forward chaining may lead search to a dead-end.

Example:

Rule 1 – $a \wedge b \rightarrow c$

Rule 2 – $d \wedge e \rightarrow f$

Rule 3 – $f \wedge t \rightarrow g$

In fact base

a
b
d
e
t
c
f

Rule 1 is a and b implies c, rule 2 is d and c implies t, rule 3 is f and t implies goal g. In fact base, a, b, d, e, t are true.

If we start with the start state, rule 1 and rule 2 both are enabled.

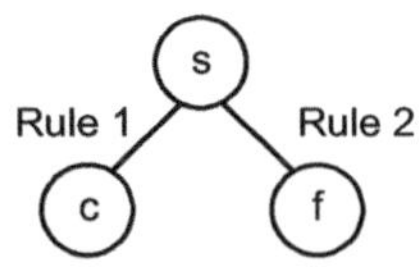

But, if we select Rule 1, which added c in the fact base, but with this we cannot reach to the goal (as f is not true). So, we need to backtrack one level up.

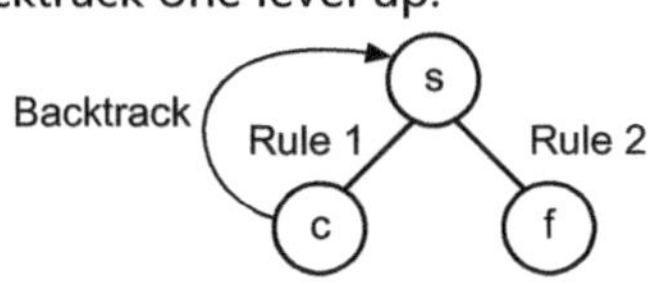

and then Rule 2 will be fired, so, f will be added in the fact base.

Now, rule 3 is fired, and goal is found.

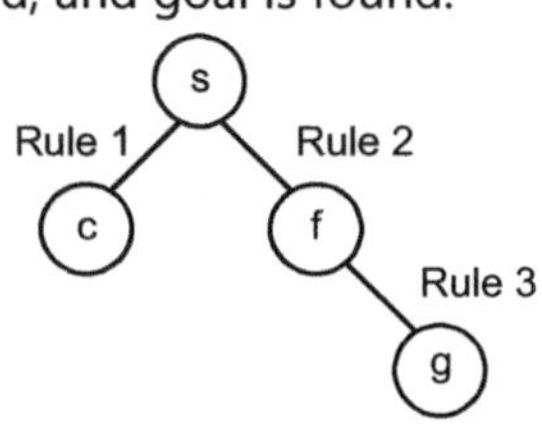

In forward chaining system, facts are held in a working memory.

Condition action rules represent actions to taken when specific facts occur in the working memory.

If condition THEN action.

Actions are nothing but adding and deleting facts from working memory.

Forward Chaining Algorithm:

- Repeat
- Find all rules which have satisfied conditions given facts in working memory.
- Choose one, using conflict resolution strategies.
- Perform actions in conclusion, probably modifying working memory.
- Until no rules can fire, or "halt" symbol added to working memory.

5.15 BACKWARD CHAINING RESOLUTION

Here, we start with the goal and try to prove the goal using the given facts.

Example:

We have the rules

Rule 1 – $a \wedge b \wedge c \Rightarrow e$

Rule 2 – $e \wedge f \rightarrow g$

Rule 3 – $g \wedge b \rightarrow x$

x is a goal

In fact base

a
b
c
f

In the fact base a, b, c, f are true initially.

Here the objective is to prove x.

We start with the goal x, x is true, when g and b are true.

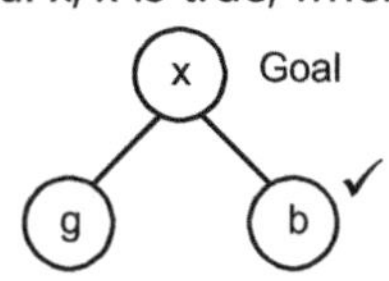

Here, be is already true, but to prove g, e and f must be true.

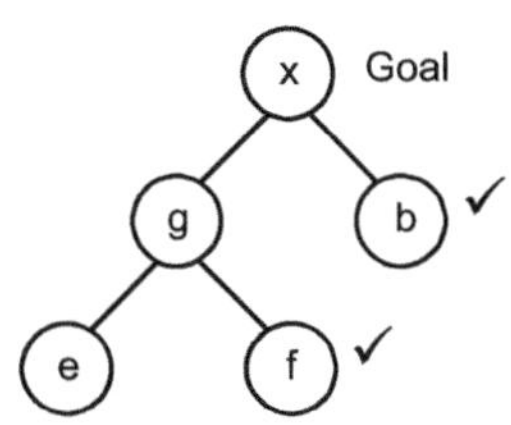

f is already true, to prove e. The a, b, c must be true.

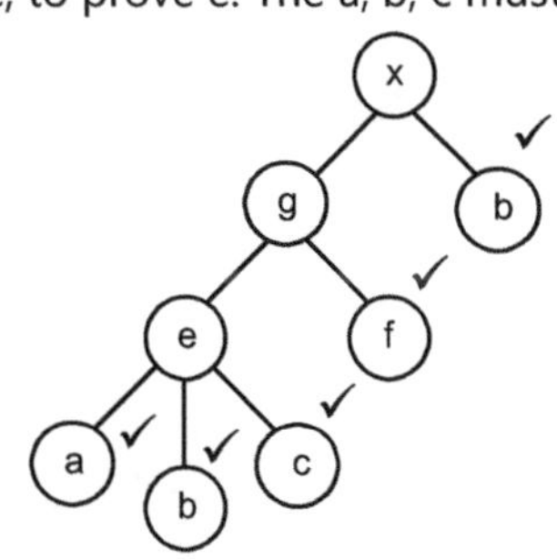

a, b, c are true in the back base. So, e and f are true.

So, g is true and b is already true. So, x is proved.

Backward chaining is very much goal driven as compared to forward chaining.

Basic Algorithm:

To prove goal G:

- If G is in the initial facts (base fact) it is proven.
- Otherwise, find a rule, which can be used to conclude G and try to prove each of the rule's conditions.

EXERCISE

1. Explain syntax and semantics of FOL.
2. Explain knowledge engineering in FOL.
3. Explain the Kinship domain with FOL.
4. Explain connections between ∃ and ∀.
5. Explain BNF for FOL.
6. Explain Propositional versus FOL with example.
7. Explain Forward and Backward chaining.
8. Convert following sentences into FOL:
   (i) All humans are mammals.
   (ii) Some humans are male.
   (iii) Nisha likes everything.
   (iv) Everyone likes everyone.
   (v) Everyone is liked by everyone.
   (vi) Everybody sleeps.
9. Explain the following sentences in first order logic:
   (i) A whale is a mammal.
   (ii) John knows Jann'e Father.
   (iii) If it is raining, then the ground is wet.
   (iv) If the switch is on and the light is off then the light-bulb is broken.
   (v) All computers have processors.

✠ ✠ ✠

UNIT VI

UNCERTAINTY

6.1 QUANTIFYING UNCERTAINTY

- Agents must handle uncertainty with partial observability, non-determinism or combination of both. Sometimes an agent may never know for certain what state it's in or where it will end up after a sequence of actions.
- Problem solving agents and logical agents designed to handle certainty by keeping track of a belief state a representation of the set of all possible world states that it might be in and generating a contingency plan that handles every possible situation that its sensors may report during execution. It has certain disadvantages :
  - ➢ Here logical agent consider every logical possible explanation for the observation no matter how unlikely it happens. This makes structure of agent large and complex.
  - ➢ A correct contingent plan that handles every event can grow arbitrarily large.
  - ➢ Sometimes there is no plan that is guaranteed to achieve goal.
  - ➢ Consider an example of automated taxi which has the goal of delivering a passenger to the airport on time.
- The agent forms a plan Ago, that involves leaving from go minutes before the flight departs and driving at a reasonable speed. Even though the airport is only about 5 mile distance, a logical agent will not be able to conclude with certainty that plan ago will get us to airport in time. It reaches the weaker conclusions that the car does not break down or run out of gas and I don't get into an accident and there are no accident on the bridge and the plane does not leave early.
- None of these conditions can be deduced for sure, so the plans success can not be inferred. This is called the qualification problem for which there is no solution available.
- The performance measure includes getting to the airport in time for the flight avoiding a long, unproductive wait at the airport, and avoiding speeding tickets along the way. The right things to do – rational decision therefore depends on both the relative importance of various goals and likelihood that and degree to which they will be achieved.

6.2 ACTING UNDER UNCERTAINTY

- One problem with the logical agent approach is that agents almost never have access to the whole truth about their environment. Some sentences can be ascertained directly from the agent's percepts and others can be inferred from current and previous percepts together with knowledge about the properties of the environment. The agent must therefore act under **Uncertainty**.
- Uncertainty can also arise because of incompleteness and incorrectness in the agent's understanding of the properties of the environment. The qualification problem says that many rules about the domain will be incomplete, because there are too many conditions to be explicitly enumerated, or because some of the conditions are unknown. For example, the agent wants to drive someone to the airport to catch the flight and is considering a plan ago that involves leaving home 90 minutes before the flight departs and driving at a reasonable speed. Even though the airport is only about 15 miles away, the agent will not be able to reach definite conclusion such as "Plan ago will get us to airport in time", but rather only the weaker conclusion such as "Plan ago will get us to the airport in time, as long as my car does not break down or run out of gas and I don't get into accident and there are not accident on the bridge and the plane doesn't leave early and there's no earthquake, ..."
- A logical agent necessarily achieve that plan ago will necessarily achieve the goal and that makes it difficult for the logical agent to conclude that plan ago is the right thing to do.
- Let us consider that Ago is in fact the right things to do. It means that out of all the possible plans that could be executed, Ago is expected to maximize the agent's performance measure, given the information it has about the environment. The performance measure includes:
  - ➢ Getting to the airport in time for the flight.
  - ➢ Avoiding along, unproductive wait at the airport.
  - ➢ Avoiding speeding tickets along the way.

- The information the agent has cannot guarantee any of these outcomes for Ago, but it can provide some degree of belief that they will be achieved.
- Other plan such as A_{120} will increase the agent's belief that it will get to airport on time, but also increase the likelihood of a long wait.
- The right things to do, the **Rational Decision,** therefore depends on both the relative importance of various goals and the likelihood that, and degree to which, they will be achieved.

6.2.1 Handling Uncertain Knowledge

- Consider a dental diagnosis system using first order logic, we might propose rules such as

  $\forall$ P Symptom (P, Tooth ache) $\Rightarrow$ Disease (P, Cavity)
- The problem is that this rule is wrong. Not all patients will toothaches have cavities, some of them may have gum disease, or impacted wisdom teeth, or one of several other problems.

  $\forall$ P Symptom (P, Tooth ache) $\Rightarrow$ Disease (P, Cavity) $\vee$
  Disease (P, Gum disease)
  $\vee$ Disease (P, Impacted wisdom)
- Unfortunately, in order to make the rule true, we have to add an almost unlimited list of possible causes. We would try learning the rule into a causal rule.

  $\forall$ P Disease (P, Cavity) $\Rightarrow$ Symptom (P, Toot ache)
- But this rule is not right either, not all cavities cause pain. The only way to fix the rule is to make it logically exhaustive to extend the left-hand to cover all possible reasons why a cavity might or might not cause a toothache. even then, for the purpose of diagnosis one must also take into account the possibility that the patient may have a toothache and a cavity that are unconnected.
- Trying to use first-order logic to cope with a domain like medical diagnosis fails for three main reasons:
  1. **Laziness:** It is too much work to list the complete set of antecedents or consequents needed to ensure an exception less rule and too hard to use the enormous rules that result.
  2. **Theoretical Ignorance:** Medical science has no complete theory for the domain.
  3. **Practical Ignorance:** Even if we know all the rules, we may be uncertain about a particular patient because all the necessary tests have not or cannot be run.
- The agent's knowledge can at best provide only a **Degree of Belief** in the relevant sentence. our main tool for dealing with degrees of belief will be **Probability Theory**, which assigns a numerical degree of belief between 0 and 1 to sentences.
- Probability provides a way of summarizing the uncertainty that comes from our laziness and ignorance. The probability could be derived from statistical data or from some general rules or from a combination of evidence sources.
- A probability of 0 for a given sentence corresponds to an unequivocal belief that the sentence is false, while a probability of 1 corresponds to an unequivocal belief that the sentence is true. Probabilities between 0 and 1 correspond to intermediate degrees of belief in the truth of the sentence. The sentence itself is in fact either true or false. It is important to note that a degree of belief is different from a degree of truth. If an agent assigns a probability of 0.8 to a sentence, then the agent expects that in 80% of cases that are indistinguishable from the current situations as far as the agent's knowledge goes, the sentence will turn out to be actually true. Thus the probability theory makes the same ontological commitment as logic namely that facts either do or do not held in the world. Degree of truth as held in the world. Degree of truth as opposed to degree of belief is the subject of **Fuzzy Logic**.
- Suppose that the agent has drawn a card from a shuffled pack. Before looking at the card, the agent might assign a probability of 1/52 to its being the ace of shades. After looking at the card, on appropriate probability for the same proposition would be 0 or 1. Thus an assignment of probability to a proposition is analogous to saying whether or not a given logical sentence is entailed by the knowledge base, rather than whether or not it is true. Just an entailment status can change when more sentences are added to the knowledge base, probabilities can change when more evidence is acquired.
- All probability statements must therefore indicate the evidence with respect to which the probability is being assessed. As the agent receives new percepts its probability assessment are updated to reflect the new evidence. Before the evidence is obtained, we talk about **Prior** or **Unconditional Probability**; after the evidence is obtained, we talk about **Posterior** or conditional probability.

6.2.2 Uncertainty and Rational Decisions

- A logical agent typically has a single goal and executes any plan that is guaranteed to achieve it. An action can be selected or rejected on the basis of whether or not it achieves the goal, regardless of what other actions achieve. When uncertainty enters the picture this is no longer the case. Consider again the Ago plan for getting to the airport. Suppose it has a 95% chances of succeeding. Does this mean it is a rational choice? Obviously, the answer is 'Not'. There might be other plans, such as A_{120}, with higher probabilities of success. if it is vital not to miss, the flight, then it might be worth risking the too longer wait at the airport. In most circumstances this is not a good choice, because although it almost guarantees getting there on time, it involves an intolerable wait.
- To make such choices, an agent must first have preferences between the different possible outcomes of various plans. A particular outcome is a completely specified state, including such factors as whether or not the agent arrives in time and the length of the wait at the airport. We will be using **Utility Theory** to represent and reason with preferences. The term utility is used here in the sense of the quality of being useful not in the sense of the electric company or water works. Utility theory says that every state has a degree of usefulness, or utility to an agent and that the agent will prefer states with higher utility.
- The utility of a state is relative to the agent whose preferences the utility function is supposed to represent. There is no accounting for taste or preferences. You can say agent's preference are odd but cannot say it is irrational.
- It is also interesting that utility theory allows for altruism. It is perfectly consistent for an agent to assign high quality to state where the agent itself suffers a concrete loss but others profit. Here 'concrete loss' must denote a reduction in 'personal welfare' of the kind normally associated with altruism or selfishness - wealth, prestige, comfort and so on rather than a loss of utility per sec. Therefore utility theory is necessarily 'selfish' only if one equates a preference for the welfare of others with selfishness, conversely altruism is only inconsistent with the principle of utility maximization if one's goals do not include the welfares of others.
- Preferences as expressed by utilities are combined with probabilities in the general theory of rational decisions called decision theory.

  Decision theory = Probability theory + Utility theory
- The fundamental ideal of decision theory is that an agent is rational if and only if it chooses the action that yields the highest expected utility, averaged overall the possible outcomes of the action. This is called the principle of Maximum Expected Utility (MEU). Probabilities and utilities are therefore combined in the evaluation of an action by weighting the utility of a particular outcome by the probability that it occurs.

6.2.3 Design for a Decision Theoretic Agent

- The structure of an agent that uses decision theory to select actions is identical, at an abstract level, to that of logical agent. Program 6.1 shows what needs to be done.

Program 6.1 : A Decision Theoretic Agent

```
function DT-AGENT(percept) returns an action
    static: a set probabilistic beliefs about the state of the world
    calculate updated probabilities for current state based on
        available evidence including current percept and previous action
    calculate outcome probabilities for actions,
        given action descriptions and probabilities of current states
    select action with the highest expected utility
        given probabilities of outcomes and utility information
    return action
```

6.3 BASIC PROBABILITY NOTATION

- Now, we have setup the general framework for a rational agent, we will need a format language for representing and reasoning with uncertain knowledge. My notation for describing degrees of belief must be able to deal with two main issues: the nature of the sentence to which degrees of belief are assigned and the dependence of the degree of belief on the agent's state of knowledge.

6.3.1 Prior Probability/Unconditional Probability

- We will use the notation P(A) for the unconditional or prior probability that the proposition A is true. For example, if a cavity denotes the proposition that a particular patient has a cavity,

  P(Cavity) = 0.1

  means that in the absence of any other information, the agent will assign a probability of a 0.1 to event of the patient's having a cavity. It is important to remember that P(A) can only be used when there, is no other information. As soon as some new information B is known, we have to reason with unconditional probability of A given B instead of P(A).
- The proposition that is the subject of a probability statement can be represented by a proposition symbol, as in P(A) example. Proposition can also include equalities involving so called random variables. For example, if we are concerned about the random variable weather we might have,

  $$P(\text{Weather} = \text{Sunny}) = 0.7$$
  $$P(\text{Weather} = \text{Rain}) = 0.2$$
  $$P(\text{Weather} = \text{Cloudy}) = 0.08$$
  $$P(\text{Weather} = \text{Snow}) = 0.02$$
- Each random variable X has a domain of possible values (x_1, ..., x_n) that it can take on. We will usually deal with discrete sets of values although continuous random variables can also be used. We can view proposition symbols as random variables as well, if we assume that they have a domain (true, false). Thus, the expression P(cavity) can be viewed as shorthand for P(cavity = true). Similarly, P(¬ cavity) is shorthand for P(cavity = false). Usually, we will use the letters A, B and so on for Boolean random variables, and the letters X, Y and so on for multivalued variables.
- Sometimes, we will want to talk about the probabilities of all the possible values of a random variable. In this case, we will use an expression such as P(weather), which denotes a vector of values for the probabilities of each individual state of the weather. Given the preceding values, for example, we would write

  P(Weather) = {0.7, 02, 0.08, 0.02}
- This statement defines a probability distribution for the random variable weather.
- We will also use expressions such as P(Weather, Cavity) to denote the probabilities of all combination of the values of a set of random variables. In this case, P(Weather, Cavity) denotes a 4 × 2 table of probabilities.
- We can also use logical connectives to make more complex sentence and assign probabilities to them. For example,

  $$P(\text{Cavity} \land \neg \text{Insured}) = 0.06$$

  says there is 6% chances that a patient has a cavity and has no insurance.

6.3.2 Conditional Probability

- Once the agent has obtained some evidence concerning the previously unknown propositions making-up the domain, prior probabilities are no longer applicable. Instead, we use conditional or posterior probabilities with the notation P(A | B). This is read as 'the probability of A given that all we know is B'. For example,

  $$P(\text{Cavity} \mid \text{Tooth ache}) = 0.8$$
- Indicates that if a patient is observed to have a toothache and no other information is yet available, then the probability of the patient having a cavity will be 0.8. It is important to remember that P(A | B) can say only be used when all we know is B. As soon as we know C, then we must compute P(A | B ∧ C) instead of P(A | B). A prior probability P(A) can be though of as a special case of conditional probability P(A), where the probability is conditioned on no evidence.
- We can also use the P notation with conditional probabilities. P(X | Y) is a two-dimensional table giving the values of $P(X = x_i \mid Y = y_i)$ for each possible, i, j. Conditional probabilities can be defined in terms of unconditional probabilities.

  The equation

  $$P(A \mid B) = \frac{P(A \land B)}{P(B)} \qquad \dots (6.1)$$

  holds whenever P(B) > 0. This equation can also be written as

  $$P(A \land B) = P(A \mid B)\, P(B)$$

  which is called the product rule.
- The product rule easier to remember, it comes from the fact that for A and B to be true, we need B to be true and then A to be true given B. We can also have it the other way around

  $$P(A \land B) = P(B \mid A)\, P(A)$$

- We can also extend our P notation to handle equations like these, providing a welcome degree of conciseness. For example, we might write

$$P(X, Y) = P(X | Y) P(Y)$$

which denotes a set of equations relating the corresponding individual entries in the table. Thus one of the equations might be

$$P(X = x_i \wedge Y = y_2) = P(X = x_1 | Y = y_2) P(Y = y_2)$$

- In general, if we interested in the probability of a proposition A and we have accumulated evidence B, then the quantity we must calculate is P(A | B). Sometimes we will not have this conditional probability available directly in the knowledge base and we must resort to probabilistic inference.
- Probabilistic interference does not work like logical inference. It is tempting to interpret the statement P(A | B) = 0.8 to mean "whenever B is true, conclude that P(A) is 0.8". This is wrong on two counts: first P(A) always denotes his prior probability of A, not the posterior given some evidence, second, the statement P(A | B) = 0.8 is only applicable when B is the only available evidence. When additional information C is available, we must calculate P(A | B ∧ C), which may bear little relation to P(A | B). In the extreme case, C might tell us directly whether A is true or false.

6.4 INFERENCE USING FULL JOINT DISTRIBUTIONS

- The probabilities inference is used here which computes the posterior probabilities for query propositions given observed evidence. Here the full joint distribution is used as the knowledge base from which answers to all questions may be decided.
- Consider an example in which domain consisting of three Boolean variables toothache, cavity and catch is used.
- The full joint distribution table is shown in Table 6.1 below.

Table 6.1 : A Full Joint Distribution for Toothache, Cavity, Catch

	Toothache		~ Toothache	
	Catch	~ Catch	Catch	~ Catch
Cavity	0.108	0.012	0.072	0.008
¬ Cavity	0.016	0.064	0.144	0.576

- Notice that probabilities in the joint distribution sum to 1. To calculate the probability of proposition simply identify those possible words in which the proposition is true and add up their probabilities. For example, there all 6 words in which cavity ∨ toothache holds.

P(cavity ∨ toothache) = 0.108t 0.012 t

0.072 + 0.008 + 0.016 + 0.064 = 0.28

Addition of the first row entries gives the unconditional or marginal probability of the cavity.

P(cavity) = 0.108 + 0.012 + 0.072 + 0.008 = 0.2

- This process is called marginalization, we can write the general marginational rule for any sets of variables Y and Z.

$$P(Y) = \sum_{z \in Z} P(Y, z)$$

where, $\sum_{z \in Z}$ means sum over all possible combinations of values of the set of variables z, which is abbreviate as Σ_z leaving Z implicit. Hence

$$P(\text{cavity}) = \sum_{z \in \{\text{catch,toothache}\}} P(\text{cavity}, z)$$

- A variant of this value involves conditional probability instead of joint probability using product rule

$$P(Y) = \sum_{z} P(Y|z) P(z)$$

- This rule is called conditioning conditional probability can be defined in terms of unconditional probabilities as follows :

$$P(a|b) = \frac{P(a \wedge b)}{P(b)}$$

Further evaluating the expression from the full joint distribution. Consider an example to compute the probability of a cavity, given evidence of toothache as follows :

$$P(\text{cavity} | \text{toothache}) = \frac{P(\text{cavity} \wedge \text{toothache})}{P(\text{toothache})}$$

$$= \frac{0.108 + 0.012}{0.108 + 0.012 + 0.016 + 0.064}$$

$$= 0.6$$

- The similar formula can be applied to find the probability that there is no cavity, given a toothache.

$$P(\neg \text{cavity} | \text{toothache}) = \frac{P(\neg \text{cavity} \wedge \text{toothache})}{P(\text{toothache})}$$

$$= \frac{0.016 + 0.064}{0.108 + 0.012 + 0.016 + 0.064} = 0.4$$

- The two values sums to 1.0. Here the term $\frac{1}{P(\text{toothache})}$ remain constant.

- It can be viewed as a normalization constant for the distribution P(cavity | toothache) ensuring that it adds up to 1.

  We can write two equation in one

  P(cavity | toothache) = $\propto$ P (cavity, toothache)

  = $\propto$ [P(cavity, toothache, catch) + P(cavity, toothache, $\neg$ catch)

  = $\propto$ [(0.108 + 0.016) + (0.012 + 0.064)]

  = $\propto$ (0.12, 0.08) = (0.6, 0.4)

  We can calculate P(cavity | toothache) even if we don't know the value of P(toothache). We add value 0.12 and 0.08. These are the correct relative proportion, but they don't sum to 1 so we normalize them by dividing each one by 0.12 + 0.08 getting the true probabilities of 0.6 and 0.4.

  Here we extract a general inference procedure. Query involves a single variable $\times$ (cavity in the example). Let E be the list of evidence variables. Let r be the list of observed values for them and let Y be the remaining unobserved variables. The query P(X|e) and can be evaluated as

  $$P(X|e) = \propto P(X, e) = \propto \sum_{y} P(X, e, y)$$

  where the summation is over all possible ys. Notice that together the variables X, E and Y constitute the complete set of variables for the domain, so P(X, e, y) is simply a subset of probabilities from the full joint distribution.

6.5 INDEPENDENCE

- The full joint distribution is expanded by adding a fourth variable, weather. The full joint distribution then becomes P(toothache, catch, cavity, weather) has 2 $\times$ 2 $\times$ 2 $\times$ 4 = 32 entries. It contains 4 editions, one for each kind of weather. We can construct the product rule for finding (toothache, catch, cavity, cloudy) and P(toothache, catch, cavity) relationship.

  P = (toothache, catch, cavity, cloudy)

  = P (cloudy \ toothache, catch, cavity) = P(cloudy) ... (6.2)

  For this we can deduce,

  P(toothache, catch, cavity, cloudy) = P(cloudy P(toothache, catch, cavity)) ... (6.3)

  A similar equation exists for every entry in P(toothache, catch, cavity, cloudy) = P(cloudy) P(toothache, catch, cavity) ... (6.4)

- A similar equation exists for every entry in P(toothache, catch, cavity, weather). We can write the general equation

  P(toothache, catch, cavity, weather) = P(toothache, catch, cavity) P(weather) ... (6.5)

- Thus the 32 element table for four variables can be constructed from one 8 element table and one 4 – element table.
- The property used in equation 6.2 is called independence. In particular the weather is independent of one's dental problem independence between prepositions a and b can be write as

  $$P(a \mid b) = P(a) \text{ or } P(b|a) = P(b)$$

  or $$P(a \wedge b) = P(a)\, P(b)$$

- All these forms are equivalent. Independence between variables X and Y can be written as follows :

  $$P(X|Y) = P(X) \text{ or } P(Y|X) = P(Y)$$

  or $$P(X, Y) = P(X) \quad P(Y)$$

- Independence assertions are usually based on knowledge of the domain.
- As the toothache weather examples shows they can dramatically reduce the amount of information necessary to specify the full joint distribution. If the complete set of variables can be divided into independent subsets, then the full joint distribution can be factored into separate joint distribution can be factored into separate joint distribution on those subsets.

6.6 BAYE'S RULE AND ITS USE

- Recall the two forms of the product rule

  $$P(A \wedge B) = P(A \mid B)\, P(B)$$

  $$P(A \wedge B) = P(B \mid A)\, P(A)$$

  Equating the two right-hand sides and dividing by P(A), we get

  $$\boxed{P(B \mid A) = \frac{P(A \mid B)\, P(B)}{P(A)}} \quad \text{... (6.6)}$$

- This equation is known as Baye's rule. This simple equation underlies all modern AI systems for probabilistic inference. The more general case of multivalued variables can be written using the P notation as follows

  $$P(Y \mid X) = \frac{P(X \mid Y)\, P(Y)}{P(X)}$$

  where again this is to be taken as representing a set of equations relating corresponding elements of the tables. We will also have occasion to use a more general version can conditionalized on some background evidence E:

$$P(Y \mid X, E) = \frac{P(X \mid Y, E)\ P(Y \mid E)}{P(X \mid E)}$$

6.6.1 Applying Baye's Rule

- On the surface, Baye's rule does not seem very useful. It requires three terms:
  - ➢ a conditional probability
  - ➢ two unconditional probability - just to compute one conditional probability.
- Baye's rule is useful in practice because there are many cases where we do have good probability estimates for these three numbers and need to compute the fourth. In a task such as medical diagnosis, we often have conditional probabilities on casual relationships and want to derive a diagnosis. A doctor knows that the disease meningitis causes the patient to have stiff neck, say 50% of the time. The doctor also knows some unconditional facts: the prior probability of a patient having meningitis is 1/50,000 and the prior probability of any patient having a stiff neck is 1/20. Letting S be the proposition that the patient has a stiff neck and M be the proposition that the patient has meningitis we have,

$$P(S \mid M) = 0.5$$
$$P(M) = 1/50{,}000$$
$$P(S) = 1/20$$
$$P(M \mid S) = \frac{P(S \mid M)\ P(M)}{P(S)} = \frac{0.5 \times 1/50{,}000}{1/20}$$
$$= 0.0002$$

- That is we expect only one in 5000 patients with a stiff neck to have meningitis. Notice that even though a stiff neck is strongly indicated by meningitis (probability 0.5), the probability of meningitis in the patient remains small. This is because the prior on stiff necks is much higher than that for meningitis.
- One obvious question to ask is why one might have available the conditional probability in one direction but not the other. In the meningitis case, perhaps the doctor knows that 1 out of 5000 patients with stiff necks has meningitis and therefore has no need to use Baye's rule.
- Unfortunately, diagnostic knowledge is often more tenuous that causal knowledge. If there is a sudden epidemic of meningitis, the unconditional probability of meningitis, P(M), will go up.

6.6.2 Normalization

- Consider the following equation for calculating the probability of meningitis of meningitis given a stiff neck

$$P(M \mid S) = \frac{P(S \mid M)\ P(M)}{P(S)}$$

- Suppose we are also concerned with the possibility that the patient is suffering from whiplash W given a stiff neck

$$P(W \mid S) = \frac{P(S \mid W)\ P(W)}{P(S)}$$

- Comparing these two equations, we see that in order to compute the relative likelihood of meningitis and whiplash, given a stiff neck, we need not assess the prior probability P(S) of a stiff neck. To put numbers on the equations, suppose that $P(S \mid W) = 0.8$ and $P(W) = 1/1000$.

  Then $\frac{P(M \mid S)}{P(W \mid S)} = \frac{P(S \mid M)\ P(M)}{P(S \mid W)\ P(W)} = \frac{0.5 \times 1/50{,}000}{0.8 \times 1/1000} = \frac{1}{80}$

- That is whiplash is 80 times more likely than meningitis, given a stiff neck.
- In some cases, relative likelihood is sufficient for decision-making, but when as in this case, the two possibilities yield radically different utilities for various treatment actions, are needs exact values in order to make rational decisions. It is still possible to avoid direct assessment of the prior probability of the 'symptoms', by considering an exhaustive set of cases. For example,

$$P(M \mid S) = \frac{P(S \mid M)\ P(M)}{P(S)}$$
$$P(\neg M \mid S) = \frac{P(S \mid \neg M)\ P(\neg M)}{P(S)}$$

- Adding these two equations and using the fact that $P(M \mid S) + P(\neg M \mid S) = 1$, we obtain

$$P(S) = P(S \mid M)\ P(M) + P(S \mid \neg M)\ P(\neg M)$$

  Substituting into the equation for $P(M \mid S)$, we have

$$P(M \mid S) = \frac{P(S \mid M)\ P(M)}{P(S \mid M)\ P(M) + P(S \mid \neg M)\ P(\neg M)}$$

- This process is called normalization, because it treats $1 \mid P(S)$ as a normalizing constant that allows the conditional terms to sum to 1. Thus in return for assessing the conditional probability $P(S \mid \neg M)$, we can avoid assessing P(S) and still obtain exact probabilities from Baye's rule. In general, multivalued case we obtain the following form for Baye's rule:

$$P(Y \mid X) = \alpha\ P(X \mid Y)\ P(Y)$$

  where α is the normalization constant needed to make the entries in the table $P(Y \mid X)$ sum to 1.

6.7 THE WUMPUS WORLD REVISITED

- To solve the probabilistic reasoning problems in the wumpus world the ideas explained above can be utilized. Uncertainty arises in the wumpus world because the agent's sensors give only partial information about the world. The wumpus world is a cave consisting of rooms connected by passage ways. Lurking somewhere in the cave is the terrible wumpus, a beast that eats anyone who enters its room. A situation in which each of the three reachable squares – [1, 3], [2, 2] and [3, 1] might contain a pit. Pure logical inference can conclude nothing about which is most likely to be safe, so a logical agent might have to choose randomly. Here probabilistic agent can do much better than the logical agent. Our aim is to calculate the probability that each of the three square contains a pit. The relevant properties of the wumpus world are that (1) a pit causes breezes in all neighboring squares and (2) each square other than [1, 1] contains a pit with probability 0.2. The first step is to identify the set of random variables we need :
  - ➢ As in the propositional logic case, we want one Boolean variable P_{ij} for each square, which is true i_{ff} square [i, j] actually contains a pit.
  - ➢ We also have Boolean variable B_{ij} that are true i_{ff} square [i, j] is breezy; we conclude these variables only for the observed square – e.g. [1, 1], [1, 2] and [2, 1].
- The next step is to specify the full joint distribution $P(P_{1,1}, \ldots P_{4,4}, B_{1,1}, B_{1,2}, B_{2,1})$ applying the product rule, we have

  $P(P_{1,1}, \ldots P_{4,4}, B_{1,1}, B_{1,2}, B_{2,1}) = P(B_{1,1}, B_{1,2}, B_{2,1} \mid P_{1,1}, \ldots P_{4,4})\ P(P_{1,1} \ldots P_{4,4})$
- This decomposition makes if easy to see what the joint probability value should be. The first term is the conditional probability distribution of a breeze configuration; given a pit configuration, its values are 1 if the breeze are adjacent to the pits and 0 otherwise. The second term is the prior probability of a pit configuration. Each square contains a pit with probability 0-2, independently of the other square hence,

  $$P(P_{1,1,\ldots} P_{4,4}) = \prod_{i,j=1,1}^{4.4} P(P_{i,j})$$

  For a particular configuration with exactly n pits $P(P_{1,1}, \ldots P_{4,4}) = 0.2^n \times 0.8^{16-n}$

6.8 PROBABILISTIC REASONING

- Probabilistic reasoning summarises uncertainties arising in environment from the different sources in fast and derives portable outcomes. The environment may be static. The past experience represents statements or hypothesis. Whenever a new statement is generated on the basis of previous facts it can also be referred to as hypothesis. Let us try to differentiate between logical and probabilistic reasoning. In case of logical reasoning, the hypothesis could be right or wrong. But in case of probabilistic reasoning, the possible truth of hypothesis is calculated.
- Bayesian inference falls in probabilistic reasoning. We have already discussed Baye's theorem. The prior probabilities are simplified with the use of Bayesian network. One of the major advantage of Bayesian network is the simplicity in calculation of the probabilities with the representation of large variables.
- So we can always say that the Bayesian network is important in inferring for future. But it has some drawbacks. It is feasible in small and medium sized network. With the large and complex network the number of variables and the relationships are increased and the CPT calculations exits for each node. So these calculations can be handled with machine learning algorithm.
- In connection with belief networks, it involves two tasks-learning the parameters and learning the structure. In structure learning the relationships among variables are identified from historic data on the basis of their conditional independence, with the underlying concept to maximise the posterior probability. An exhaustive search process is required to find out possible relationship that is exponential in the number of variables. In case of parameters learning, the CPT associated with the variable are computed. In case of discrete values, probability values are used whereas in case of continuous value attributes, Gaussian distributions are used as probability values.
- Once the BN is built, we can infer. Since the computation is very complex with BN, there are different approaches that are used for inferring viz top-down and bottom-up. In top down, effects are predicted with prior knowledge of causes, whereas in bottom up, it is from evidence to cause. The most common algorithm that is used is bucked elimination, where the elimination of unobserved variables takes place by the calculation of inference equation and its

elimination. Markov chain simulation-Markov chain Monte Carlo algorithm uses random sampling in generation of next states to infer. So all these approaches are useful in case of static environment. In next section the probabilistic reasoning under dynamic condition is shown.

6.8.1 Probabilistic Reasoning Over Time

- A dynamic environment can be imagined as a collection of small fragments taken at regular interval of time from a larger one. So at every interval it has a set of random variables, some of which are observed and some are not. The length of the time slice or the interval is dependent on the problem, and is discrete in nature. Mapping it symbolically, we can say X_t represents the set of unobserved variables at time t and ε_t represents the set of observable evidence variables.
- An observation at time t is E_t, which has values e_t. Relating this to the example of traffic, ε_t contains an evidence that person is late and X_t contains whether there is traffic jam. Further we can say that X_1, X_2 and X_3 are the unobserved state variables ε_1, ε_2 and ε_3 are the evidence variables representing the case of whether the person is late or not at the different time slice.
- Once we have variables defined, it is important to model the environment. We can represent the relationship graphically following the caused order. So as cause precedes the effect, the variables can be placed in the causal order for each time slice as it is done in BN. Hence in dynamic environment dynamic BN is used, where the nodes are random variables over time t. Since each time, slice has its own state and evidence, the relationship are more unbound and complex. Further every variable in every time slice has its own CPT, so large CPT could be created, where there exists large number of parents as well. In order to limit the CPT, it is assumed that the law which governs the process of change in environment does not change.

6.8.2 Markov Assumption

- Let us first try to understand and resolve the problem of unbounded number of parents. Parents of every node are limited to a finite number by the Markov assumption. Markov assumption states that any state depends on the finite history of states. Processes satisfying these assumptions are called Markov chains.
- Simplest version of Markov chain is the first order Markov process. In this case the current state depends only on its previous state. The BN structure for the first order Markov process is shown in Fig. 6.1.

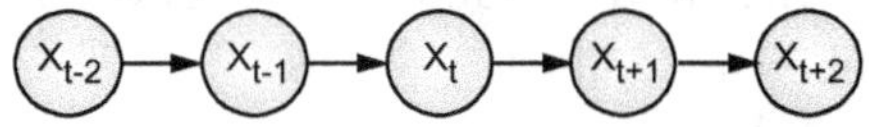

Fig. 6.1 : First order Markov process

- To add further we also assume that the evidence E_t depends only on the current state, so we have

  $P(\varepsilon_{t\,|\,X_{0:t}}, \varepsilon_{0:t-1}) = P(\varepsilon_t \mid X_t)$

  This conditional distribution $P(\varepsilon_t|X_t)$ is referred to as sensor model.
- Further the second order Markov process states that the current state depends on previous two states.

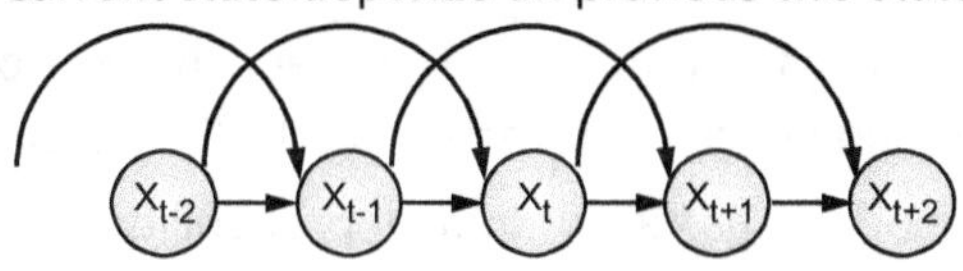

Fig. 6.2 : Second order Markov process

Models :

- In this dynamic environment, the network model and the inference is carried. Out using three different models – hidden Markov Model (HMM) Kalman filter and Dynamic Bayesian Network (DBN).
- Let us proceed with HMM. In many cases all the variables in the problem domain are not visible or observable. In such cases instead of DBN, HMM is used. HMM describes the temporal probabilistic model, where the state of the process is described by 0 single discrete structure.
- Kalman filter assumes that the values of random variables are continuous and its associated probability distribution is Gaussian. To explain it we consider an environment, where in crowed a familiar face is seen by you. You scratch your head to recollect where you had met that person earlier or whether you know him. You still try further to locate that face in the crowed. So that you do not lose the track and are able to infer. This problem is an inference, where a noisy model exists.

6.9 REPRESENTING KNOWLEDGE IN AN UNCERTAIN DOMAIN

Representing Knowledge in an Uncertain Domain using Bayesian Network :

- We saw that independence and conditional independence relationship among variables can greatly reduce the number of probabilities that need to be specified in order to define the full joint distribution.

The data structure is used to represent the dependencies among variables. This data structure is called as a Bayesian Network. It can represent any full joint probability distribution. Below Bayesian Network is described in depth.

- A Bayesian network is a directed graph in which each node is annotated with quantitive probability information.

The Specifications are Given Below :

- Each node corresponds to random variable which may be discrete or continuous.
- A set of directed links or arrows connects pairs of nodes. If there is an arrow from node X to node Y, X is said to be a parent of Y. The graph has no directed cycles and hence is a Directed Acyclic Graph (DAG).
- Each node X_i has a conditional probability distribution $P(X_i \mid \text{parents } (X_i))$ that quantifies the effect of the parents on the node.
- The meaning of arrow is that X has a direct influence on Y_1 which suggests that causes should be parents of effects. It is usually easy for a domain expert to decide what direct influences exists in domain.
- Consider the following example. You have a new burglar alarm installed at home. It is fairly reliable at detecting burglary, but also responds on occasion to minor earthquakes. You also have two neighbors, John and Mary who have promised to call you at work when they hear the alarm. John nearly always calls when he hears the alarm, but sometimes confuses with the telephone ringing with the alarm and calls then too. Many on the other hand likes rather loud music and often misses the alarm together. Given the evidence of who has or who has not called, we would like to estimate the probability of burglary.

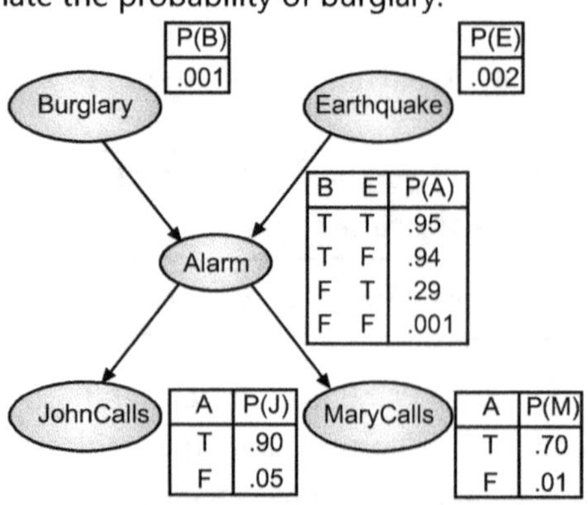

Fig. 6.3 : Bayesian network simulation for Burglary alarm

- Bayesian network for this domain is shown in above Fig. 6.3. The network structure shows that burglary and earthquake directly affect the probability of the alarms going off but whether John and Mary call depends on the alarm. The network thus represents our assumptions that they do not perceive burglaries directly; they do not notice minor earthquake and they do not confer before calling.
- The conditional distributions are shown as a conditional probability table or CPT. This form of table can be used for discrete variables. Each row in a CPT contains the conditional probability of each node value for a conditioning case. A conditioning case is just a possible combination of values for parent nodes. A node with no parents has only one row, representing the prior probabilities of each possible value of the variable.
- Notice that the network does not have nodes corresponding to Mary's currently listening to loud music or to the telephone ringing and confusing John. These factors are summarized in the uncertainty associated with the links from alarm to John calls and Mary calls.
- The probabilities actually summarize a potentially infinite set of circumstances in which the alarm might fail to go off (e.g. high humidity, power failure, dead battery, cut wires, a dead mouse stuck inside the bell etc.) or John or Mary might fail to call and report it (out to lunch, on vacation, temporarily deaf, passing helicopter etc.). In this way a small agent can cope with a very large world, at least approximately. The degree of approximation can be improved if we introduce additional relevant information.

6.10 THE SEMANTICS OF BAYESIAN NETWORKS

There are two ways in which we can understand Semantics of Bayesian networks:

1. See the network as representation of the joint probability distribution. This is useful in understanding how to construct networks.
2. See the networks as an encoding of a collection of conditional independence statements. This is useful in designing inference procedures. However, the two ways are equivalent.

Representing the Full Joint Distribution:

- We explain it, by calculating the probability that the alarm has sounded, but neither the burgulary nor an earthquake has occurred, and both Arisha and Bobby telephone you.

  $P(j \wedge m \wedge a \wedge \neg b \neg e) = P(j \mid a)\ P(m \mid a)\ P(a \mid \neg b \wedge \neg e)\ P(\neg b)\ P(\neg e)$

  $= 0.90 \times 0.70 \times 0.001 \times 0.999 \times 0.998 = 0.00062$

  We can generalise the example by writing:

  $$P(x_t, \ldots, x_m) = \prod_{j=1}^{n} P(x_i \mid \text{parents } (x_i))$$

  where parents (x) denotes the specific values of the variables in the parents (x).

- If the Bayesian network is a representation of the joint distribution then it too can be used to answer any query, as earlier in the case of inference through probabilities. This does it really so and that too more efficiently. An extension of Baylsian network is called Decision Net Work or Influence Diagram.

6.11 EFFICIENT REPRESENTATION OF CONDITIONAL DISTRIBUTIONS

- For a smallish k which has maximum number of parents, node requires up to $O(2^k)$ numbers for filling in CPT which has all the possible conditioning cases. This is the worst case scenario in which parent child relationship is arbitrary. Such relationship are clled as a canonical distribution.
- Simplest example is a deterministic node. A deterministic node has its value specified exactly by the value of parents which does not contain any uncertainty. The relationship can be logical one or numerical. If we consider example of parent Canadian, U. S., Mexican and the child node North America, the child is the disjunction of parent. It is an example of logical relationship. The numerical example is that in which parent nodes are the prices of a particular, model of car at several dealers and child node is the price that a bargain hunter heats.
- Uncertain relationship has attribute of noisy logical relationship. The example is the noisy OR which is extension of logical OR. In propositional logic, we may say that fever is true iff cold, flue or malaria is true. The noisy OR model allows for uncertainty about ability of each parent to cause the child to be true.
- The casual relationship between child and parent may be inhibited and 50 patient could have cold but not fever. Model contains two assumptions first it assumes that all the possible causes are listed (in case of miscellaneous cause, it can be added and called as a leak node). Second it assumes that inhabitation of parent and child is independent of whatever inhabits.
- In general, noisy logical relationship in which a variable depends on k parents can be described with O(k) parameters instead of $O(2^k)$ for the full conditional probability table.
- Bayesian net with continuous variables many real world problem contains continuous quantities that have an infinite number of possible values. Hence it is impossible to specify conditional probability of such variables with the help of discretization (dividing up possible values into a fixed set of interval), we can handle continuous variables. But it can cause loss of accuracy and very large CPT. The most common solution is to define standard families of probability density function that are specified by a finite number of parameters. e.g. Gaussian distribution. Another solution is to define non parametric representation.
- Network with discrete and continuous variables is called a hybrid Bayesian. Hence we need to use conditional distribution for continuous variable given discrete or continuous parents.

6.12 INFERENCE IN BAYESIAN NETWORKS

Here inference in Bayesian Network is in two parts

1. Exact inference in Bayesian Network
2. Approximate inference in Bayesian Network

6.13 EXACT INFERENCE IN BAYESIAN NETWORKS

- The basic task for any probabilistic inference system is to compute the posterior probability distribution for a set of query variables, given some observed events.
- In the burglary network, we might observe the event in which 'John calls = True and Mary calls = true'. We could then ask for say the probability that burglary has occurred.

  P(Burglary John Calls = true, Mary calls = true)

  = (0.284, 0.716)

Here we see exact algorithm for computing posterior probabilities and will consider the complexity of this task.

Inference by Enumeration

- Any conditional probability can be computed by summing terms from the full joint distributions. More specifically, a query P(X|e) can be answered using following equation.

$$P(X|e) = \propto P(x,e) = \propto \sum_{y} P(X, e, y)$$

- Now a Bayesian network gives a complete representation of the full joint distribution. A Bayesian network gives a complete representation of the full joint distribution. Therefore a query can be answered using a Bayesian network by computing sums of products of conditional probabilities from the network.
- Consider the query P(Burglary | John calls = true, Mary calls = true). The hidden variables for this query are earthquake and alarm. We have

$$P(B|j,m) = \propto P(B, j, m) = \propto \sum_{e} \sum_{a} P(B,j,m,e,a)$$

- The Bayesian network then gives is an expression in terms of CPT entries. Here we do this for Burglary = true.

$$P(b|j,m) = \propto \sum_{e} \sum_{a} P(b)\, P(e)\, P(a)\, P(a|b,e)\, P(j|a)\, P(m|a).$$

- To compute this expression, we have to add four terms, each computed by multiplying five numbers. In the worst case, where we have to sum out almost all the variables, the complexity of the algorithm for a network with n Boolean variables is $O(n_2^n)$.

  An improvement can be obtained from the following simple observations : The P(b) is constant term and can be moved outside the summations over a and e and the P(e) term can be moved outside the summation over a. Hence we have

$$P(b|j, m) = \propto P(B) = \sum_{e} P(e) \sum_{a} P)a|b,e\_ P(j|a)\, P(m|a)$$

- This expression can be evaluated by looping through the variables in order, multiplying CPT entries as we go. For each summation we also need to loop over the variables possible values. The structure of this computation as shown we obtain $P(b|j,m) = \propto \times 0.00059224$. The corresponding computation for 7b yields $\propto \times 0.0014919$; hence

$$P(B|j,m) = \propto (0.00059224, 0.0014919)$$
$$\approx <0.284, 0.716>$$

- That is, the chance of burglary, given calls from both neighbors is 28%. Note that the tree in Fig. 6.3 makes explicit the repeated sub-expression evaluated by algorithm. The product P(j|a) P(m|a) and P(j|┐a) P(m|┐a) are computed twice, once for each value of e. The next section describes general method that avoids, such wasted computations.

The Variable Elimination Algorithm :

- The algorithm can be improved substantially by eliminating repeated calculations of the kind illustrated in Algorithm. The idea is simple : do the calculation once and save the results programming. Here variable elimination algorithm is explained. Variable elimination works by evaluating expression in right-to-left order i.e. bottom up. Intermediate results are done only for those portions of the expression that depend on variable.
- Consider the example for burglary network we evaluate the expression

$$P(B|j,m) = \propto \underbrace{P(B)}_{f_1(B)} \sum_{e} \underbrace{P(e)}_{f_2(E)} \sum_{a} \underbrace{P(a|B,e)}_{f_3(A,\,B,\,E)} \underbrace{P(j|a)}_{f_4(A)} \underbrace{(m|a)}_{f_5(A)}$$

- Here the factors $f_4(A)$ and $f_5(A)$ corresponding to P(j/G) and P (m|a) depend just on A because J and m are fixed by the query. They are therefore two element vectors :

$$f_4(A) = \begin{pmatrix} P(j|a) \\ P(j|┐a) \end{pmatrix} = \begin{pmatrix} 0.90 \\ 0.05 \end{pmatrix}$$

$$f_5(A) = \begin{pmatrix} P(m|a) \\ P(m|┐a) \end{pmatrix} = \begin{pmatrix} 0.70 \\ 0.01 \end{pmatrix}$$

  $f_3(A,B,E)$ will be a 2 × 2 × 2 matrix, which is hard to show on the printed page. In terms of factors, the query expression is rewritten as

$$P(B|j,m) = \propto f_1(B) \times \sum_{e} f_2(E) \times \sum f_3(A,B,E) \times f_4(A) \times f_5(A)$$

  Where 'X' operator is not ordinary matrix multiplication but instead the pointwise product operation.

- The process of evaluation is a process of summing out variables (right to left). From pointwise products of factors to produce new factors, eventually yielding a factor that is the solution i.e. the posterior distribution over the query variable.

The Steps are as Follows :

- First we sum out A from the product of f_3, f_4 and f_5. This gives us a new 2×2 factor f_6 (B,E) whose indices range over just B and E.

$$f_6(B,E) = \sum_a f_3(A,B,E) \times f_4(A) \times f_5(A)$$

$$= (f_3(a,B,E) \times f_4(a) \times f_5(a)) + f_3(7a,B,E) \times f_4(\neg a) + f_5(\neg a)$$

Now we are left with expression

$$P(B|j,m) = \propto f_1(B) \times \sum_e f_2(E) \times f_6(B,E)$$

- Next we sum out E from the product of f_2 and f_6

$$f_7(B) = \sum_e f_2(E) \times f_6(B,E)$$

$$= f_2(e) \times f_6(B,e) + f_2(7e) \times f_6(B,7e)$$

This leaves the expression

$$P(B|j,m) = \propto f_1(B) \times f_7(B)$$

- Which can be evaluated by taking the pointwise product and normalizing the result.
- Examining this sequence, we see that two basic computational operations are required (1) Pointwise product of pair of factors (2) Summing out a variable from a product of factors. These operations are described further.

Operations on Factors :

- The pointwise product of two factors f_1 and f_2 yields a new factor f whose variables are the union of the variables in f_1 and f_2 and whose elements are given by the product of the corresponding elements in the two factors. Suppose the two factors have variables $Y_1 \ldots Y_K$ in common. Then we have

$$f(X_1 \ldots X_j, Y_1 \ldots Y_k, Z_1 \ldots Z_l) = f_1(X_1 \ldots X_j, Y_1 \ldots Y_k)\ f_2 (Y_1 - Y_k, Z_1 - Z_l)$$

- If all the variables are binary, then f_1 and f_2 have 2^{j+k} and 2^{k+l} entries, respectively and the point wise product has 2^{j+k+l} entries.

For example, given two factors f_1 (A,B) and f_2 (B,C), the point wise product $f_1 \times f_2 = f_3(A,B,C)$ has $2^{1+1+1} = 2^3 = 8$ entries as shown in following Table 6.2.

Table 6.2 : Illustrating Pointwise Multiplication : $f_1(A,B) \times f_2(B,C) = f_3(A,B,C)$

A	B	f₁(A, B)	B	C	f₂(B, C)	A	B	C	F₃(A, B, C)
T	T	.3	T	T	.2	T	T	T	$.3 \times .2 = .06$
T	F	.7	T	F	.8	T	T	F	$.3 \times .8 = .24$
F	T	.9	F	T	.6	T	F	T	$.7 \times .6 = .42$
F	F	.1	F	F	.4	T	F	F	$.7 \times .4 = .28$
						F	T	T	$.9 \times .2 = .18$
						F	T	F	$.9 \times .8 = .72$
						F	F	T	$.1 \times .6 = 0.6$
						F	F	F	$.1 \times .4 = .04$

- Note that the factor resulting from a pointwise product can contain more variables than any of the factors being multiplies and that the size of a factor is exponential in the number of variables. This is where both space and time complexity arise in the variable elimination algorithm.
- Summing out a variable from product of factors is done by adding up the submatrices formed by fixing the variable to each of its value in turn. For example, to sum out A from $f_3(A,B,C)$ we write

$$f(B,C) = \sum_a (A,B,C) = f_3(a,B,C) + f_3(\neg a,B,C)$$

$$= \begin{pmatrix} .06 & .24 \\ .42 & .28 \end{pmatrix} + \begin{pmatrix} .18 & .72 \\ .06 & .04 \end{pmatrix} = \begin{pmatrix} .24 & .96 \\ .48 & .32 \end{pmatrix}$$

- The only trick is to notice that any factor that does not depend on the variable to be summed out can be moved outside the summation. For example,

If we were to sum out E First in the burglary network, the relevant part of the expression would be

$$\sum_e f_2(E) \times f_3(A,B,E) \times f_4(A) \times f_5(A) = f_4(A) \times f_5(A) \times \sum_e f_2(E) \times f_3(A,B,E)$$

- Now the pointwise product inside the summation is computed and the variable is summed out of the resulting matrix.
- Note that matrices are not multiplied until we need to sum out a variable from the accumulated product. At that point we multiply just those matrices that include the variable to be summed out.

The Complexity of Exact Inference :

- The complexity of exact inference in Bayesian networks depends strongly on the structure of the network. The Burglary network shown early belongs to the family of networks in which there is at most one undirected path between any two nodes in the network. These are called singly connected networks or polytrees and they have particularly nice property. The time and space complexity of exact inference in polytree is linear in the size is defined as the number of CPT entries.

- For multiply connected networks variable elimination can have exponential time and space complexity in the worst case even when the number of parents per node is bounded.

Clustering Algorithm :

- The variable elimination algorithm is simple and efficient for answering individual queries if we want to compute posterior probabilities for all the variables in a network, however it can be less efficient. For example in a polytree network one would need to issue O(n) queries coasting O(n) each for a total of $O(n^2)$ time.
- Using clustering algorithm this time can be reduced to O(n). For this reason these algorithms are widely used in commercial Bayesian networks tools.
- The basic idea of clustering is to join individual nodes of the network to form cluster nodes in such a way that the resulting network is a polytree.

6.14 APPROXIMATE INFERENCE IN BAYESIAN NETWORKS

- Given the intractability of exact inference in large, multiply connected networks, it is essential to consider approximate inference methods. This section describes randomized sampling algorithms, also called Monte Carlo algorithm that provide approximate answers whose accuracy depends on the number of samples generated. Monte Carlo algorithms are used in many branches of science to estimate quantities that are difficult to calculate exactly. In this section, we are interested in sampling applied to the computation of posterior probabilities. We describe two families of algorithms
  1. Direct sampling
  2. Markov Chain sampling

1. Direct Sampling Method

- The primitive element in any sampling algorithm is the generation of samples from known probability distribution. Given a source of random numbers uniformly distributed in the range [0, 1], it is a simple matter to sample any distribution on a single sample any distribution on a single variable, whether discreate or continuous.
- The simplest kind of random sampling process fro Bayesian kind of random sampling process for Bayesian network generates events from a network that has no evidence associated with it. The idea is to sample each variable in turn in topological order. The probability distribution from which the value is sampled is conditioned on the values already assigned to the variables parent.

Program 6.2 : Sampling Algorithm that Generates Events from Bayesian Network

```
function PRIOR-SAMPLE(bn) returns an event sampled from the prior specified by bn
inputs : BN, A Bayesian network specifying joint distribution P(X1, ..., Xn)
    x ← an event with n elements
    foreach variable Xi in X1, ..., Xn do
    x[i] ← a random sample from P(Xi | parents (Xi))
return x
```

2. Inference by Markov Chain Simulation

- Markov Chain Monte Carlo (MCMC) algorithm work quite differently from rejection sampling and likelihood weighting. Instead of generating each sample from scratch, MCMC algorithm generate each sample from scratch MCMC algorithms generate each sample by making random change to the preceding sample.
- It is therefore helpful to think of an MCMC algorithm as being in a particular current state specifying a next state by making random changes to the current state. Here a particular form of MCMC called Gibbs sampling, which is especially well suited for Bayesian network.

Gibbs Sampling in Bayesian Network

- The Gibbs sampling algorithm for Bayesian network states with an arbitrary state and generates a next state by randomly sampling a value for one of the non-evidence variables X_i. The sampling for X_i is done conditioned on the current values of the variables in the Markov blanket of X_i. The algorithm therefore wanders randomly around the state space-the space of possible complete assignments flipping one variable at a time, but keeping the evidence variables fixed.

Temporal Model

We have understood techniques for probabilistic reasoning in the context of static worlds, in which each random variable has a single fixed value. A changing world is modeled using a variable for aspect of the world state at each point in time.

6.15 RELATIONAL AND FIRST-ORDER PROBABILITY MODELS

- The FOL has representational advantages over prepositional logic.
- Bayesian network has the set of random variables fixed and finite and each has a fixed domain of possible values. It limits the applicability of the Bayesian network. If the way is found in which we can combine probability these with the expressive power of first order representation the range of problems that can be handled is increased.

Possible Worlds :

- Probability model defines a set Ω of possible worlds with a probability P(w) for each worlds a. In case of Bayesian network, the possible worlds are assignment of values to variables.
- For the Boolean case, the possible worlds are prepositional logic. For the first order logic, it is all possible worlds to those of FOL. This model also needs to define a probability for each such possible world, like, Baysian networks. We can obtain the probability of any first order logical sentence ϕ as, a sum over the possible worlds where it is true.

$$P(\phi) = \Sigma P(w)$$

- Conditional probabilities $P(\phi|e)$ can be obtained similarly. Thus we can obtain answer from the given model for any given question. Here the problem is that the set of first order model, is infinite relational probability model is one approach to deal with this problem. The idea is to borrow not from the standard semantics of first order logic but from the database semantics.

Relational Probability Models :

- Like FOL, RPM have constants, functions and predicate symbol. We will assume a type signature for each function, that is a specification of the type of each argument and the function value. If the type of each object is known many spacious possible worlds are eliminated by this mechanism. To complete the RPM, we have to write the dependencies that govern these random variables.
- We can redefine the model by introducing a context specific independence to reflect the fact that dishonest customers ignore quality when giving a recommendations. Here kindness plays no role in thir decisions.

6.16 OTHER APPROACHES TO UNCERTAIN REASONING

The problem with probabilistic approach to uncertain reasoning is that they did not scale up because of the exponential number of probabilities required in the full joint distribution. And hence variety of alternatives were tried for a variety of reasons:

1. **Default Reasoning:**

   Probability theory is essentially numerical whereas human judgmental reasoning is more qualitative. Certainly, we are not consciously aware of doing numerical calculations of degrees of belief. One should also not that qualitative reasoning mechanisms can be built directly on top of probability theory, so that the "no numbers" argument against probability has little force. Nonetheless some qualitative schemes have a good deal of appeal in their own right. One of the most well studied is default reasoning which treats conclusions not as "believed to a certain degree", but as believed until a better reason is found to believe something else.

2. **Rule Base Approach:**

   In this approach certain logical rule base systems are made. They are successful but add a sort of 'fudge factor' to each rule to accommodate uncertainty.

3. **Representing Ignorance:**

   One area that we have not addressed so far is the question of ignorance; as opposed to uncertainty. Consider flipping a coin. If we known the coin to be fair then a probability of 0.5 for head is reasonable. If we know the coin is biased but we do not know which way then 0.5 is the only reasonable probability. The Dempster-shafer theory uses interval - valued degree of belief to represent on agent's knowledge of the probability of a proposition other methods using second order probabilities are known.

4. Probability makes the same ontological commitment as logic; the events are true or false in the world, even if the agent is uncertain as to which is the cases. Researchers in fuzzy logic have proposed on ontology that allows vagueness; that an event can be 'sort of' true, vagueness and uncertainty are in fact orthogonal issues.

6.16.1 Default Reasoning

- Consider example, when one sees a car parked on the street, one would normally be willing to accept that it has four wheels even though only 3 are visible. Probability theory can certainly provide a conclusion that the fourth wheel exists with high probability on the other hand introspection suggests that the possibility of the car not having four wheels does not even arise unless some new evidence presents itself.
- Thus it seems that the four-wheel conclusion is reached by default, in the absence of any reason to doubt it. If new evidence arrives such as if one seems the owner carrying a wheel and notices that the car is jacked up then the conclusion can be retracted. This kind of reasoning is said to exhibit non-monotonicity because the set of belief does not grow monotonically over time as new evidence arrives. First order logic on the other hand, exhibits strict monotonicitly.
- Reasoning schemes such as default logic, non-monotonic logic and circumscription are designed to handle reasoning with default rules and retraction of beliefs.

Still there certain technical issues with default reasoning:

- What is the semantic status of default rules? 'cars have four wheels' is false, what does it mean to have it in one's knowledge base? What is a good set of default rules to have? Without a good answer to these questions default reasoning systems will be non-modular and it will be hard to develop a good knowledge engineering methodology.
- What happens when the evidence matches the premises of two default rules with conflicting conclusions? In some schemes one can express priorities between rules, so that one rule takes precedence. Specifically preference is a commonly used form of priority in which a special case rule, takes precedence over the general case. "Three-wheeled cars have three wheels" takes precedence over "cars have four wheels".
- Sometimes a system may draw a number of conclusions on the basis of a belief that is later retracted. How can a system keep track of which conclusions need to be retracted as a result? Conclusions that have multiple justifications, only some of which have been abandoned, should be retained, whereas those with no remaining justifications should be dropped.
- How can beliefs that have default status be used to make decisions? This is probably the hardest issue of default reasoning. Decisions often involve trade-offs and one therefore needs to compare the strength of belief in the outcomes of different actions.

No default reasoning system has successfully addressed all of these issues.

6.16.2 Rule Based Methods for Uncertain Reasoning

In addition to monotonocity, logical reasoning systems have three other important properties the probabilistic reasoners lack:

- **Locality:** In logical systems, whenever we have a rule of the form A $\Rightarrow$ B, we can conclude B given evidence A, without worrying about any other rules. In probabilistic systems, we need to consider all of the available evidence.
- **Detachment:** Once a logical proof is found for a proposition B, the proposition can be used regardless of how it was derived. That is, it can be detached from its justification. In dealing with probabilities, on the other hand, the source of the evidence for a belief is important for subsequent reasoning.
- **Truth Functionality:** In logic, the truth of complex sentences can be computed from the truth of the components. Probability combination does not work this way, except under strong independence assumption.

  These properties confer obvious computational advantage. There have been several attempts to device uncertain reasoning schemes by attaching degrees of belief to propositions and rules in what is essentially a logical system. This means treating degree of belief as a generalized truth value, in order to retain truth functionality. That is, each proposition is assigned a degree of belief and the degree of belief in, say AV B is a function of the belief in A and the belief in B.

The bad news for truth functional system is that the properties of locality, detachment and truth functionality are simply not appropriate for uncertain reasoning.

How it is possible that the truth functional systems were ever considered useful? The answer lies in restricting the tasks required of them and in carefully engineering the rule base so that undesirable interactions do not occur. The most famous example of a truth functional system for uncertain reasoning is the certainty factors model, which was developed for the MYCIN medical diagnosis program and widely used in expert systems of the late 1970s.

6.16.3 Representing Ignorance: Dempster - Shafer Theory

- The Dempster - Shafer theory is designed to deal with the distinction between uncertainty and ignorance. Rather than computing the probability of a proposition, it computes the probability that the evidence supports the proposition. This measure of belief is called a **Belief Function** written Bel (X).
- Consider coin flipping for an example of belief functions. Suppose a shady character comes up to you and offers to bel you 110 that this coil will come up heads on the next flip. Given that the coin may or may not be fair what belief should you ascribe to the event of it coming up heads? Dampster - Shafer theory says that because you have no evidence either way, you have to say that the belief Bel (Heads) = 0 and also that Bel ($\neg$ Heads) = 0. This makes Dempster - Shafer reasoning systems skeptical in a way that has some intuitive appeal. Now suppose you have an expert at your disposal who testifies with 90% certainty that the coin is fair. Then Dempster - Shafer theory gives Bel (Heads) = $0.9 \times 0.5 = 0.45$ and likewise Bel ($\neg$ Heads) = 0.45. There is still a 0.1 gap, that is not accounted for by evidence. "Dempster Rule" shows how to combine evidence to give new values for Bel and Shafer's work extends this into a complete computational model.
- One interpretation of Dempster - Shafer theory is that it defines a probability interval - the interval for Heads is [0, 1] before our expert testimony and [0.45, 0.55] after. The width of the interval can be a good aid in deciding when we need to acquire more evidence, it can tell you that the expert's testimony will help you if you do not know whether the coin is fair, but will not help you if you have already determined that the coin is fair.

6.16.4 Representing Vagueness: Fuzzy Set and Fuzzy Logic

- Fuzzy set theory is a means of specifying how well an object satisfies a vague description. For example, consider the proposition "Nate is tall". Is this true, given that Nate is 5' 10"? Most people would hesitate to answer 'true' or 'false', preferring to say 'sort of'. Note that this is not the question of uncertainty about the external world. We are sure of Nate's height. Rather it is a case of a vagueness or uncertainty about the meaning of the linguistic term tall. Hence most people says that fuzzy set theory is not a method for uncertain reasoning at all.
- Another way to think of this is as similarly to a proptotype - how close is Nate to our prototype for tall person? We could express this in logical notation by making tall person a constant and having a function similarly that compares things to it.

  Similarity (Nate, Tall Person) = Sort of
- Fuzzy set theory takes a slightly different approach. It treats Tallperson as a fuzzy predicate and says that the truth value of TallPerson (Nate) is a number between 0 and 1, rather than being just true or false. The name 'Fuzzy Set' derives from the interpretation of the predicate as implicitly defining a set of its members, a set that does not have sharp boundaries. Consider a Kernel with 60 rott weilers and 40 retrievers. If we pick a dog at random, the probability of it being a rottweiler is 0.6, this is uncertainty. The uncertainty can be resolved by looking at the dog. But if a rottweiler and retrievers were to mate, then the puppies would be half rottweiler half retriever. There is no uncertainty here, no additional evidence we can gather to determine the breed of puppies. Rather, this is a case of fuzziness at the boundary between two breeds.
- Fuzzy logic takes a complex sentence such as TallPerson (Nate) $\vee$ Smart (Nate) and determines its truth value as a function of the truth values of its components. The rules for evaluating the fuzzy truth T, of a complex sentence are

$$T(A \wedge B) = \min(T(A), T(B))$$
$$T(A \vee B) = \max(T(A), T(B))$$
$$T(\neg A) = 1 - T(A)$$

- Fuzzy logic is therefore a truth functional system and is thus subject to all the usual problems. It has the additional problem that it is inconsistent with normal propositional or first-order logic. In any logic, we have to ensure that standard equivalences such as $A \vee \neg A \Leftrightarrow True$ hold, but in fuzzy logic,

  $$T(A \vee \neg A) \neq T(True)$$

- Despite these serious semantic difficulties, fuzzy logic has been very successful in commercial applications particularly in control systems for products such as automatic transmission trains, video cameras and electric shavers.

EXERCISE

1. Explain Bay's rule and its uses.
2. Describe design for decision theoretic agent.
3. Explain the term prior probability and conditional probability.
4. Explain quantifying uncertainty.
5. What is the conditional probability.
6. Explain inference using full joint distribution.
7. Explain in brief independence.
8. Explain Bayesian network.
9. Explain rule based methods for uncertain reasoning.

✠ ✠ ✠

Paper- I

Time : 3 Hrs. **Marks : 60**

Instructions to the candidates :

(1) Each Question carries 12 Marks.

(2) Attempt any five questions from the following.

(3) Illustrate your answers with neat sketches, diagram etc., wherever necessary.

(4) If some part or parameter is noticed to be missing, you may appropriately assume it and should mention it clearly.

1. Attempt the following questions

(a) Explain desirables properties of AI internal representation and AI software. **[6]**

(b) What is AI? State various characteristics of AI? **[6]**

2. Attempt any two of the following

(a) Explain the structure of agents in AI. **[6]**

(b) What is problem? What are basic elements needed fir solving single-state problem. **[6]**

(c) Explain Informed (Heuristic) search strategies. **[6]**

3. Attempt the following questions

(a) Explain backtracking search for CSPs. **[6]**

(b) Define in brief local consistency and its types. **[6]**

4. Attempt any two of the following

(a) Write a note on : Adversarial search. **[6]**

(b) What is Alpha-Beta pruning? **[6]**

(c) Explain Game three. **[6]**

5. Attempt the following questions

(a) Explain Propositional versus FOL with example. **[6]**

(b) Explain knowledge engineering in FOL. **[6]**

6. Attempt the following questions

(a) Explain Bay's rule and its uses. **[6]**

(b) Explain quantifying uncertainty. **[6]**

Paper- I

Time : 3 Hrs. **Marks : 60**

Instructions to the candidates :

(1) Each Question carries 12 Marks.

(2) Attempt any five questions from the following.

(3) Illustrate your answers with neat sketches, diagram etc., wherever necessary.

(4) If some part or parameter is noticed to be missing, you may appropriately assume it and should mention it clearly.

1. Attempt the following questions

(a) Explain the nature and scope of AI. Why game playing problems are considered as AI problem. **[6]**

(b) Explain the concept of Rationality. **[6]**

2. Attempt any two of the following

(a) Explain Breath-first search with example. **[6]**

(b) Define Heuristic functions. **[6]**

(c) Explain problem solving agents. **[6]**

3. Attempt the following questions

(a) Explain local search for CSPs with example. **[6]**

(b) What is the structure of problem. **[6]**

4. Attempt any two of the following

(a) Explain Mini-Max algorithm with example. **[6]**

(b) Explain Mini-Max with Tic-Toc-Toe. **[6]**

(c) Write a short note on games. **[6]**

5. Attempt the following questions

(a) Explain the Kinship domain with FOL. **[6]**

(b) Explain BNF for FOL. **[6]**

6. Attempt any two of the following questions

(a) Explain in brief independence. **[6]**

(b) What is the conditional probability. **[6]**

(c) Explain Bayesian network. **[6]**

✠ ✠ ✠

www.ingramcontent.com/pod-product-compliance
Lightning Source LLC
LaVergne TN
LVHW062207171026
850499LV00044B/1876
9789389944105